THE GUANTÁNAMO EFFECT

FOREWORD BY THE *Honorable Patricia M. Wald*

Human Rights Center, UNIVERSITY OF CALIFORNIA, BERKELEY

International Human Rights Law Clinic

UNIVERSITY OF CALIFORNIA, BERKELEY, SCHOOL OF LAW

IN PARTNERSHIP WITH *Center for Constitutional Rights*

THE
GUANTÁNAMO
EFFECT

EXPOSING THE CONSEQUENCES
OF U.S. DETENTION AND INTERROGATION PRACTICES

LAUREL E. FLETCHER + ERIC STOVER

STEPHEN PAUL SMITH, ALEXA KOENIG,
ZULAIKHA AZIZ, ALEXIS KELLY, SARAH STAVETEIG,
NOBUKO MIZOGUCHI

UNIVERSITY OF CALIFORNIA PRESS   BERKELEY LOS ANGELES LONDON

University of California Press, one of the most distinguished
university presses in the United States, enriches lives around
the world by advancing scholarship in the humanities, social
sciences, and natural sciences. Its activities are supported by
the UC Press Foundation and by philanthropic contributions
from individuals and institutions. For more information,
visit www.ucpress.edu.

University of California Press
Berkeley and Los Angeles, California

University of California Press, Ltd.
London, England

Library of Congress Cataloging-in-Publication Data

The Guantánamo effect : exposing the consequences of
U.S. detention and interrogation practices / Laurel E.
Fletcher . . . {et al.}.
    p.   cm.
    Originally published as an electronic resource: ISBN
9780976067733. Guantánamo and its aftermath. Berkeley,
CA : Human Rights Center, University of California,
Berkeley ; International Human Rights Law Clinic,
University of California, Berkeley, School of Law, [2008].
    Includes bibliographical references and index.
    ISBN 978-0-520-26176-1 (cloth : alk. paper)
    ISBN 978-0-520-26177-8 (pbk. : alk. paper)
    1. War on Terrorism, 2001—Prisoners and prisons,
American.   2. Guantánamo Bay Detention Camp.
3. Prisoners of war—Cuba—Guantánamo Bay Naval Base.
4. Detention of persons—Cuba—Guantánamo Bay Naval
Base.   I. Fletcher, Laurel E.
HV6432.G826   2009
355.7′1—dc22   2009007947

Manufactured in the United States of America
18   17   16   15   14   13   12   11   10   09
10   9   8   7   6   5   4   3   2   1

This book is printed on Cascades Enviro 100, a 100% post
consumer waste, recycled, de-inked fiber. FSC recycled certified and processed chlorine free. It is acid free, Ecologo
certified, and manufactured by BioGas energy.

To the memory of my parents, Daniel and Eleanor Fletcher

LAUREL E. FLETCHER

For Richard Pierre Claude

ERIC STOVER

CONTENTS

ACRONYMS AND ABBREVIATIONS

ARB	Administrative Review Board
BSCT	Behavioral Science and Consultation Team
CCR	Center for Constitutional Rights
CIA	Central Intelligence Agency
CITF	Criminal Investigative Task Force
CSRT	Combatant Status Review Tribunal
DOD	Department of Defense
DOJ	Department of Justice
FBI	Federal Bureau of Investigation
FM	Field Manual (Army)
GC	Geneva Conventions
HRC	Human Rights Center, University of California, Berkeley
ICRC	International Committee of the Red Cross
IHRLC	International Human Rights Law Clinic, University of California, Berkeley, School of Law
IRF	Immediate Reaction Force
JAG	Judge Advocate General

MP	Military Police
NLEC	No Longer an Enemy Combatant
OIG	Office of the Inspector General
OLC	U.S. Office of Legal Counsel
POW	Prisoner of War
PTSD	Post-Traumatic Stress Disorder
SERE	Survival, Evasion, Resistance, and Escape
SOP	Standard Operating Procedure

FOREWORD

This sobering report by researchers at the University of California, Berkeley, adds a new chapter to the chronicle of America's dismal descent into the netherworld of prisoner abuse since the tragic events of September 11, 2001. Carefully researched and devoid of rhetoric, it traces the missteps that disfigured an internationally admired nation and tainted its self-proclaimed ideals of humane treatment and justice for all. Through the voices of detainees formerly held at U.S. detention facilities in Afghanistan and Guantánamo Bay, Cuba, the report provides new insights into the lingering consequences of unjust detention and the corrupted processes developed in the desperate months following 9/11.

In Afghanistan, military codes and international treaties fell victim to the innovative and sometimes bizarre thinking of a small band of Administration officials who needed a place where they could hold detainees indefinitely and beyond the reach of civilian courts. In that place, Guantánamo, men who posed no serious security threat to the United States—estimated by government sources at one-third to one-half of the total detainee population—suffered equally with Taliban fighters and Al Qaeda terrorists. Effective screening processes to separate the innocent from the dangerous (or even those with vital information relevant to future attacks against the United States) were nonexistent or, when belatedly instituted under pressure of a pending lawsuit, proved flagrantly unconstitutional. Of the more than 770 detainees who have endured Guantánamo in its nearly seven-year lifetime, over 500 have been released without formal charges or trial. So far, of the 200 or more who remain in detention, only 23 have been charged with a crime. Stalwart defenders of the detention program claim vital information has been elicited; they just can't tell us what it is.

There are bound to be casualties when any nation veers from its domestic and international obligations to uphold human rights and international humanitarian law. Those casualties are etched on the minds and bodies of many of the 62 former detainees interviewed for this report, many of whom suffered infinite variations on physical and mental abuse, including intimidation, stress positions, enforced nudity, sexual humiliation, and interference with religious practices. Indeed, I was struck by the similarity between the abuse they suffered and the abuse we found inflicted upon Bosnian Muslim prisoners in Serbian camps when I sat as a judge on the International Criminal Tribunal for the former Yugoslavia in The Hague, a U.N. court fully supported by the United States. The officials and guards in charge of those prison camps and the civilian leaders who sanctioned their establishment were prosecuted—often by former U.S. government and military lawyers serving with the tribunal—for war crimes, crimes against humanity and, in extreme cases, genocide.

There are now more than 500 Guantánamo "veterans" living in 30 countries. A majority of those interviewed for this report harbor distinctly negative views of the United States. Only six of the 62 former detainees have regular jobs. Many have lost homes, businesses, and assets, while others have been shunned by their neighbors or even suspected of being American spies. The "stigma of Guantánamo" infects their future prospects. Two-thirds of the former detainees report residual psychological and emotional trauma. With the exception of a program instituted in Saudi Arabia, no meaningful help has been forthcoming from public or private sources to reintegrate former detainees into their communities. Nor have their U.S. captors apologized—let alone provided compensation—for their treatment.

Beginning with the Lieber Code in the American Civil War, the U.S. military championed the concept of humane and responsible behavior toward captured combatants and civilians in times of war. That there must be individual responsibility for violations of international humanitarian norms was the singular contribution of military law to the Nuremberg Principles. For over a century, the U.S. Army Field Manual has set out clear directions for the conduct of military personnel toward prisoners in their custody. But when the "gloves came off" at the direction of civilian and Pentagon leaders after 9/11 (against the express will of the military Judge Advocate General Corps and some courageous military advisors), the tradition of the military also became a casualty. Within months, high-level officials in the departments of Justice and Defense had approved "enhanced" interrogation techniques and sidestepped our obligations under the Geneva Conventions. Soon thereafter, interrogation became the *raison d'être* for U.S. detention facilities in Afghanistan and later Guantánamo, where military officers were consigned to holding hearings on the status of detainees who stood before them shackled, often unable to understand the proceedings, without access to lawyers or the power to call witnesses of their own.

Even the U.S. Federal Courts have been affected by these policies. The Bush Administration's initial attempts to bar the courts from overseeing the treatment of Guantánamo detainees failed—but only after several years of unsupervised abuse. Former detainees interviewed for this report commented that the sense of "futility" that pervaded the camp was perhaps the most demoralizing aspect of their detention—for a long time there appeared no way out, no fair hearing nor neutral magistrate before whom to plead innocence or mistaken capture. Denying Guantánamo detainees any outside contacts was a purposeful tactic meant to increase their dependence on their captors and to encourage confessions. Hunger strikes and suicide attempts (labeled "manipulative self-injurious behavior") became the only recourse of detainees until lawyers finally appeared on the scene and courts intervened.

A tragic time indeed. The authors of this report conclude by proposing remedial measures apart from the widely agreed upon recommendation to close Guantánamo. So far, no impartial and thorough investigation of those responsible for the abuses documented here and in other reports has taken place, although the plethora of published stories, documentaries, and exposés provide some likely suspects. The authors urge formation of an "independent, nonpartisan commission" to investigate and publicly report on the treatment of detainees in Afghanistan, Guantánamo, Iraq, and other locations. They wisely recommend such a commission be armed with subpoena power, full access to classified material, and the power to determine whether further criminal investigations of those allegedly responsible are warranted. They also insist that the work of the commission must not be limited by the grant of pardons or other shields from accountability. The focus of such a commission should be retrospective—to determine what went wrong and why, and who was responsible—as well as prospective—to recommend new polices and best practices for screening, detaining, and interrogating those who pose a serious threat to the nation's security.

We, as a nation, must not only remember our past but strive not to repeat it. This report makes an invaluable start in that direction.

The Honorable Patricia M. Wald

The Honorable Patricia M. Wald served on the United States Court of Appeals for the District of Columbia Circuit (1979–99) and the International Criminal Tribunal for the former Yugoslavia (1999–2001). Judge Wald was also a member of the President's Commission on the Intelligence Capabilities of the U.S. Regarding Weapons of Mass Destruction (2004–5).

PREFACE

We don't own the problem [of Guantánamo]—it was created
by the previous Administration. But we'll be held accountable
for how we handle this.[1]
Gregory B. Craig, White House Counsel

"The United States will not torture," President Obama declared two
days into his administration.[2] On January 22, 2009, at a ceremony in the
White House with Vice President Biden and former military officers at
his side, the new president signed a series of executive orders that mandated the review of the 245 detainees remaining in U.S. custody in
Guantánamo Bay, Cuba, established an interagency panel to examine
America's interrogation methods, and ordered the detention facility
closed within a year.[3] In one of his first official acts as President, Obama
fulfilled a campaign promise and reaffirmed the vision of change that
had swept him into office months earlier.

But the president left unresolved many questions about detainee
treatment and how he would address the legacy of Guantánamo and its
pernicious effects on the men who had passed through its gates. And
though he directed the Central Intelligence Agency (CIA) to shut what
remained of its network of secret prisons, he left himself leeway to rein-
state certain aspects of the CIA's program, including interrogation
methods that a number of current and retired military officers and FBI
agents have fiercely criticized as tantamount to torture.

Indeed, a week prior to Obama's announcement, Susan J. Crawford,
a Pentagon official in charge of deciding whether to bring detainees

before military commissions, had concluded that the techniques military interrogators used on a Saudi national over a 51-day period from November 2002 to January 2003 at Guantánamo amounted to torture. "Shocked" and "embarrassed" by the discovery, Crawford chose not to refer the case for prosecution. "The techniques they used were all authorized," she told Bob Woodward of the *Washington Post*,

> but the manner in which they applied them was overly aggressive and too persistent. You think of torture, you think of some horrendous physical act done to an individual. This was not any one particular act; this was just a combination of things that had a medical impact on him, that hurt his health. It was abusive and uncalled for. And . . . clearly coercive. It was the medical impact that pushed me over the edge [to call it torture].[4]

Former General Counsel of the U.S. Navy Alberto J. Mora concurred. In testimony before the Senate Committee on Armed Services, he declared that the use of "so-called 'harsh' techniques" at Guantánamo and other detention facilities "was a mistake of massive proportions." Drawing on basic legal distinctions, he urged the senators to focus their inquiry "not merely on banning torture, but banning cruelty." He added:

> The choice of the adjectives "harsh" or "enhanced" to describe these interrogation techniques is euphemistic and misleading. The more precise legal term is "cruel." Many of the "counter-resistance techniques" authorized for use in Guantánamo in December 2002 constitute "cruel, inhumane, and degrading" treatment that could, depending on their application, easily cross the threshold of torture.[5]

In the pages that follow, we tell the story of 62 of the over 500 detainees who were detained initially in Afghanistan and Pakistan (some having been falsely identified or sold into captivity) and incarcerated in U.S. detention facilities at Kandahar or Bagram Air Base in Afghanistan, and then at Guantánamo until their eventual release. Treatment of the detainees in these facilities varied from individual to individual, but the *totality of their experience*—or what we refer to in this book as the "Guantánamo Effect"—reflects just the kind of issues Susan Crawford and Alberto Mora raise about the legality and morality of detention and interrogation policies under the Bush Administration.

The Guantánamo Effect was not brought about by "excesses" committed by individual guards and interrogators—although they may have been contributing factors in particular instances—but rather by a camp system designed to help interrogators break the will of detainees. Life for detainees "inside the wire," as soldiers referred to the camp, was one of isolation and arbitrary and harsh treatment, punctuated by moments of terror and despair. Interrogators used guards and medical personnel to identify and exploit vulnerabilities of detainees. Guards, acting either under orders or on their own initiative, humiliated and dehumanized detainees, frequently disrupted their sleep, and desecrated the Quran. And, if minor infractions were committed, they often placed detainees in solitary confinement for days and weeks on end. The operating assumption was that camp conditions should serve to weaken the defenses of detainees and enable interrogators to break them down psychologically.

As months of incarceration turned into years, the *cumulative effect* of indefinite detention, abusive interrogations, and prolonged isolation at Guantánamo began to exact an increasing psychological toll on many detainees, our interviews and other reports indicate. Psychological damage, as doctors who treat victims of torture and prisoner abuse have long recognized, can result not only from *individual acts of extreme cruelty* (such as waterboarding) but from the cumulative nature of *seemingly less severe acts*, such as sleep deprivation, stress positions, and sexual humiliation, especially when applied in sequence and in combination, with one technique intensifying the effects of the others, over long periods of time. The stress and suffering produced by these cumulative acts can be further compounded by the ongoing uncertainty of indefinite detention.

The Guantánamo Effect did not end at the U.S. naval base in Guantánamo Bay, Cuba. Many former detainees told us the emotional and psychological problems brought on by their incarceration followed them home. Guantánamo, they said, shrouded them in "guilt by association," even though they had never been tried or convicted of a crime, and inhibited their ability to reintegrate with their families and communities and to find meaningful employment.

And so the question remains: how will we as a nation address the legacy of this dark period? Major General Antonio Taguba, the retired two-star army general who investigated abuses at Abu Ghraib and an outspoken critic of the Bush Administration's detention and interrogation polices, put it this way:

> How do we come to terms with those that were cruelly mistreated and were innocent, never charged, were illegally detained, and never compensated for their suffering? This is not a political issue, but a moral and ethical dilemma which has far-reaching implications.[6]

Confronting the Guantánamo Effect, as we suggest in this book, requires a willingness to examine not only specific acts of torture and cruelty but a wide range of policies and practices aimed at breaking the bodies and minds of real and imagined enemies. In April 2009, President Obama released legal memos describing the interrogation techniques approved by the Bush administration with a statement that this disclosure was required by law but was not a precursor to prosecutions.[7] However, a full and open inquiry into the Bush Administration's detention and interrogation policies could establish a public record of what took place, rending the veil of denial and impunity held up by those who ordered, planned, and carried out illicit acts, and could result in institutional reforms to ensure that the means used to protect U.S. national security are consistent with basic human rights and our obligations under domestic and international law.

Should we as a society fail to investigate thoroughly how we have treated detainees in recent years and to pursue appropriate criminal prosecutions of those responsible, we not only shirk our obligation to uphold human rights but also imperil our future. Societies that fail to confront their past transgressions may repeat them. Indeed, history will judge us by the actions we take—or neglect to take—to rectify the Guantánamo Effect.

Laurel E. Fletcher and Eric Stover
March 2009

Chapter 1

INTRODUCTION

"The New Paradigm"

On September 20, 2001, nine days after the attacks on the World Trade Center and the Pentagon, President George W. Bush announced that the United States was engaged in a "war on terror" unlike any conflict it had ever faced.[1]

The cornerstone to winning this war would be obtaining information from known and suspected terrorists. Four days earlier, Vice President Dick Cheney had explained in an interview on NBC's *Meet the Press* that to defeat America's new enemy,

> We'll have to work sort of the dark side. . . . We've got to spend time in the shadows in the intelligence world. A lot of what needs to be done here will have to be done quietly, without any discussion, using sources and methods that are available to our intelligence agencies—if we're going to be successful. That's the world these folks operate in. And, so it's going to be vital for us to use any means at our disposal basically, to achieve our objectives.[2]

Cheney's cloak-and-dagger description belies the extensive legal scaffolding that would be erected over the next two years to justify the unprecedented use of "enhanced interrogation techniques"—many of which appear to contravene domestic and international prohibitions against prison abuse and torture.

Within days of 9/11, the Bush Administration began developing what came to be known as "the New Paradigm" for the "war on terror."[3] Under it, the president authorized, in Jane Mayer's words, "a new, ad hoc system of detention and interrogation that operated outside any previously known coherent body of law."[4] The central feature of this new project would be the authority to use more flexible methods of interrogation on suspected terrorists, tactics believed to yield higher value intelligence.[5] As former U.S. Undersecretary of Defense for Policy Douglas Feith bluntly put it: "Intelligence is in the heads of these people. We need to extract it."[6]

But who were the subjects of these methods of "extraction"? How would they be identified, apprehended, and treated once in detention? What methods of interrogation would be used on them? And what would become of them once the "intelligence" had been extracted?

In this book we attempt to answer these questions through interviews with 62 former detainees held in U.S. custody in Afghanistan and Guantánamo Bay, Cuba, as well as 50 U.S. government officials, representatives of nongovernmental organizations, attorneys representing detainees, and former U.S. military and civilian personnel who had been stationed in Guantánamo or Afghanistan. We draw on this wealth of information, supplemented by and compared to what has appeared in media reports and publications by U.S. government and nongovernmental organizations, to develop as comprehensive a picture as possible of life inside U.S. detention facilities—Guantánamo especially—and the effects of incarceration on the lives of former detainees and their families. It should be noted that we only were able to interview detainees who had been released, not those remaining in U.S. custody in Guantánamo or other locations. With so much still unknown, it is not yet possible to provide a full accounting of what has taken place in Guantánamo or other detention centers. Our hope is that further investigations and studies will follow.

"THE NEW PARADIGM" TAKES SHAPE

The Administration's first known foray into the "dark side" took place on September 17, 2001, when President Bush issued a secret directive granting the Central Intelligence Agency (CIA) authority to set up detention facilities known as "black sites" outside the United States, and employ what he would term "an alternative set of interrogation procedures" on suspected terrorist leaders taken into its custody.[7] Word of this new directive was kept secret until October 2001, when a senior U.S. official told the *Washington Post* that President Bush had directed the CIA to "undertake its most sweeping and lethal covert action since the agency was founded in 1947." "The gloves are off," the official said. "The president has given the agency the green light to do whatever is necessary. Lethal operations that were unthinkable pre–September 11th are now under way."[8]

The Administration then turned to determining what rules would apply to detention and treatment of those captured under this new paradigm. Since 1950, the Third Geneva Convention, also known as the Geneva Convention Relative to the Treatment of Prisoners of War (POWs), had established the rules governing the capture and detention of enemy fighters. The Third Geneva Convention, signed by 195 countries including the United States, defines who is considered a "combatant" and how disputes about this status are to be resolved, and it sets forth an elaborate regime for how POWs are to be treated during confinement. It also limits the questioning of POWs, prohibits "physical or mental torture" and "any other form of coercion to secure from them information of any kind whatever,"[9] and provides that prisoners who refuse to divulge information "may not be threatened, insulted, or exposed to any unpleasant or disadvantageous treatment of any kind."[10]

In early January 2002, lawyers in the U.S. Office of Legal Counsel (OLC) of the Department of Justice (DOJ) prepared a series of memoranda arguing that the Third Convention did not apply to members of Al Qaeda or the Taliban captured in the war in Afghanistan or other locations.[11] On January 25 of that year, Alberto Gonzales, then White House Counsel, sent a memorandum to the president claiming that the "war on terror" had rendered "obsolete Geneva's strict limitations on [the] questioning of enemy prisoners."[12] He recommended that the president explicitly deny Al Qaeda and Taliban prisoners the protection of the Third Geneva Convention to "preserve flexibility" and "reduce the threat" that administration officials and military personnel would later be prosecuted for war crimes.[13] In what the historian Arthur Schlesinger characterized as "the most dramatic, sustained, and radical challenge to the rule of law in American history,"[14] President Bush formally endorsed Gonzales' recommendation in a memorandum issued a few days later.[15] The president announced that those taken into U.S. custody would not be considered POWs but would be treated "humanely and, to the extent appropriate and consistent with military necessity, in a manner consistent with the principles" of the Third Geneva Convention.[16] The Administration designated those taken into custody as "unlawful enemy combatants," a category not recognized in the Geneva Conventions.[17]

GUANTÁNAMO BAY

In addition to the CIA's secret detention centers or "black sites," the Administration needed to find a secure location to keep enemy prisoners captured in Afghanistan. It had to be a place where detainees could be held and interrogated for indefinite periods of time far from the reach of civilian courts, with their more exacting standards of evidence and emphasis on protecting defendants' rights. In October and November 2001, an inter-agency task force, comprising lawyers from the White House and the departments of Defense, State, and Justice, debated various options. "The one thing we all agreed on was that any detention facility should be located outside the United States," writes John Yoo, a former Department of Justice lawyer who served on the task force.[18]

We researched whether the courts would have jurisdiction over the facility, and concluded that if federal courts took jurisdiction over . . . camps, they might start to run them by their own lights, substituting familiar peacetime prison standards for military needs and standards. We were also strongly concerned about creating a target for another terrorist operation. . . . No location was perfect, but the U.S. Naval Station at Guantánamo Bay, Cuba, seemed to fit the bill.[19]

For much of its 110-year history, the U.S. naval base at Guantánamo Bay has served as a refueling station,[20] and in recent decades also as a center for processing predominately Cuban and Haitian refugees. The first detainees, transferred from U.S. custody in Afghanistan, arrived at Guantánamo on January 11, 2002, and were locked in a facility called Camp X-Ray, a series of small, outdoor cages built specifically for the new arrivals. After three months, X-Ray was closed, and the detainees were moved to a new and larger facility, Camp Delta.

Since early 2002, a number of government departments and agencies—principally the Department of Defense (DOD), the Federal Bureau of Investigation (FBI), and the CIA—have dispatched interrogators to Guantánamo. Operating under varying rules and with different goals and guidelines, these institutions repeatedly clashed over their disparate views of acceptable and effective interrogation techniques.[21] Traditionally, the FBI's primary focus has been on domestic law enforcement, which emphasizes obtaining information for use in investigating and prosecuting past or future crimes. The FBI has repeatedly stated that the most effective way to obtain accurate information is to use rapport-building interview techniques.[22] For its part, the DOD, which is bound by directives from the Secretary of Defense and interrogation regulations set out in the U.S. Army Field Manual, traditionally engages in interrogations to meet short-term, time-sensitive military objectives.[23] In addition to direct questioning, the Field Manual, according to the U.S. Department of Justice, "permits military interrogators to utilize methods that, depending on the manner of their use, might not be permitted under FBI polices, such as 'Fear Up

Few principles are as well settled in international law as those that outlaw the abuse and torture of prisoners.[1] Prohibitions against torture and inhuman treatment are included in, among other international agreements, the Universal Declaration of Human Rights,[2] which the UN General Assembly adopted at the close of the Second World War and the United States helped to draft; the International Covenant on Civil and Political Rights,[3] which the United States ratified in 1992; the Geneva Conventions of 1949,[4] which the United States ratified in 1955; and the United Nations Convention Against Torture,[5] which the United States ratified in 1994. The prohibition against torture has long been part of customary international law and has risen to the level of *jus cogens,* meaning that it is now a "higher law" that cannot be violated by any State.[6]

The prohibitions against torture and other forms of inhuman treatment

---

[1]See Jaffer and Singh, *Administration of Torture,* 3; Physicians for Human Rights, *Broken Laws, Broken Lives: Medical Evidence of Torture By U.S. Personnel and Its Impact,* June 2008, 95–98.

[2]Universal Declaration of Human Rights, G.A. Res. 217A, at 71, U.N. GAOR, 3d Sess., 1st plen. mtg., U.N. Doc. A/810 (1948).

[3]International Covenant on Civil and Political Rights, art. 7, Dec. 16, 1966, 999 U.N.T.S. 171, *entered into force* Mar. 23, 1976.

[4]Article 3 in each of the conventions ("Common Article 3") prohibits "violence to life and person, in particular murder of all kinds, mutilation, cruel treatment and torture" and "outrages upon personal dignity, in particular humiliating and degrading treatment." See, for example, Article 3 of Geneva Conventions III.

[5]U.N. Convention Against Torture and Other Cruel, Inhuman, or Degrading Treatment or Punishment, G.A. Res. 39/46, U.N. GAOR. 39th Sess. Supp. No. 51, *entered into force* June 26, 1987, U.N. Doc. A/Res/39/46, available at http://www.unhchr.ch/html/menu3/b/h_cat39.htm (accessed September 12, 2008).

[6]One of the principal judicial rulings in this regard is *Filartiga v. Pena-Irala,* 630 F.2d 876, 884 (2d Cir. 1980), *remanded to* 577 F. Supp. 860 (E.D.N.Y. 1984). The court noted: "[T]he torturer has become like the pirate and slave trader before him *hostis humani generis,* an enemy of all mankind." Ibid., 890.

(Harsh),' defined as exploiting a detainee's pre-existing fears including behaving in an overpowering manner with a loud and threatening voice."[24]

Less is known about the CIA's role in interrogations generally and especially at Guantánamo, although it seems certain that the agency has maintained a secret detention center there and that its agents have used highly coercive interrogation methods, including torture and cruel and inhuman treatment, on alleged Al Qaeda members.[25] On October 2, are firmly embedded in U.S. law.[7] U.S. laws prohibiting torture and inhuman treatment include the Torture Victims Protection Act (1991),[8] the Torture Convention Implementation Act (1994),[9] the War Crimes Act (1996),[10] the Detainee Treatment Act (2005),[11] the Military Commissions Act (2006),[12] as well as the Fifth, Eighth, and Fourteenth Amendments of the U.S. Constitution. The War Crimes Act, which applies to any circumstance "where the person committing such war crime is a member of the Armed Forces of the United States or a national of the United States," criminalizes "torture" and "other cruel or inhuman treatment."[13]

[7]In this regard, the United States submitted the following statement to the UN Committee against Torture in 2002: "Torture is prohibited by law in the United States. It is categorically denounced as a matter of policy and as a tool of state authority.... Every act of torture within the meaning of the Convention is illegal under existing federal and state law, and any individual who commits such an act is subject to penal sanctions as specified in criminal statutes.... Torture cannot be justified by exceptional circumstances." *United States of America, Consideration of Reports Submitted by State Parties under Article 19 of the Convention,* UN Committee against Torture, Add., at ¶¶ 6, 100, U.N. Doc. CAT/C/28/Add. 5, 2000, available at http://www1.umn.edu/humanrts/cat/cat-reports2000 .html (accessed September 12, 2008).

[8]Torture Victims Protection Act of 1991, Pub. L. No. 102–56, 106 Stat. 73 (1992) (codified at 28 U.S.C. § 1350 [2007]).

[9]Torture Convention Implementation Act of 1994, Pub. L. No. 103–236, 106 Stat. 463 (1994) (codified at 18 U.S.C. §§ 2340, 2340A [2004]).

[10]War Crimes Act of 1966, Pub. L. 104–192, § 2(a), 110 Stat. 2104, Aug. 21, 1966 (codified as amended at 18 U.S.C. § 2441 [2006]).

[11]Detainee Treatment Act of 2005, Pub. L. No. 109–148, 119 Stat. 2739 (2005) (to be codified in scattered sections of 10, 28, and 42 U.S.C.).

[12]Military Commissions Act of 2006, Pub. L. No. 109–366, 120 Stat. 2600 (2006). (Amending 18 U.S.C. § 2441).

[13]War Crimes Act § 2(a). However, the Military Commissions Act, passed in 2006, contains broad exceptions to criminal liability under the War Crimes Act. Military Commissions Act of 2006, Pub. L. No. 109–366, 120 Stat. 2600–2636 (2006). For example, the Military Commissions Act modified the War Crimes Act so that only "grave breaches" of Common Article 3 could give rise to prosecution, whereas before, prosecutions could be brought for any violation of Common Article 3. 120 Stat. 2632 § 6(a)(2).

2002, CIA counterterrorism lawyer Jonathan Fredman explained the Agency's thinking on the parameters of CIA interrogations to a group of military and intelligence officials gathered at Guantánamo: "The CIA is not held to the same rules as the military. . . . [Torture] is basically subject to perception. If the detainee dies you're doing it wrong."[26] (See Appendix A for minutes of the meeting.)

By end of summer 2002, the Chairman of the Joint Chiefs of Staff had concluded that interrogations at Guantánamo had not provided as much information as they had hoped and recommended the Army and FBI develop "a new plan to exploit detainee vulnerabilities."[27] To develop these methods, the Pentagon looked to a program designed to train U.S. military personnel to withstand interrogation by enemy Captors. Known as "Survival, Evasion, Resistance, and Escape" (SERE), the program subjects military personnel to stress positions, forced exercise to the point of exhaustion, sensory deprivation or sensory overload, and other forms of psychological duress—all to prepare them for the possibility of abuse and torture by foreign intelligence services.[28] (See Appendix B for description of SERE techniques.)[29] On September 16, 2002, a delegation of Guantánamo interrogators traveled to a SERE conference at Fort Bragg, North Carolina, run by the Joint Personnel Recovery Agency (JPRA), which administers the training program for the military.[30] Two months later, a team of SERE instructors traveled to the naval base to train their counterparts in these techniques.

On September 26, 2002, a group of the most important lawyers in the Bush Administration flew to Guantánamo. The group included Cheney's aide David Addington, White House counsel Alberto Gonzales, and Secretary of Defense Donald Rumsfeld's top counsel, William J. Haynes II. During their visit, the delegation toured Camp Delta, met with military commanders, and observed at least two interrogations.[31] On October 11, 2002, Guantánamo commanders sent a request up the chain-of-command to have the SERE techniques and other "enhanced" interrogation methods—some of which were already in use at the base—officially approved.[32]

At the same time, some military officers at Guantánamo were growing concerned that the International Committee of the Red Cross (ICRC), the Geneva-based humanitarian organization that regularly visited the naval base, might learn about the military's more aggressive interrogations. For example, on October 2, 2002, Lieutenant Colonel Diane Beaver of the Army's Judge Advocate General Corps (JAG) told a group of military and intelligence officials gathered at Guantánamo that harsher interrogation techniques would require greater secrecy. "We may need to curb the harsher operations while ICRC is around," she told the group, according to minutes of the meeting. "It is better not to expose them to any controversial techniques. . . . This would draw a lot of negative attention."[33] (See Appendix A.)

"ENHANCED" INTERROGATION TECHNIQUES

The Bush Administration's argument for authorization of harsh interrogation techniques can be traced to a legal memorandum that Assistant Attorney General Jay S. Bybee co-wrote with John Yoo in August 2002.[34] Contrary to all previous definitions of torture in international law, the memo opined that abuse does not rise to the level of torture under U.S. law unless such abuse inflicts pain "equivalent in intensity to the pain accompanying serious physical injury, such as organ failure, impairment of bodily function, or even death."[35] Mental torture required, in this legally dubious view, "suffering not just at the moment of infliction but . . . lasting psychological harm, such as seen in mental disorders like post-traumatic stress disorder."[36] To qualify as torture, the infliction of pain had to be the "precise objective" of the abuse rather than a by-product. An interrogator could know that his actions could cause pain, but "if causing such harm is not the objective, he lacks the requisite specific intent" to be found guilty of torture.[37] The memo, in blatant disregard of the U.S.'s obligations under international law, also asserted that domestic laws banning torture could not constitutionally be applied to interrogations ordered by the president in his capacity as commander-in-chief of the armed forces and that the torture of suspected terrorists for interrogation purposes would be lawful if justifiable on grounds of "necessity" and "self-defense."[38]

By late 2002, FBI agents assigned to Guantánamo had begun raising questions to FBI headquarters regarding the interrogation techniques being used by the military. Similarly, a number of officials with the U.S. military and its JAG Corps were questioning the "legal propriety" and negative public impact of the more coercive interrogation methods used at Guantánamo.[39] As each branch of the military was consulted about the proposed expansion of interrogation techniques, they uniformly expressed their concerns.[40] (See Appendix C.)[41] Despite their consistent calls for a considered, in-depth legal and policy analysis, Secretary of Defense Rumsfeld issued a directive, prepared by Department of Defense General Counsel William J. Haynes II, on December 2, 2002, authorizing isolation for thirty days at a time, twenty-four-hour interrogations, and the exploitation of "individual phobias (such as fear of dogs) to induce stress."[42] He also authorized interrogators to deprive detainees of light and auditory stimuli, forcibly strip them naked, hood them and subject them to "stress positions."[43] Some of these methods were adapted from the SERE program, and many of them went far beyond those permitted in the Army Field Manual.

On the same day Rumsfeld issued his directive, the commander of the DOD Criminal Investigative Task Force (CITF) prohibited his agents from participating in interrogations at Guantánamo that employed "any questionable techniques . . . and to withdraw from any environment or action which he/she feels is inappropriate."[44] On December 17, 2002, Naval Criminal Investigative Service (NCIS) personnel with the CITF informed the navy's general counsel, Alberto J. Mora, that detainees were being subjected to "physical abuse and degrading treatment" at Guantánamo and in Afghanistan.[45] Three days later, Mora approached the Defense Department's general counsel, William Haynes, to express concerns about Rumsfeld's December 2 directive. Mora warned Haynes that interrogation methods authorized by Rumsfeld for use at Guantánamo "could rise to the level of torture," and "expressed surprise that the Secretary had been allowed to sign it."[46]

On January 15, 2003, Rumsfeld withdrew the December 2 directive[47] and established a working group to look into the development of new interrogation techniques. On April 4, 2003, the group submitted its report, evaluating and proposing thirty-five interrogation methods.[48] Two weeks later, on April 16, Rumsfeld, relying largely on the legal reasoning in the Bybee-Yoo memo of August 2002, issued a new directive endorsing twenty-four of the thirty-five, including environmental manipulation, sleep adjustment, and extended isolation.[49]

GOVERNMENT INVESTIGATIONS OF ABUSE

In recent years, several U.S. departments and agencies have investigated reports of detainee abuse in U.S. detention facilities in Afghanistan, Iraq, Guantánamo, and other locations. In addition to criminal investigations, the Department of Defense has conducted several major reviews of detainee interrogations.[50] A 2004 Pentagon review of 187 DOD investigations found that 71 (38%) had resulted in a finding of substantiated detainee abuse, including six cases involving detainee deaths.[51] Another review in 2005 concluded that abuses did take place at Guantánamo, but the Army Field Manual on interrogations authorized most of these actions, despite their offensiveness.[52]

More recently, in May 2008, the Office of the Inspector General of the Department of Justice issued a 437-page report entitled *Review of the FBI's Involvement in and Observations of Detainee Interrogations in Guantánamo Bay, Afghanistan, and Iraq* (OIG/DOJ Report).[53] DOJ investigators had interviewed or surveyed 450 FBI employees who had been detailed to Guantánamo at various times. Approximately 240 of the agents said "they never observed nor heard about potentially abusive treatment of detainees at GITMO." Over 200 agents, however, said "they observed or heard about various rough or aggressive treatment of detainees, primarily by military interrogators. The most frequently reported techniques included sleep deprivation or disruption, prolonged shackling, stress positions, isolation, and use of bright lights or loud music."[54] According to the OIG/DOJ Report, the FBI "decided in the summer of 2002 that it would not participate in joint interrogations of detainees with other agencies in which techniques not allowed by the FBI were used."[55]

Taken together, these reports suggest sharp disagreements between U.S. departments and agencies over the frequency and systematic nature of detainee abuse and the propriety of certain interrogation methods used on detainees in Guantánamo and elsewhere.[56]

As of October 2008, a small number of low-level military personnel have been prosecuted for their involvement in abuse of detainees in Afghanistan and Iraq; none has been prosecuted for alleged detainee abuse at Guantánamo. No officials in the military or civilian chains of command have been prosecuted for their roles in abuses. Meanwhile, no independent commission has reviewed U.S. detention and interrogation practices since the attacks of September 11, 2001. Nor has there been an assessment of what has happened to the more than 500 detainees released from Guantánamo and returned to their countries of origin or third countries.

THE DETAINEE STUDY

To fill this void, our three organizations joined together in 2006 to conduct a study of detainees previously held in U.S. custody in Afghanistan and Guantánamo Bay, Cuba. To take advantage of our organizations' discrete areas of expertise, we agreed that the two UC Berkeley institutions—the Human Rights Center (HRC) and the International Human Rights Law Clinic (IHRLC)—would conduct the research, analyze the data, and write up the study findings, while the Center for Constitutional Rights (CCR) would help Berkeley researchers gain access to former detainees, provide expertise, and assist with review of the final analysis. The UC Berkeley institutions made all final decisions regarding the text.

Research for the report began in August 2006 and ended in October 2008. By then, over 770 detainees were known to have been held at the naval base in Guantánamo Bay. Of these, approximately 520 had been released or transferred to the custody of other governments.[57] The researchers gathered three sets of original data using both qualitative and quantitative methods in an effort to develop a comprehensive picture of life inside Guantánamo and the effect of incarceration on the lives of detainees and their families. The first data set consisted of in-depth interviews with 62 former detainees living in nine countries. The second consisted of in-depth interviews with 50 key informants, including U.S. government officials, representatives of nongovernmental organizations, attorneys representing detainees, and former U.S. military and civilian personnel who had been stationed in Guantánamo or Afghanistan. The third data set involved an analysis of 1,215 coded media reports concerning Guantánamo.

The primary objectives of the study were to:

- Develop a record of the experience of detention and interrogation by detainees formerly held in U.S. custody in Afghanistan and Guantánamo;

- Assess how their incarceration and treatment had affected their ability to rebuild their lives and reintegrate with their families and communities; and

- Compare those data with information on detention and interrogation procedures in documents released by the Department of Defense and reports published by the U.S. government, independent organizations, and the media. (See the Bibliography for a select list.)

Interviews with Former Detainees

Researchers conducted in-depth interviews with 62 former detainees in nine countries. The data constitute an extensive body of direct testimony about their detention, their treatment in U.S. custody in Afghanistan and Guantánamo, and their experiences since release.[58] To protect respondents, interviews were conducted anonymously and thus the names of respondents are not provided in the book. Interviewers followed a detailed protocol, reviewed and approved by UC Berkeley's Committee for Protection of Human Subjects. The interview questionnaire was developed in collaboration with researchers familiar with the institutional settings at Guantánamo.[59] Professional translators were used to conduct interviews where the researcher did not speak the respondent's language.

All interviews were transcribed. The transcriptions were then coded using Atlas.ti, a software program used widely in the social sciences for coding qualitative data. The coding was both deductive, employing predetermined codes generated from the interview questions, and inductive, allowing researchers to identify salient themes and patterns in the data throughout the coding process.[60] In all, over 200 codes were developed and tagged, resulting in 2,179 pages of coded data. The codes included a range of topics, including, for example, basic demographic information, circumstances of detention, types of interrogation methods used, treatment of the Quran, and treatment of detainees in U.S. custody prior to Guantánamo, access to medical care, and reunification with family members. Researchers reviewed the codes to find subject clusters where former detainees related similar or dissimilar experiences. In this sense, the coding served as an index of common experiences.

Interviews with Key Informants

Fifty interviews were conducted with key informants as a means to understand further the detainees' accounts and gather additional information for the study. Eighteen interviews were conducted with attorneys who have represented 164 of the approximately 430 detainees who have had legal representation. Eleven interviews were conducted with U.S. government officials. Four interviews were conducted with U.S. personnel formerly stationed at Guantánamo. One interview was conducted with an Army officer serving in Afghanistan. Finally, 16 interviews were conducted with former U.S. government officials and representatives of international and U.S.-based nongovernmental organizations. Key informants provided information on their experiences and interactions with detainees inside Guantánamo, the development and implementation of government policies, and their perspectives on the efficacy of those policies. The key-informant interviews, like those with former detainees, were conducted using detailed interview protocols, approved by UC Berkeley. Interviews were anonymous unless the key informant wished to be identified.

The Media Database

The third set of original data comprised information drawn from 1,215 media reports on released detainees, entered into an Oracle relational database. The media reports were published before 2007 by one or more of seven internationally prominent news outlets.[61] This database enabled researchers to use quantitative methods to identify patterns and trends in the demographic composition of former detainees, reported conditions at Guantánamo, and circumstances of release. The data were compared to interview data and secondary sources. (Throughout the book, we also refer to media reports published in 2007 and 2008; however, these reports were not entered into the database.)

The database used a controlled vocabulary designed by the researchers. The database design and coding process utilized principles for quantitative analysis of human rights violations developed by the Human Rights Data Analysis Group.[62] The high level of detail in the protocol enabled the translation of every item of relevant information from the text of each media report into the database variables. After data entry was complete,[63] the data were downloaded and analyzed with the R statistical package.[64] Media reports about each detainee were then merged to obtain the most complete information possible. The database captured the names of over two-thirds (219) of the 310 detainees known to have been released from Guantánamo by December 2006.[65]

Limitations of the Study

The combined methods of inquiry of former detainee interviews, key informant interviews, and media database analysis provide a triangulated view of former detainees' experiences and concurring evidence that increases the validity of the findings. Researchers designed the methodologies and questionnaires to reduce any potential bias or threat to the study's reliability and validity. Nevertheless, possible limitations must be acknowledged.

First, the findings presented in this book are limited to our interview sample. The researchers used a convenience sample for former detainee interviews because of the lack of public information on and access to former detainees. The sample was not random and the data may not reflect the actual population of those released from Guantánamo.[66] The pool of respondents was limited to released detainees in countries that were accessible, for a variety of reasons, to researchers. In addition, the voluntary nature of the interviews may have created a selection bias, with particular sub-groups of the detainee population being more or less willing to speak with U.S. researchers.

Second, the detainee interviews covered sensitive subjects including violations of human rights and abusive treatment, trauma, opinions about the U.S. government, and treatment by national governments. It is possible that respondents did not answer truthfully or fully because they feared reprisals or stigmatization or because they were reminded of experiences too painful or traumatic to talk about with strangers.[67] Anonymity and confidentiality were stressed in the consent form and names were never recorded, so former detainees may have been able to be more forthcoming with researchers than with journalists on certain topics.[68] Moreover, the concurrence of evidence through the three methods of inquiry reduced the risk of systematic error.

Third, U.S. citizens or residents, often using professional translators as mediators, conducted all of the interviews of former detainees. It is possible that the presence of U.S. researchers may have created additional bias, particularly to questions regarding opinions about or treatment by the United States and its representatives. Similarly, the interviewer's gender or other personal characteristics may have made respondents reluctant to report particular incidents of abuse or discuss especially sensitive topics, such as sexual humiliation, psychological problems, family relations, or economic hardships.

Finally, researchers were unable to verify the accounts reported in interviews with former detainees and key informants. Indeed, the purpose of the research was not investigatory in nature but sought to identify patterns in the experiences of former detainees and, where possible, to compare these data to incidents and trends in the media database and secondary sources.

We believe the interview data, taken as a whole, are accurate and reliable for several reasons. First, many of the respondents, now located in various countries around the world and reportedly not in touch with one another, related similar incidents and experiences. Second, conclusions were based on significant patterns rather than on the reports of any individual respondent. Interviewers also insisted that respondents—both former detainees and key informants—only relate incidents they had either experienced or directly witnessed. Thus, the analysis of the interview and media data was based entirely on such direct reports. Finally, we found a high degree of consistency when comparing the patterns and trends in the interview data with data on detention and interrogation procedures in documents released by the Department of Defense and reports published by the U.S. government, independent organizations, and the media.

Chapter 2

AFGHANISTAN

The Long Journey Begins

On October 7, 2001, nearly four weeks after the attacks on the Twin Towers and the Pentagon, the United States launched its war in Afghanistan. As cruise missiles blanketed Taliban positions around Kabul, Jalalabad, and Kandahar and FA-18 Hornets made daily sorties seeking out Al Qaeda strongholds in the Tora Bora Mountains, thousands of civilians, as well as foreign and Afghani fighters, crossed the border region into Pakistan. Many became trapped in the borderlands, as the United States dropped leaflets promising generous rewards for "al-Qaeda and Taliban murderers."[1] Some sought shelter with local Pakistani tribesmen, while others made their way to safe houses, the homes of relatives and friends, or resettled in cities and towns deep inside Pakistan.

As word of the cash payments circulated through the borderlands, local militia and village leaders began seizing those fleeing and turned them over to the Pakistani army. Pakistan President Pervez Musharraf later wrote in his autobiography, *In the Line of Fire: A Memoir,* that Pakistani troops took 689 Al Qaeda suspects into custody after 9/11, and subsequently turned over 369 to the Central Intelligence Agency, which paid "millions of dollars" in exchange.[2] At the same time, security forces in other countries began detaining suspected militants at the

رهبران طالبان و القاعده

دطالبان او القاعده مشرانو

تا ۵ ملیون دالر جائزه در مقابل ارائه معلومات
موثق در باره محل بود و باش و یا دستگیری
رهبران طالبان و القاعده پرداخته میشود.

تر ۵ ملیون دالر جائزه دهغه موثق معلومات دپاره
چه د طالبان او القاعده مشرانو د نیولو او یا
استوگنئ ځای وشی ورکول کیږی.

Figure 1. Afghanistan bounty leaflet. "Reward for information leading to the whereabouts or capture of Taliban and Al Qaeda leadership."

request of the United States, some of whom were turned over to U.S. authorities.

Over a third of the 62 respondents in our study said they knew, either from personal observation or being told by U.S. or Pakistani officials, they had been sold to the United States. One former detainee said villagers had offered him and his companions a place to rest and then handed them over to Pakistani soldiers. "We thought they were being kind, and then they tricked us," he said. "They sold us for money, and the next thing we knew we were in American custody. . . . Nobody had any evidence on us, nobody checked to see if we had weapons or if we were fighting or dangerous." Another respondent described hearing American voices counting out money as he and other detainees, hooded

Figure 2. Afghanistan bounty leaflet. Front: "Get wealth and power beyond your dreams. Help the Anti-Taliban Force rid Afghanistan of murderers and terrorists." Back: "You can receive millions of dollars for helping the Anti-Taliban Forces catch Al Qaeda and Taliban murderers. This is enough money to take care of your family, your village, and your tribe for the rest of your life. Pay for livestock, doctors, schoolbooks, and housing for all your people."

and shackled, waited to be loaded onto a plane that he was sure was bound for Afghanistan. "We could hear [the Americans] counting money and saying to the Pakistanis: 'Each person is $5,000. Five persons, $25,000. Seven persons, $35,000.'"

In Afghanistan, thirteen of our respondents said they were arrested in raids by U.S. forces or were turned over to the Americans by Afghan soldiers. Some said they were detained because of mistaken identities, while others said they were detained for possessing weapons, which many claimed were ubiquitous and needed for personal protection. In one case, the possession of a passport was enough to raise suspicion. This respondent said American soldiers took possession of his briefcase while searching his home. Inside was his Afghan passport with a Saudi visa. He explained to his U.S. captors that it was a legal passport and visa, but the soldiers still detained him. "After I was taken to Kandahar, I told them, 'Look in the passport, if the passport is illegal, if the visa is illegal, it's your right to hold me. But if it is not illegal and illicit, please release me.'"

Other respondents said personal feuds or failure to pay bribes to local officials led to their arrests. As one respondent put it: "Of course people gave wrong information to the U.S. troops. People just did whatever they wanted, especially if there was money involved." Another respondent believed his fate was tied to a local conflict in the area where he lived: "It was just a business. People were sold to the U.S. soldiers. In my case, I had personal feuds with people where I was living." A third was handed over to American soldiers after he refused to give his car to Afghan soldiers at a checkpoint in Gardez; he heard later that the provincial governor had received $500 for turning him over to the Americans. Another respondent said he had been arrested because he refused to turn over a satellite phone, while yet another said he was detained at a checkpoint for possessing binoculars, which he used for hunting birds.

The first stop on the way to Guantánamo for all of the respondents in our study was at one of two U.S. detention facilities located near the Afghan cities of Kandahar and Bagram.[3] The detention center at Kandahar was a makeshift camp of tents, airport buildings, and Quonset huts at the city's airport. From early October 2001, when the first interrogators arrived, it served as a clearinghouse for detainees captured in Afghanistan and other countries.[4] The second prison, at Bagram Air Base north of Kabul, remained open as of October 2008 and plans for its expansion suggest it is likely to be operational for years to come. Built by the Soviets as an aircraft machine shop in 1979, the Bagram Theater Internment Facility is a long, squat, concrete building with rusted metal sheets where windows once were. When U.S. troops took it over in early December 2001, they retrofitted the building with five large wire pens and a half dozen $9' \times 7'$ plywood isolation cells. The facility was expected to hold detainees while they were interrogated and screened for possible shipment to Guantánamo Bay. However, the transfer of detainees to Guantánamo largely stopped in September 2004, and

In the half century between the end of the Second World War and the events of September 11, 2001, the U.S. military had maintained detention facilities in six wars and military operations overseas.[1] In these conflicts stated U.S. military policy was to apply the Geneva Convention Relative to the Treatment of Prisoners of War (GC III) and the Geneva Convention Relative to the Protection of Civilian Persons in Time of War (GC IV) and other relevant conventions and international instruments.[2] The nation's most recent use of wartime detention facilities, prior to the war in Afghanistan and the second Iraq war, was during Operation Desert Storm in 1991.[3] In this conflict, the U.S. and its allies captured 86,743 Iraqis. A total of 69,820 POWs and civilian internees were marshaled through U.S.-operated facilities in Iraq, Kuwait, and Saudi Arabia between January 19, 1991, and May 2, 1991.[4] The transfer of prisoners back to their home countries was so well organized that officials of the International Committee of the Red Cross stated that the handling of Iraqi prisoners was the best they had observed under the Third Geneva Convention.[5] The same could not be said of later detentions in Afghanistan, Iraq, and elsewhere.

[1]James F. Gebhardt, "The Road to Abu Ghraib: U.S. Army Detainee Doctrine and Experience," *Military Review* (January–February 2005): 44–50.

[2]Ibid., 48.

[3]Ibid., 92–93.

[4]Ibid., 92.

[5]Ibid., 92–93.

caused the numbers at Bagram to swell. Today the internment facility holds about 630 mostly Afghani detainees.[5] All told, U.S. forces have held tens of thousands of detainees in Kandahar and Bagram, with fewer than 800 known detainees being transferred to the detention facility at Guantánamo Bay.[6]

KANDAHAR AND BAGRAM: THE ARRIVAL

Chris Mackey, a U.S. Army interrogator at Kandahar and Bagram and co-author of *The Interrogators: Task Force 500 and America's Secret War Against Al Qaeda*, describes how detainees were processed after their arrival at the Kandahar facility:

As always, it happened at night. A cargo plane touched down in darkness, its lights doused to avoid attack, and lumbered across the rutted runway toward what had once been the passenger terminal of the Kandahar airport. Its rear ramp lowered, revealing a ragged train of enemy fighters in bare feet and rags, emerging like aliens in the red-hued light of the cargo hold. Their heads were covered in burlap bags, but their breath was still visible in the frigid air. Some were wounded, others had relieved themselves, and all stank. They were bound together in long chains. As they were spirited down the ramp, if one were to stumble, he would pull the others down with him.[7]

Once on the tarmac, military police, flashlights in hand and shouting commands and obscenities, surrounded the detainees and led them into a barbered-wire enclosure the size of a football field that was illuminated by floodlights. "With a mighty *thud*," writes Mackey, "the prisoners were hurled, one by one, into a three-sided sandbag 'pin-down.' Rubber-gloved MPs armed with surgical scissors made them lie on their stomachs and began cutting away the rags."[8] Respondents found these events especially humiliating. Recalled one former detainee:

They used a thin sort of wire or string that was connected to our upper arms and then pulled us like a bunch of animals. When the wire tightened it cut off your blood circulation and your arm became useless. . . . You couldn't see, so you had no way of knowing how many were behind you or in front of you. . . . It felt as if we were a bunch of headless animals.

Another respondent put it this way:

I think the first thing the American soldiers wanted was to show that they were in total control of the situation. After that, they wanted to humiliate us. Yes, humiliation was clearly the objective. . . . If they put you naked in front of other people, if they put things up your ass, they can destroy your dignity. . . . It's as if they're telling you: "We're human beings, but you're just animals."

Several former detainees described a similar experience at Bagram. "When I arrived at Bagram," one said,

I was surrounded by six or seven American soldiers and a translator. One of the soldiers untied my hands and cut off my trousers and shirt. It is a very big insult for us Afghans, especially for Pashtuns, and even to those who are our enemies they would never do that—take off our clothes in front of other people. At that time I prayed to my God to just give me death. I wanted to die, not to be seen in this condition.

Some respondents recalled that when their hoods were removed on arriving at Bagram, looming in front of them was a large American flag with two hand-painted images of the New York Police Department and New York Fire Department insignias, iconic reminders of September 11. Before being stripped of their clothing, detainees were often subjected to what the guards called "shock of capture" to soften up new arrivals. Guards blasted loud music and allowed barking dogs near the detainees to create a sense of dread and terror. Some were taken directly into interrogation, while others were held in isolation cells for 24 hours before being questioned.[9]

At Kandahar, soldiers took the naked detainees from the pin-down to a large tent where a doctor performed a quick medical examination. The procedure ended with a rectal search. "One MP would put his knee into the back of one of the prisoner's knees while the other put his hand on the prisoner's neck and pushed it down until the prisoner was properly positioned," writes Mackey. "The doctor's probe always prompted new shrieks from prisoners convinced they were about to be raped."[10] From there, detainees were forced face down onto "a dusty, stained mat at the end of the tent."[11]

> It was like one of those pictures from Abu Ghraib. Most of us were naked, and they would pile us up one on top of the other. I still had my pants on, but the guys on top of the pile were completely naked. . . . [T]hey told us, "if you move we will shoot you." So we didn't move. We just stayed where we were. They kept sending people in and piling them on top of us. And nobody dared to move.

Eventually, one of the MPs would remove the shackles and coat the detainees with lice powder and send them to the next step in the process. After detainees were photographed, fingerprinted, and shaved of their hair and beard, they were given a thin pale blue jumpsuit, long underwear, a pair of rubber boots, two blankets, and, in some cases, a *bakol*, or Afghan cap. They would also be issued an Enemy Prisoner of War card with a number written on the back. This number would be scrawled across the front and back of their jump suits and serve as their "identifier" from then on. Then the hood would go back on their heads and they would be escorted to the main prison compound.[12]

From the processing area, detainees were taken into a large building, which housed the "general population," or to a smaller facility made of corrugated sheet metal with an earthen floor. Detainees in this latter group were placed in makeshift single cells divided by concertina wire. Each cell contained a latrine bucket and a plastic water bottle. Detainees were often moved between the two facilities or taken to other sites.[13] One respondent recalled spending several months in the so-called "Prison of Darkness" before being transferred to Bagram.[14] He described being held in a dark cell in a building where guards constantly played loud music. Both the guards and interrogators, he said, "covered their faces all the time." He was in a place, one of the guards told him, "that is out of the world. A place where no one knows where you are and no one is going to defend you."

In the "general population" area, groups of eight or nine detainees would be placed in a communal cell with one or two latrine buckets. Initially they were not allowed to speak to one another, and they were to stay seated at all times. Over time, this rule was relaxed, and detainees could pray together as a group.

DAILY LIFE

Daily life for detainees at Kandahar was one of tedious routine punctuated by arbitrary and humiliating treatment—guards shouting obscenities at them, taking photographs and video taping them for their personal use, and so on. Meals usually consisted of military-rationed Meals Ready to Eat (MREs). Detainees had to eat the food right out of the envelopes, squeezing the sauces and processed meat products into their mouths.

Night and day, guards walked down the rows of cells, stopping to discipline or pull a detainee for interrogation. Often they would use dogs to intimidate detainees. "I was lying face down," recalled a former Kandahar detainee, "and the MP came over and stepped on my back. Then a dog appeared next to me, with its mouth and one of its legs right up against my face. I was sure he was going to bite me, so I closed my eyes and just lay there quietly." Another detainee said the dogs occasionally did attack: "They would sometimes hold a dog close to you and let it bark, just to frighten you. But it happened sometimes that a dog might come too close and become excited and then bite someone on the leg."

At night, detainees found it difficult to sleep. During the winter months when the temperature could drop well below freezing, the two-blanket ration provided little insulation against the cold cement floors. Soldiers would occasionally wake up detainees for strip-searches or play loud rock music. Detainees held in the concertina-wire cages on Bagram's first floor complained they were bombarded with light around the clock: "During the night, we had to sleep with our faces facing the soldiers so they could see us. We were not allowed to pull the blanket over our faces or turn away to the other side. There were floodlights everywhere, and when we turned our faces in any direction, it just seemed as if the light was always there."

When a detainee was pulled out for night interrogation, all his cellmates were awakened and forced into a corner as the detainee was removed from the cell, often with excessive force. Writes one former detainee in his memoir of life in Bagram: "The [military] escort team . . . stormed in and put me in handcuffs and shackles. One of them punched me in the back with his fist. The other picked me up in his arms. One of them grabbed my hair from behind and pushed my head down. I was frog-marched out."[15]

Every two or three weeks, representatives from the International Committee of the Red Cross (ICRC) would come to Kandahar and Bagram as part of their mandate to visit detainees and prisoners in connection with armed conflict or political upheavals anywhere in the world. Visits are carried out according to standard procedures, which are made clear to the detaining authorities. In addition to acting as a courier for letters between detainees and their families, ICRC delegates register and interview prisoners; inspect detention facilities; and provide a confidential report to the authorities, underlining problems and requesting improvements where necessary.[16]

Former detainees at Kandahar and Bagram gave varying accounts of the role the ICRC played at the prisons. Two respondents said U.S. military personnel barred ICRC representatives from visiting certain detainees. Recalled one former detainee: "When the Red Cross came to our prison cell, they found no one because beforehand they would transfer us to a hidden place." Another respondent, who said he also was hidden during ICRC visits, speculated that "U.S. soldiers were thinking, 'If this guy sees the ICRC he's going to tell them everything.'" He was able to speak to ICRC officials, he added, only after other detainees gave a note to a visiting ICRC delegation alerting them to his presence. Other respondents believed the ICRC was incapable of improving their situation. "The Red Cross had no power whatsoever to help us," said one respondent. Another recalled, when he complained of the constantly blaring music detainees were subjected to, the ICRC delegate gave a helpless laugh and told him his organization was "unable to do anything" about the situation.

Other former detainees observed that guards treated them better during ICRC visits. Recalled one respondent, "[The] only time we felt that we had enough to eat was when Red Cross people came." During one such visit, he remembered being served rice and meat, fare normally reserved for military personnel. Another former detainee said an ICRC delegate had intervened to get him shoes and socks, while yet another credited the Red Cross with eliminating a lice infestation. For some, the ICRC visits also offered a glimmer of hope: "We knew that we were not completely forgotten . . . that there was someone, some organization that was trying to do something. We were somehow comforted by that."

Nudity

Of the many abuses endured at Kandahar and Bagram, one of the most humiliating was forced nudity.[17] Many respondents said the humiliation of strip searches and the disgrace of collective showers, defecation in public, and other forced exposures offended both their personal dignity and their identity as Muslims. The Quran itself cautioned against nudity, a state considered impure.[18] A Muslim's life, according to Tunisian professor of sociology Abdelwahab Bouhdiba, is "a succession of states of purity. . . . The impure man comes dangerously close to evil. . . . The angels who normally keep watch over man and protect him leave him as soon as he ceases to be pure. So he is left without protection, despiritualized, even dehumanized."[19]

Moazzam Begg, in his memoir *Enemy Combatant: My Imprisonment at Guantánamo, Bagram, and Kandahar,* further explains why he and his fellow detainees found public nudity especially humiliating: "These were men who would never have appeared naked in front of anyone, except their wives; who had never removed their facial hair, except to clip their moustache or beard; who never used vulgarity, nor were likely to have had it used against them. I felt that everything I held sacred was being violated, and they must have felt the same."[20]

Several respondents echoed this sentiment. "The greatest violence I suffered was nudity," said one former detainee. "After that, if they killed us, it wouldn't have been any sorrow for me." Another said, "The worst experience for me was being forced to take off my clothes and then having my picture taken. You know, we are Afghans and Muslims . . . I would rather be killed than to be treated in that way." Some remarked further on how offensive it was to have female soldiers observe them while they were bathing. "Some women soldiers were there," a former detainee said. "They were looking at us and laughing while we were naked. We were just like monkeys inside the bathrooms."

Desecration of the Quran

Twelve respondents related incidents of guards at Kandahar and Bagram desecrating the Quran. To Muslims, the text in its original Arabic is considered the literal word of God, revealed to Muhammad through the angel Gabriel, and a source of divine guidance and direction for mankind. Intentionally insulting the Quran is considered blasphemous and, in some countries, desecrating a copy of the Quran is punishable by imprisonment.[21]

"One day I was reciting the Holy Quran," a former Bagram detainee recalled. "The soldier ordered me not to recite it. But I refused. I said, 'No, this is my religious book, I respect it, I want to recite it.' Then the soldier snatched it and threw it outside my cell where it stayed for almost three days until another soldier came and took it away." A former Kandahar detainee related an incident in which a soldier seized a copy of the Quran as if it were a football and kicked it in the direction of another soldier, who picked it up and "put it in a latrine bucket, saying this is where it belonged." Another former Kandahar detainee said he and his cellmates pleaded with a guard to stop sitting on the Quran; instead, the soldier opened the book and spat on it.

Another respondent recalled an incident one morning at Kandahar when a soldier dropped a Quran into a container which was used to remove human waste. "I was sitting about forty meters away . . . and a soldier picked up someone's Quran, showed it to us, and dumped it into the container where the waste was being dumped," he said. "We tried to tell him to stop, and we were shouting. . . . And then all these soldiers came, with weapons, holding their weapons up to us like they were going to shoot us right there. So we stopped."

Physical Abuse

Once detainees are dehumanized, physically and psychologically, abusing them is more inviting to their guards, several studies demonstrate.[22] This phenomenon is known in psychology as "force drift." In his July 2004 memorandum criticizing the Pentagon's use of coercive interrogation techniques, then general counsel of the U.S. Navy Alberto J. Mora describes the phenomenon as the use of force to extract information that continues to escalate into harsher and harsher methods. "If some force is good," he writes, "[interrogators] come to believe . . . the application of more force must be better. Thus, the level of force applied against an uncooperative witness tends to escalate such that, if left unchecked, force levels, to include torture, could be reached."[23]

One of the first public reports of serious physical abuse came in March 2003, when the *New York Times* reported that two detainees had died in custody at Bagram the previous December.[24] Mullah Habibullah, a 30-year-old detainee, died on December 3, 2002. A 20-year-old Afghan taxi driver named Dilawar died one week later, on December 10. Both men had been beaten repeatedly while they were handcuffed and shackled with their arms extended over their heads. The initial Bagram press release failed to mention the overhead shackling or beatings,[25] even though military autopsy reports had found "blunt force injuries to the lower extremities" in both cases and deemed the deaths "homicides." Habibullah's autopsy showed extensive bruises and abrasions on his chest, arms, and head, as well as deep contusions on his calves, knees, and thighs. His left calf was marked by what appeared to have been the sole of a boot. His death was attributed to a blood clot, probably caused by the severe injuries to his legs, that traveled to his heart and blocked blood flow to his lungs. Dilawar's autopsy revealed similar injuries. The young man's legs, in the words of the Air Force medical examiner who performed his autopsy, had been hit so many times the tissue was "falling apart" and "had basically been pulpified."[26]

One of our respondents said he witnessed the violent death of a young Afghan detainee in Bagram. "He was beaten so badly that he died in front of my eyes in the morning at 2 o'clock," he recalled. "I was the last person that was with him. So we were also expecting to die like him because there was no food and no sleep. We were saying since they killed him why wouldn't they kill us too?"

Based largely on a 2,000-page confidential file of the Army's criminal investigation into the deaths of Dilawar and Habibullah (the "Bagram file"), the *New York Times* described repeated incidents of detainee abuse that had occurred at Bagram between the summer of 2002 and spring of 2003. Incidents of assault included striking shackled detainees, sleep deprivation, stress positions, prolonged hanging by the arms, beatings, use of dogs to terrorize detainees, and sexual abuse.[27] One of the harshest forms of assault was the "common peroneal strike," a potentially disabling blow to the side of the leg, above the knee, implicated in the deaths of Dilawar and Habibullah.[28] According to guards and interrogators stationed at Bagram, detainees considered important or troublesome were often handcuffed and chained to the ceilings and doors of their cells.[29]

Many respondents described similar forms of physical abuse. Six of the 31 former detainees held at Bagram described being chained to the ceiling in isolation cells or holding pens for prolonged periods.[30] Next to the interrogation rooms was a chalkboard where guards wrote the number of hours detainees were to be suspended by handcuffs from the ceiling and allowed to rest on the floor.[31] Detainees were reportedly unshackled and the "sleep deprivation" charts erased during ICRC visits.[32]

A former detainee related how he and others in his cell were repeatedly shackled to a wire hung from the ceiling over a period of eight to nine days at Bagram:

> When they brought me food, they would untie my hands from the ceiling and hand me a plate. But it was difficult moving the food into my mouth because my hands were still tied together. If some of the [guards] were treating me okay, they would tell me, "Sit on the floor and eat your meal." . . . Sometimes I fell asleep, and I would think I was just dreaming about all these things. Some of the soldiers who were guarding us weren't very nice. They would untie our hands from the ceiling, and make us do pushups while our hands were still tied to each other. Because we had handcuffs on, we were unable to do the pushups. And so they would beat us and yell, "Do the pushups!"

Another former Bagram detainee reported being suspended upside down as a punishment for talking. "The guards came and told me, 'You talk a lot. We should do something with you.' Then they chained me to the ceiling, with my head towards the floor. I was chained there for a long time, maybe three to four hours." Other respondents described being slammed into walls, intentionally pushed down stairs, or subjected to prolonged stress positions. "When the guards took me to the toilet," a former Bagram detainee recalled, "they often knocked me against the walls. Sometimes they made me sit at the top of the stairs and told me to touch my hands to my feet. Then they kicked me down the stairs." On another occasion, soldiers tied his hands to the ceiling and used his stomach as a punching bag. "Two or three times I fainted, and they took me to the hospital," he said. "After I got better they brought me back [to the cell] and tied me up to the ceiling just as before." One former Kandahar detainee said guards stuck his head in water.[33] Others said they were forced to kneel or stand with their arms outstretched at their sides or behind their heads for long periods of time, often for minor violations, such as talking to other detainees.

Detainees were also assaulted during transfer to and from interrogations. "From your tent to the interrogation tent you could be beaten up," said a former detainee held in the Kandahar facility. "Then when you got to your tent, you might be forced to kneel down, and you know, they would hit you with the butt of the gun, or punch you, kick you, or pull your hair." On the way to the interrogation rooms, detainees were often forced to move in a "run-shuffle" motion, which caused their leg shackles to scrape against their ankles, causing them to bleed. Nearly all of the study respondents mentioned the pain caused by shackling; two respondents, interviewed several years after their release from Guantánamo, still bore visible scars caused by their handcuffs or leg shackles.

INTERROGATION

From the onset of the war in Afghanistan until its revision in September 2006, the Army Field Manual 34-52 (FM 34-52) officially defined the "interrogation mission" and set out the rules and regulations that were supposed to guide U.S. army interrogators in battlefield human intelligence operations.[34] Issued in September 1991, the 177-page manual describes how to conduct interrogations in accordance with the Geneva Conventions and U.S. domestic law. The manual "expressly prohibits acts of violence or intimidation, including physical or mental torture, threats, insults, or exposure to inhumane treatment as a means of or aid to interrogation." Torture is defined in the manual as "the infliction of intense pain to body or mind to extract a confession or information, or for sadistic pleasure." FM 34-52 provides examples of physical torture, including "forcing an individual to stand, sit, or kneel in abnormal positions for prolonged periods of time" and "any form of beatings." It also defines coercion "as actions designed to unlawfully induce another to compel an act against one's will." Examples of coercion include "threatening or implying physical or mental torture to the subject, his family, or others to whom he owes loyalty" and "intentionally denying medical assistance or care in exchange for the information sought or other cooperation." Interrogators who violate these prohibitions, the manual warned, may be subject to prosecution under the Uniform Code of Military Justice.[35] Indeed, FM 34-52 cautioned interrogators to think before they leapt into potentially illegal situations:

> In attempting to determine if a contemplated approach or technique would be considered unlawful, consider these two tests:
>
> - Given all the surrounding facts and circumstances, would a reasonable person in the place of the person being interrogated believe that his rights, as guaranteed under both international and U.S. law, are being violated or withheld, or will be violated or withheld if he fails to cooperate.
> - If your contemplated actions were perpetrated by the enemy against U.S. POWs [Prisoners of War], you would believe such actions violate international or U.S. law.
>
> If you answer yes to either of these tests, do not engage in the contemplated action. If a doubt still remains as to the legality of a proposed action, seek a legal opinion from your servicing judge advocate.[36]

Thus, if interrogators had doubts about engaging in a particular act, they were supposed to seek legal advice. According to Mackey, the job of interrogation at Bagram involved two main objectives. First, interrogators were to perform "intelligence triage," extracting tactical information to help commanders in the conflict zone.[37] "Soldiers are dying, get the information. That's all you're told: Get the information," is how one former interrogator at Bagram put it.[38] Second, interrogators were to decide who would be sent to Guantánamo. The Pentagon determined the criteria for transfer, but their guidelines were broad. All Al Qaeda, Taliban, non-Afghan foreign fighters, and "any others who may pose a threat to U.S. interests, may have intelligence value, or may be of interest for U.S. prosecution" were to be transferred.[39] Interrogators had limited time to conduct screening processes, and hundreds of detainees were sent through the facilities in the first few months after the U.S. invasion. Michael Gelles, a Navy psychologist involved in screening detainees, described the process as "pure chaos."[40] Fearful of making a mistake and releasing dangerous or valuable detainees, interrogators often signed off on the transfer of detainees they thought might be innocent. This became a dire situation for the affected detainees, given the reality that "once a prisoner's name was on a manifest for Cuba, it was next to impossible to get the name off."[41]

Interrogations at Kandahar and Bagram took place on a daily basis—sometimes two or three times a day for a single individual, though some detainees might be left to go several days before being questioned again. Sessions could last five minutes, an hour, ten hours or more. One or two military interrogators conducted the interrogations. But there were also times when CIA interrogators would observe or participate. Sometimes CIA personnel would deliver a detainee or, just as likely, turn up with a name and, if the person was found, spirit him away to a secret, unspecified location.[42] At least one of the study respondents believed he had been held in a secret detention center operated by the CIA in Afghanistan.

Several respondents described being physically abused or threatened during interrogation sessions. A former detainee described an encounter with interrogators at Bagram:

One of the Americans was wearing only shorts. The other had a big chain which he moved back-and-forth in his hands. They looked like hungry tigers. They had tattoos of snakes and scorpions, and of tigers and the teeth of tigers. The guy who had the chain, he just kept staring at me. The first question they asked me was what my name was. Then the American soldier in shorts came and grabbed me by the neck and hit my head against the wall. And he was shouting very loudly, "You are a liar!"

In another instance, a respondent described being interrogated during surgery: "So there were two guys interrogating me and there was the doctor operating on the back, and of course it hurt, I could feel, I could feel, it was not extremely painful because I was half unconscious, but not fully. And at the same time they were asking me questions, and always about bin Laden, and nothing else."

Some interrogators threatened detainees with physical or mental torture, harm to their families, or death. "[The interrogators] never told us anything," a respondent said. "And if they told us something, then they lied. They said, 'You are going to be shot, you are going to be killed, you will get an injection, or we will hang you.' Stuff like that." A former detainee said, "Two or three times I was told by interrogators at Bagram that if I didn't cooperate, they would send me to a place where I would never come back alive." Another respondent said, "[The interrogators] told me I would spend the rest of my life in Bagram and Guantánamo. . . . I felt I would be much luckier if I died. . . . It was really difficult because we saw that there was no law there."

During one interrogation session, a former detainee was shown photographs of his family: "They waved a phone in front of me and said, 'They're just a phone call away.' Then they asked, 'Do you know where they are? Do you think they're safe?'" During his interrogation, he heard a woman screaming in a nearby room. "That was the worst," he said. "Worse than all of the humiliations, than being punched or kicked or beaten, worse than the terror of having to wear a hood and being forced to kneel on the ground and being dragged around. . . . Listening to the sound [of that woman screaming] . . . made me think there was a possibility that my family had been affected. That was the worst."

TRANSPORT TO GUANTÁNAMO

Most respondents said they learned about Guantánamo's existence from their interrogators and guards. Yet they were never informed why they were being transferred. It was a place, many were told, from which they would never return. Rumors spread through the detention centers about the fate of those who had been taken to the camp. One respondent recalled seeing a stack of orange clothing in the corner of a tent at Kandahar: "I started thinking, you know, whenever they distributed those orange outfits [to the detainees], they never came back. I realized these were the outfits worn by criminals in the United States. And that most of them had been sentenced to death." He recalled seeing convicted terrorist Timothy McVeigh on CNN being taken to his execution in the same orange clothes. It was then that he realized he was headed to Guantánamo, where he believed he, too, would be executed.

Before being loaded onto military planes bound for Guantánamo, detainees were taken to a room or tent and stripped and shaved. A guard told one former detainee that it was a precaution in case they tried to hide a pin or a minute weapon in their hair.[43] "It was so hot," one respondent said, "[I was] having difficulties breathing because we were hooded, and we sat like that for two or three hours. Finally, they dragged us in to another room and . . . made us strip naked and took pictures." During this process, detainees were individually searched. They were then given a set of orange clothes, as well as an orange hat and jacket, and heavily shackled. Handcuffs and ankle shackles were locked to a chain around the waist. "They put mask and goggles on first, and then they took us to a room where they put earplugs in our ears. We waited a long time in that place."

"Before we were taken to the plane," explained one, "we were taken to a room and made to sit on metal chairs. Our hands were tied, and when the soldiers passed by, they just hit us in the forehead as if we were animals." Several others described the treatment they received prior to boarding the plane as the worst they experienced at Kandahar or Bagram. In the words of one respondent:

> We were taken to a room and forced to sit cross legged . . . we were insulted so much in that room. We were beaten on the back and insulted with words like "fuck you, shut up, don't talk." And we sat in that position for about three or four hours. . . . Eventually we started to cry because of the pain and grief we were receiving.

According to another former detainee, "when they took us [to] the plane, they boarded us like sheep. Our hands were tied, and we couldn't do anything."

Over a quarter of the respondents said they were drugged prior to the flight. Some recalled being given pills, while others said they felt something like a patch being placed behind one of their ears. "I wasn't able to move," said a former detainee. "I couldn't tell exactly what it was . . . I felt in a daze and very heavy. My nose was blocked, I could hardly breathe." After arriving in Guantánamo, this man recalled being subjected to a medical exam and "that's when they removed the patch." For some the drugs were a blessing: "I pleaded for medication because it was so painful. I asked to be drugged, and eventually they did. So I woke up in Guantánamo in a daze."

Many respondents complained about their treatment on the flight. All detainees were short shackled to ensure limited movement. "It is what is called the 'three-piece suit,'" explained one former detainee. "It means shackling the hands to a chain at the waist, with another chain running from the waist to the feet shackles. Also earmuffs are placed over the ears, black eye goggles over the eyes, and a facemask placed over your head. Then you are put in an excruciatingly painful position on the airplane and made to stay like that for 36 hours." Some said they were chained to seats in the cargo plane, while others said they were chained to the floor. They were given little to eat; some respondents

mentioned receiving an apple or a sandwich, both of which were difficult to eat given the restraints. It was so cold on the plane, "we were just
shaking the whole way," reported one former detainee. Some said the
trip was so unbearable they didn't think they would survive: "There was
goggles put over my face, there was a strap of plastic that was holding
the goggles on. A bit of the ear was tucked in like this. It was the worst
pain ever. I just wanted to die."

Due to the restraints and medications, going to the bathroom during
transport was an ordeal. Recalled one respondent:

> At one point I asked to go to the bathroom. I can remember a female escort-
> ing me. It was two soldiers—a male and a female. And the doors were open.
> They left the doors open and they took your trousers down for you. So this
> woman was taking my pants down for me. And I needed to take a pee basi-
> cally. And I was standing there for maybe 10 minutes. And I couldn't relieve
> myself at all, I just couldn't. She was watching me from behind, and I knew
> that she was watching me. And for that reason, my body kind of just like, it
> was not, nothing was happening. And the thing was, I needed to go to the
> toilet for a long time. And now my bladder, my stomach, was really hurting.
> And, you know, I was in such pain that I couldn't relieve myself. . . . So I went
> and sat back down, and after a couple more hours I asked to go again. And
> this time it took me like about 10, 20 minutes again. . . . But by the time I
> relieved myself, it was all over the place. It was all over me because I could-
> n't see what I was doing. . . . The plane was moving, so it went all over me.
> So I sat back down. . . . It was really humiliating. . . . Just imagine a woman
> being there, and she had to go to the toilet in front of all men.

The vast majority of respondents reported that the cargo plane
touched down en route to Guantánamo. Some speculated, given the
weather conditions and distance they had traveled, that the plane
stopped in Turkey or possibly Germany. Recalled one respondent: "In
the middle of the trip, we had to change planes. The plane landed and a
couple of soldiers lifted us from a sitting position and took us off to
another plane."

Upon final arrival in Guantánamo, a rear ramp opened at the back of
the cargo plane and detainees were off-loaded onto the tarmac. Most

respondents were terrified of what awaited them in this strange new place, but initially at least they were relieved to move their legs and escape the painful positions in which they had been held.

At least one former detainee, however, was hopeful. "When it was my turn to be taken out of the plane, I could just see [some of my surroundings] from the corner of the goggles I was wearing. When I saw the American flag, I thought, 'We're in America now. They're going to treat me well here.'"

Chapter 3

GUANTÁNAMO

Pushed to the Breaking Point

On January 11, 2002, a cargo plane holding 20 detainees from Afghanistan landed at the U.S. naval base in Guantánamo Bay, Cuba, the first of many detainee transfers that eventually swelled the camp population at its height to over 600. Hooded and wearing earmuffs, detainees felt a blast of hot, humid air as they were escorted off the plane by U.S. soldiers, hustled onto a bus, and transported across the water by a ferry to a large building, part of the detention center located on the southeast corner of the 45-square-mile base. Once inside, detainees encountered a beehive of activity similar to their processing at Kandahar and Bagram. Camp personnel removed their outer clothing and earmuffs, lowered their goggles, and cut off their clothes. "[S]omeone was taking fingerprints," a former detainee recalled.

> There was another person swabbing for DNA. Someone's snapping photos. And someone else was doing the internal examination and other stuff. There were so many soldiers watching or standing around, I don't know what they were all doing. But in front of everybody they just, like, cut off all our clothes.

Detainees were taken to communal showers, the first in months for many, where soldiers scrubbed them with stiff brushes and gave them undergarments and orange jumpsuits. The final stop was a table where

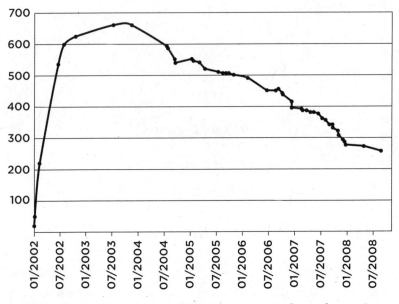

Figure 3. Reported population at Guantánamo, 2002 to September 2008.

Sources: From 2003 onward, population numbers were drawn from U.S. Department of Defense press releases (published online at http://www.defenselink.mil/releases). For 2002, population numbers were based on three sources: CNN, "Shackled Detainees Arrive in Guantánamo," January 11, 2002; Worthington, Andy, *The Guantánamo Files: The Stories of the 774 Detainees in America's Illegal Prison* (London: Pluto Press, 2007); and GlobalSecurity.org, "Guantánamo Bay Detainees," http://www.globalsecurity .org/military/facility/guantanamo-bay_detainees.htm.

the detainees were given a chance to write a letter home. One former detainee recalled his complaints to a guard that his hand shackles made it difficult to write: "I said to the guard, 'So, how am I supposed to write?' And he said: 'With your hands.' And I replied, 'Well, they're tied . . . so there's no point in me writing is there?'"

Over the next four years, U.S. military planes would deliver more than 770 detainees to the camp.[1] Most detainees were identified as nationals of Afghanistan (221), Saudi Arabia (140), Yemen (110), or Pakistan (70).[2] The camp population peaked at 660 in July 2003[3] and began to decline in November of that year (Figure 3). In October 2008, approximately 255

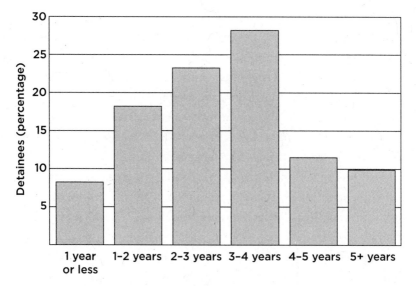

Figure 4. Length of time former detainees report spending at Guantánamo.

Source: Based on interviews with 62 former detainees conducted in 2007–2008. Interviewee sample was nonrandom and recruited through local NGOs in countries where the researchers could obtain visas. In most cases length of detention is based on self-report (and due to anonymity has not been officially verified).

Note: Afghan calendar dates were converted to Roman dates when necessary.

detainees remained at Guantánamo.[4] In addition, there is a separate facility at the base, "Camp 7," that reportedly houses approximately 15 "high value" detainees and about which little is known.[5] The average length of detention at Guantánamo of our respondents was approximately three years (36.8 months), although others, including some detainees who remain, have been held there for six years or longer (Figure 4).

CAMP MANAGEMENT

When the first detainees arrived at Guantánamo, responsibility for camp operations and interrogations was split between two units. Brigadier General Rick Baccus headed Joint Task Force 160, which administered the camp. Major General Michael E. Dunlavey commanded Joint Task Force 170, which was in charge of interrogations.[6] The two generals reportedly clashed; Baccus was accused of being "soft" on detainees and Dunlavey pressed for more stringent interrogation techniques. In November 2002, the Pentagon reorganized the camp structure and merged the administrative and interrogation task forces into a single unit, "Joint Task Force 160/170," and appointed Major General Geoffrey Miller as its commander.

Many respondents remarked that conditions changed significantly when General Miller assumed command. Miller, a two-star general from Texas with an "air of supreme confidence,"[7] developed specialized interrogation teams "that for the first time integrated military intelligence personnel with the military police guard force—blurring a line that had previously been impermeable in the Army."[8] He also employed military and civilian behavioral scientists to look for "psychological vulnerabilities, soft spots, ways to manipulate the detainees . . . to get them to cooperate, and [look] for . . . psychic vulnerabilities and cultural vulnerabilities."[9] Miller made intelligence gathering the organizing principle of the camp and in the process, turned it into what historian Alfred McCoy termed "a veritable behavioral-scientific laboratory."[10]

Miller used guards to support interrogation by having them "set the conditions" or soften up detainees before they were questioned.[11] Miller also instituted what he called a "level system," to distinguish detainees. Detainees were classified into one of four levels and issued "comfort items" and privileges based on the extent of their cooperation with interrogators. Level 1 status was for the most "compliant" detainees, who were allowed to wear a white—considered a "higher status" color in Muslim culture—jumpsuit and to possess comfort items such as a prayer mat or personal roll of toilet paper.[12] Level 4 detainees were those considered most "defiant." They wore orange jumpsuits and were denied a sheet and a mattress, which were considered comfort items.[13] Detainees could also be categorized as Level 5 for "intelligence gathering purposes"

International law provides clear guidelines for the treatment of prisoners of war. The Geneva Conventions establish that a captured soldier is not a criminal, but "merely an enemy no longer able to bear arms"[1] and as such is not subject to torture or coercion and is entitled to minimum due process protections before being sentenced.[2] President Bush determined that suspected Taliban and Al Qaeda fighters would not have the benefit of Geneva protections; nevertheless, he stated they were to be treated in a humane manner consistent with their underlying "principles."[3] In a June 2006 decision, *Hamdan v. Rumsfeld,* the Supreme Court ruled that under the Geneva Conventions Guantánamo detainees were entitled to certain minimum due process protections afforded to non-combatants facing criminal charges.[4] However, no court has ruled on whether the conditions of confinement at the base meet the Geneva Convention requirements.[5]

[1]International Committee of the Red Cross, *The Geneva Conventions of August 12, 1949, Preliminary Remarks,* 12, available at http://www.icrc.org/Web/eng/siteeng0.nsf/htmlall/57JNJG?OpenDocument&View=defaultBody&style=custo_print (accessed October 3, 2008). The Conventions require parties to a conflict to distinguish between civilians and combatants. The treatment of combatants who have been captured during conflict is governed by the Third Geneva Convention. International Committee of the Red Cross, *Convention (III) Relative to the Treatment of Prisoners of War. Geneva, 12 August 1949,* available at http://www.icrc.org/ihl.nsf/7c4d08d9b287a42141256739003e63bb/6fef854a3517b75ac125641e004a9e68 (accessed October 3, 2008). The treatment of civilians during conflict is governed by the Fourth Geneva Convention. International Committee of the Red Cross, *Convention (IV) Relative to the Protection of Civilian Persons in Time of War. Geneva, 12 August 1949,* available at http://www.icrc.org/ihl.nsf/385ec082b509e76c41256739003e636d/6756482d86146898c125641e004aa3c5 (accessed October 3, 2008). Civilians and combatants who have put down arms are to be treated humanely. Ibid., art. 3.

[2]Geneva Convention III, arts. 3, 17, 99.

[3]See *Memorandum from President George W. Bush,* February 7, 2002, reprinted in Jameel Jaffer and Amrit Singh, *Administration of Torture: A Documentary Record from Washington to Abu Ghraib and Beyond* (New York: Columbia University Press, 2007), A-6, also available at http://www.pegc.us/archive/White_House/bush_memo_20020207_ed.pdf (accessed October 8, 2008).

[4]*Hamdan v. Rumsfeld,* 548 U.S. 557 (2006), available at http://www.supremecourtus.gov/opinions/05pdf/05-184.pdf (accessed on July 15, 2008).

[5]*In Re Guantánamo Bay Litigation,* No. 1-05-cv-01509-UNA (D.D.C. 2008), Memorandum Opinion Denying the Petitioners' Motion for a Temporary Restraining Order and Denying the Petitioners' Motion for a Preliminary Injunction.

by interrogators and housed in a segregated intelligence block.[14] Miller left the naval base in March 2004 to serve in Iraq,[15] but his level system continued to be practiced at Guantánamo.

Several respondents said that after Miller's arrival at the camp interrogators seemed to have greater control of the conditions and treatment of detainees on the blocks. A respondent, reflecting the views of other former detainees, explained:

> The guards used to work together with the interrogators. Everything you did in your cage, they noted. . . . Your interrogator tells the guards what they need to do with you. For example, there's an interrogator who plays the "good guy." . . . He knows I like motorcycles. . . . So he tells me, "I have a nice motorcycle magazine. You can have it, you can keep it in your cell." So I take the magazine and go back to my cell. But he tells the guards who are taking me [out of the interrogation booth] to take the magazine away from me. So at the next interrogation he says, "What, they took your magazine away? . . . I don't know why they did that, they are bad people, they are stupid," and so on. . . . "I will get you a new magazine." And so you are supposed to think, "Oh, he's a nice guy, he's just trying to help me."

At Guantánamo there were a number of sources personnel were to rely on for knowing what procedures to follow with detainees. While the Army Field Manual and individual camp orders provided some guidance, another set of prime sources for U.S. military personnel has been the Standard Operating Procedures Manuals (SOPs) for Guantánamo, generally issued for a specific time period. They provide instructions for soldiers stationed at the site, including procedures for processing, feeding, and restraining detainees. SOPs are typically not publicly available, but the manuals for 2003 and 2004 were leaked in 2007[16] and thus provide a glimpse into day-to-day guidelines for at least those two years—a period during which most of the respondents in this study were detained at the base. In addition to these sources, authorities at the base issued more specific orders to personnel regarding camp operations and administration. Such orders were issued more frequently than SOPs; one former guard said that at times orders were updated daily or even between shifts.

The Camp Delta SOPs specified that detainees were to be placed in isolation cells for four weeks as part of a "Behavior Management Plan" as soon as they arrived at the camp.[17] Major goals of isolation were to foster detainees' dependence on their interrogators and "to enhance and exploit the disorientation and disorganization felt by a newly arrived detainee," by denying access to the Quran, mail, and by preventing visits with ICRC representatives, until interrogators decided to integrate them into the cellblocks. It was permissible, according to the SOP manuals for detainees during this period, to have "No access. No contact of any kind with the ICRC."[18]

Many respondents indeed commented that they had been held in isolation when they arrived. "There was a small window on the door [of the isolation cell], where guards slipped us our food," recalled one. "Some soldiers would leave the window open for five minutes, which would make us very happy. Sometimes at night we could hear strange voices. There was a prisoner beside my cell who became mentally ill." A few reported being put into isolation for over thirty days in conjunction with interrogation.

THE CELLBLOCKS

The detainees who arrived at Guantánamo in the early months of 2002 were initially housed in a facility called Camp X-Ray.[19] The camp consisted of 8′ × 6′ wire-mesh cages connected by a corrugated metal roof, while a row of wooden shacks served as interrogation rooms. The open cages made them feel as if they were living outdoors, several former detainees said. As one respondent put it:

> When the rain came in, it fell on our heads, even if we were standing. . . . Small animals—like scorpions, tarantulas, mice, rats, and snakes—would wander in, so we made hammocks with our sheets to sleep in, even though we weren't allowed to. . . . Each cell had two buckets. One was for water, which was full of chlorine so it was difficult to drink. The second was a latrine bucket. You had to go to the toilet in front of everybody. After a couple of days, you would stain yourself with your stuff. . . . We were given a towel, blanket, sheet, soap, and a little bottle of shampoo. The toothbrush had a sawed off handle. . . . And we lived like that for three months.

Some guards even prohibited detainees from stretching their towels across the wire walls for privacy or to shade themselves from the glaring sun. As the number of weeks grew, so did feelings of dread and hope-lessness. "I thought I was in a dream, like a nightmare," said one respondent. "I was very far away; I was in a very different climate; and I was thinking that I would never go home. I was hoping for an earthquake to either kill us all or to open up the cells."

In April 2002, Camp X-Ray was closed and the detainees were moved to Camp Delta, which would eventually contain over 800 cells. Today, Camp X-Ray is all but abandoned, filled with weeds and wasp nests.[20] Cellblocks at Camp Delta consist of two rows of shipping containers, creating 19 cellblocks with 48 cells each. Each cell has a metal bed, toilet, a sink with running water, and a single wall of green wire mesh through which detainees can see those in adjacent cells.[21] The cells offer no privacy and many respondents complained about the constant scrutiny of guards. Some respondents found conditions in Camp Delta the same as or harsher than those at Camp X-Ray. When the rains came, a respondent said, "the person at the end [of the Delta cellblock] would be in real trouble, because his cage was exposed at the side. . . . I was at the end once, and got drenched. Your towel's wet, your blanket's all wet. Your sheets are wet. You're all wet. You've got no dry clothes. Your bunk's wet, and you can't sleep." Small animals, just as at Camp X-Ray, would come into the cells. "We even had snakes coming in . . . they were grass snakes, but even so." Detainees spent virtually all their non-interrogation time in their cells. Said one former detainee: "Every week I was taken out for 15 minutes for exercise, and I was given five minutes a week to go to the shower stalls, and wash myself. . . . The whole time I was shackled."

Camp Delta itself was divided into several sub-camps, including Camp Echo and Camps 1 through 6. Camp Echo, which housed detainees the military initially designated for prosecution by specially created military commissions but later housed other detainees as well, was a collection of shacks situated in a separate part of the base.[22] Camp 3 served as a punishment unit where detainees were held in isolation.[23] In Camp 1, the cell conditions were essentially the same as in Camp 3, but detainees were housed next to one another so they could communicate.[24]

As of August 2008, Camp 4 housed approximately 75 detainees classified as most cooperative or awaiting release.[25] Detainees lived there in dormitory fashion, ten to a room; they were responsible for maintaining their own living quarters and ate communally.[26]

While none of the respondents we interviewed had spent time in Camps 5, 6, or 7, these camps were also used to house detainees. Camps 5 and 6 were constructed as permanent facilities modeled after U.S. high-security prisons. The conditions of isolation in these camps were more severe than those in mainland U.S. "super-max" facilities which often subject prisoners to near total isolation for years on end.[27] As of August 2008, a reported 50 detainees were housed in Camp 5 and 75 in Camp 6, several for over a year in one camp or the other.[28] The location of Camp 7 on the base has not been disclosed, but it allegedly houses approximately 15 detainees transferred from CIA custody and is operated by a separate command.[29]

Another detention facility at Guantánamo, known as Camp Iguana, originally housed juvenile detainees aged 13 to 15.[30] Three child detainees, all under the age of sixteen, were held there and subsequently released. Camp Iguana was shut down in the winter of 2004 but reopened in 2005 to hold detainees classified as "No Longer an Enemy Combatant," meaning they were no longer considered a security threat.[31] Several respondents remarked on the improved conditions at the new facility: the food was better, they were able to watch movies and walk outside, and they could see the ocean.

SOCIAL RELATIONS

The nearly 800 individuals known to have been held at Guantánamo since its opening have represented 46 different countries.[32] While almost all are Muslim, they otherwise have been quite diverse in languages spoken, cultural traditions, and range of opinion.[33] This diversity made for a variety in the social relations that developed among detainees within the restrictive environment of the camp.

Relations among Detainees

Many respondents commented that fate had united them to their fellow detainees. "Basically everyone in an orange jumpsuit was in the same situation as me," said one. Another said developing supportive relationships was imperative: "You empathize with the people immediately around you and if not you would go crazy immediately. It's unavoidable, just to survive." A well-educated Afghan respondent described how he used his time in Camp 4, where detainees live communally, to school fellow detainees: "I taught 24 Afghan prisoners how to read and write. Then I taught them the Quran, Arabic, English, Persian, and mathematics. So I didn't have much free time there."

For some, even those allowed to fraternize, the lack of a common language and frequent relocation of detainees reportedly made establishing friendships difficult. Indeed, one reason the military moved detainees was "to disrupt the informal leadership" that officials said developed.[34] Serious antagonisms among detainees also emerged. Three Afghan respondents described being ostracized by Arab detainees for having opposed the Taliban regime and Al Qaeda. Initially the Arab extremists refused to speak to the "non-Taliban, non-extremist" detainee, and ended by throwing human waste at him and demanding that the guards move the "infidel" from the block, only for the detainee to endure a repeat of the same process wherever in the camp the detainee was transferred.

Relations between Detainees and Guantánamo Personnel

The tightly regulated environment at Guantánamo of course heavily influenced relations between detainees and their captors. The dynamics of this relationship were initiated in Kandahar and Bagram, re-affirmed during admission processing at Guantánamo, and reified by the rules and regulations that governed the behavior of detainees and soldiers alike. The sociologist Erving Goffman in his pioneering work on closed institutions notes that in prisons, the boundary between staff and inmates is often impermeable and characterized by mutual antagonism.

"Each grouping," he writes, "tends to conceive of the other in terms of narrow hostile stereotypes, staff often seeing inmates as bitter, secretive, and untrustworthy, while inmates often see staff as condescending, high-handed, and mean."[35] Required to dress in a standard uniform and be referred to by a number rather than name,[36] detainees became depersonalized in the eyes of guards, making it easy to view the detainees as less than human. Virtually all of the former detainees we interviewed said they felt diminished and humiliated by the regime at Guantánamo. One respondent put it this way:

> They tried to do everything to push our human dignity down, to really push it down. I wouldn't go as far as saying that we were treated like animals, because we were fed and everything, but I had a feeling that this was a totally new situation for [the soldiers] and that they were experimenting on us, that they didn't know what to do. . . . They were watching us constantly and noting everything we did. It was like we were subjects of a scientific study. And we were just a number.

Harsh or arbitrary imposition of petty camp regulations at Guantánamo in the view of several former detainees served no effect but to remind detainees of their powerlessness. As one respondent explained:

> [W]e were given five minutes to bathe ourselves. When we entered the bathing area, we would apply shampoo and soap to our bodies—all of which would take one or two minutes. Three minutes were supposed to be left, but the guards would call out, "Time is up!" And we would reply, "Wait, only two minutes have passed. . . . To which the guards would reply, "No, no, no, get out, get out." Is it possible to take your clothes off in one minute? And how it is possible to apply shampoo and soap on the whole body in one minute?

Another former detainee told of this incident in his cellblock:

> So I washed my shirt. . . . And I asked a guard on the morning shift if it was okay to hang it here. And the guard said, "Sure, no problem, you can hang it there." . . . Then the afternoon guy came in and said, "Take that down. . . . You can't hang that there." So I replied, "Well, the morning guy said it was

okay." To which he said: "Well, this is the afternoon, and if the morning guy told you it was okay that's him, and this is me . . . take it down."

A former guard interviewed for this study described the role guards played in fostering animosity at the camp:

> [T]he established social rule was that we were going to be as mean as possible [to the detainees] and deny them as much as possible, that we weren't going to talk [to them] at all as human beings. . . . Whenever any of the guards talked to the detainees, they would yell for the most part. Yeah, just a generally very aggressive environment. . . . Anything that [guards] could slip in like any little hits or, you know, derisive statements, they'd do it. . . . Like every little bullshit thing that detainees did, guards would write them up for it. . . . Detainees would go back a level and lose some comfort items. Guards would just do everything to make the detainee's life worse.

Former Guantánamo personnel interviewed for this study said that relations between guards and detainees were often tense. This was especially true in the first year of the camp's operation, according to a former interpreter. She noted that guards thought "every single person there was the one who is responsible for [the 9/11 attacks]. Maybe [a guard] from New York had had a friend who died in the World Trade Center bombing . . . so they came in with lots of hatred and retaliation."[37] This tension was exacerbated by the fact that guards lacked information about the detainees. A former guard put it this way: "[T]he big dilemma for the soldiers was well, is this person genuinely and truly responsible for killing American soldiers, is this person truly and genuinely responsible for 9/11?" He noted that the guards had no access to detainee files, and that the training sessions and other information provided to orient camp personnel to the camp population portrayed detainees as "violent, dangerous people." Another interpreter related an incident in a training session in which a soldier role-played an arriving detainee by acting like "a very dangerous animal." She, too, participated in the role-playing. "I figured that at the end it had affected me a lot," she said. "You know how to shout at detainees, how to react to them. . . . It was terrible."

Respondents described various "strategies" for dealing with guards, ranging from silent submission to outright hostility. A few, however, managed to develop a rapport with some guards, confirming Goffman's observation that "every total institution seems to develop a set of institutionalized practices—whether spontaneously or by imitation—through which staff and inmates come close enough together to get a somewhat favorable image of the other and to identify sympathetically with the other's situation."[38] Such "rapport-building" was of course usually easier if the detainee spoke English. One former detainee recalled how a guard came to his cell and apologized for what the U.S. government had done to him. "But if I say anything," the guard reportedly told the former detainee, "I could end up in the cell next to you. And this is my job. I joined the army so and so years ago, and this is what I have to do."

The 2003 and 2004 SOPs at Guantánamo underscored the need from the military's point of view to maintain a psychological distance between guards and detainees. Specifically forbidden were "idle chatter and small talk" or any other form of fraternization.[39] A former guard told us that he was reassigned from his duty guarding a cellblock because he was seen as too friendly with inmates. "I just talked to them about their personal lives," he said. "That's not a breach of official camp policy, but it was a breach of many of the operating procedures of some units."

Religious Practice

The right to religious practice is recognized in almost all prison systems worldwide.[40] The Geneva Conventions stipulate that prisoners of war "shall have complete latitude in the exercise of their religious duties."[41] The U.S. military's 2004 SOP for Guantánamo's Camp Delta contained extensive regulations on the role of military personnel with respect to the religious practices of detainees. Personnel were directed to "avoid touching a detainee's [Quran] whenever possible" and admonished that "anyone disrespecting the [Quran] most likely will get no cooperation and could provoke a violent reaction from detainees."[42] If a copy of the

Quran must be handled, "clean gloves [must] be used in full view of detainees prior to handling," and care be taken "so that the right hand is the primary one used to manipulate any part of the [Quran] due to the cultural association with the left hand." The Quran furthermore should not be "placed in offensive areas such as the floor, near the toilet or sink, near the feet, or dirty/wet areas."[43] Guantánamo personnel were directed to provide each detainee with a surgical mask to be suspended from the cell wall and serve as a cradle for the Quran.

Many respondents reported that they were able to pray freely at Guantánamo. One, in particular, said a guard even woke him, as he had requested, for the pre-dawn prayer. Still, a significant number described incidents where guards disrespected the Quran or interfered with their religious practices. Such abuses included mocking detainees as they prayed, and singing, playing loud music, or conducting cell searches at prayer time. Many former detainees complained of being prevented from praying or being interrupted while praying, our database of media reports confirms.[44]

Of the 33 respondents in our study who discussed treatment of the Quran, 13 reported that they directly witnessed military personnel leave the Quran on the floor.[45] In five of these instances, respondents claimed soldiers also stepped on or kicked the Quran.

One respondent said that on several occasions guards entered his cell and picked up his Quran:

> They would open it to a certain page and look through it and then throw it very forcefully across the floor. That's very offensive to us because it's a holy book, it's a clean book, its a book that you're not supposed to touch if you haven't done your ablution. So I would tell the guards, "Let me just open it for you, please don't touch it." But they wouldn't listen to me. . . . Other times they would pour water on the Qurans or throw them on the floor, and we would bang on the cells to try to get them to stop.

Interference with religious practice and desecration of the Quran at times led to cellblock protests, hunger strikes, and attempted suicides. One former detainee described a two-week hunger strike, also mentioned by several others, organized in response to the mishandling of the Quran in Camp X-Ray in February 2002:

> One of the prisoners was praying and a soldier began banging on his cage. Our prison jumpsuits had slits in the back of the trousers, and when we prayed we would tie a towel around our waist. So this prisoner was praying with a towel on and the soldier kept banging on the cell saying "take the towel off." You have to understand that once we're praying we can't really stop until the prayer is finished. This is all taking place about 40 meters away from me, and I'm shouting to the soldier let him finish and then he'll take it off. But the soldier ignores me. . . . Eventually he opened the cage door, threw the prisoner on the floor, and took his towel off . . . and then left. That's what sparked the hunger strike.

Former Army Captain Yee, in his book about the six months he served as a Muslim chaplain at Guantánamo, confirmed some of the reports of religious abuse reported by respondents.[46] He described guards mocking detainees during prayer, intentionally stepping on the Quran during cell searches, breaking the bindings on detainees' holy books, and writing "English profanities" on the pages.[47]

In one particularly vivid incident, Yee describes what happened when detainees learned that an interrogator threw a copy of the Quran on the floor during an interrogation session and stepped on it. To protest the desecration, detainees organized a mass suicide attempt which caught the authorities by surprise:

> Once every fifteen minutes, a prisoner tried to hang himself by tying his sheet around his neck and fastening it through the mesh of the cage wall. . . . The scene was chaotic. The prisoners on the block would yell and bang their cage doors and the guards would rush up and down the corridor calling for medics and trying to shackle the man who attempted the suicide. As soon as the prisoner was taken to the hospital, another detainee would be found . . . and the chaos would start again.[48]

A respondent described his role in this incident:

> As a result of the insult of the Holy Quran I decided to commit suicide. I tried to hang myself by the neck. . . . I was then taken to the hospital. When

I was asked why I had done it, I said I couldn't tolerate the insult and desecration of the Holy Quran. . . . Afterwards when I was taken to Delta block
[for mentally ill detainees] . . . I learned 28 more people had also tried to
commit suicide like me.

Our media database also suggests a pattern of Quran abuse within
Guantánamo. That database includes reports of religious victimization
such as insults and harassment from more than ten percent of the named
former detainees. One former detainee described how he was served
alcohol-laced drinks, even though alcohol is forbidden by Islam;[49]
another said guards tried to feed him a hot plate of pork.[50] Finally,
although forced shaving was mandatory upon entry to Guantánamo, the
media database includes reports of five former detainees who said they
had been subjected to this again later simply as punishment even though
shaving is against their religion.

Against this background, it is significant that over a third of the
respondents said that their faith and practice of Islam helped them cope
with their time in detention. As expressed by one respondent: "Islam
teaches us a lot about patience and prayer. Be patient and God will take
care of you, so my faith and prayer kept me going." Others found
strength in a community of Muslims. One former detainee attributed
the survival of many to "our connection to the Holy Quran and also to
the cooperation and togetherness that we had with prisoners."

INTERROGATIONS

All former detainees we interviewed said they had been interrogated at
Guantánamo. Some said they were interrogated daily or several times a
week for weeks on end, others were questioned regularly and then the
questioning would stop and months would pass before they were sum-
moned back to the interrogation booth. By January 2005, interrogators
were reportedly questioning less than a third of detainees actively.[51]
Most respondents said multiple teams of interrogators—some in military uniform, others in civilian dress—questioned them. Some sessions

took place at night. According to Col. (Ret.) Larry C. James, an Army psychologist stationed at Guantánamo in early 2003, nighttime interrogations served "to screw with the prisoner's head, to keep him off balance when he was tired."[52] Several respondents commented that various interrogators repeated the same questions, leaving the impression that their answers had not been recorded. A former translator at the base said the rotation of interrogators was inefficient, and each new team of interrogators started from scratch, corroborating this perspective:

> Each [new interrogator] will present himself as the one who's in charge of [a detainee's] case, like "I'm the one who's going to set you free or I am the one who's going to take care of your case and close your records." Then, after a couple of months, a different person comes in and says the same thing. I was the one translating and I felt uncomfortable because, you know, I felt like I was lying, although I was just translating for them.

Camp officials used a variety of tactics, in addition to apportioning relative detainee privileges through the classification system, to induce detainees to cooperate with interrogators. One respondent described the posters mounted around the camp depicting the passage of time in the life of a family. One poster, for example, showed the life cycle of a young girl—the first frame depicted her as a little girl, the second as an adolescent female, until the last frame showed her wedding day. Above it was the caption: "When will you come home, Daddy? Cooperate and you'll see me. I'm going to get married. Where will you be?" The posters reportedly had their desired effect on detainees who had children. A respondent said he saw fathers moved to tears by the posters: "I could see by looking at prisoners who were fathers that it was affecting them. . . . And [the camp authorities] had a whole series of posters. . . . One with the mother, or the daughter, or the son."

Some respondents pointed out that guards and other camp personnel seemed to work in tandem with interrogators.[53] One former detainee said that guards on his cellblock gave him bandages to treat a wounded toe. His interrogator noticed the bandage and asked if he would like to see a doctor. The former detainee said, "No, that's all right, the guards are giving me everything I need." When he returned to his cell, the guards ordered that he return the bandages and refused to provide him with new ones.

A few said they deliberately withheld information about their medical conditions for fear that their interrogators would use it against them. General Miller's integrated approach to interrogation and camp administration relied on this information sharing. Shortly after his arrival, Col. Larry James learned that interrogators were going to the medical clinic and demanding unhindered access to detainees' medical records:

> What I discovered was that on any given day, FBI, CIA, Army, Navy, and contract interrogators would go to the hospital and demand to see detainees' records immediately. If any doctor or nurse hesitated—and they naturally would as medical practitioners—these interrogators, some of them only eighteen or twenty years old, would simply walk into the medical records room and help themselves.

Both the Army Field Manual and Geneva Conventions prohibit basing a detainee's access to medical care on his cooperation with interrogators.[54] Two former detainees said that their interrogators had in fact conditioned access to medical care on providing satisfactory answers to their questions. "I had a toothache at Camp X-Ray [and] . . . the interrogators tried to use it as a weapon," one of these detainees reported. "They said, 'If you tell me this, if you sign this, then we can help you, we can get you a dentist, or you can go home and see a dentist at home.' I never saw a dentist until they released me five years later." An attorney interviewed for this study described how his client's medical treatment was predicated on his responses during interrogations: "One of our clients [was] a double amputee and he didn't have properly fitting prosthetics and every time he asked for them he was told he'd have to get them through his interrogators—they were conditioning medical treatment on his confessing to something."

Figure 5 *(opposite)*. Criminal Investigation Task Force memo referring to the role of medical personnel in interrogations.

Rhodes, Barry A

From:	Zolper, Peter C
Sent:	Wednesday, August 27, 2003 4:02 PM
To:	Fallon, Mark
Cc:	Rhodes, Barry A

Subject: (U) RE: Counter Resistance Strategy Meeting Minutes

Classification: UNCLASSIFIED//FOR OFFICIAL USE ONLY

Barry

-----Original Message-----
From: Fallon, Mark
Sent: Wednesday, August 27, 2003 12:46 PM
To: Zolper, Peter C
Subject: FW: Counter Resistance Strategy Meeting Minutes

R/Mark Fallon
Deputy Commander/SAC

-----Original Message-----
From: Fallon Mark
Sent: Monday, October 28, 2002 4:52 PM
To: McCahon Sam
Cc: Mallow Brittain; Thomas Blaine; Johnson Scott; Smith David
Subject: RE: Counter Resistance Strategy Meeting Minutes

Sam:

We need to ensure seniors at OGC are aware of the 170 strategies and how it might impact CITF and Commissions. This looks like the kinds of stuff Congressional hearings are made of. Quotes from LTC Beaver regarding things that are not being reported give the appearance of impropriety. Other comments like "It is basically subject to perception. If the detainee dies you're doing it wrong" and "Any of the techniques that lie on the harshest end of the spectrum must be performed by a highly trained individual. Medical personnel should be present to treat any possible accidents." seem to stretch beyond the bounds of legal propriety. Talk of "wet towel treatment" which results in the lymphatic gland reacting as if you are suffocating, would in my opinion; shock the conscience of any legal body looking at using the results of the interrogations or possibly even the interrogators. Someone needs to be considering how history will look back at this.

R/Mark Fallon
Deputy Commander
Criminal Investigation Task Force

In recent years, three leading American medical and psychological associations have adopted resolutions banning or re-affirming past bans on the participation of medical and psychological personnel in interrogations. In his book *Fixing Hell,* Col. (Ret.) Larry C. James, an Army psychologist who was sent to Guantánamo in January 2003, recalled his first meeting with a fellow Army psychologist and colleague who served on the Behavioral Science and Consultation Team (BSCT),[1] a special behavioral science unit formed to work with interrogators: "[He] welcomed me as a familiar face, a fellow medical practitioner, and a superior he trusted. I could tell he needed to talk . . . Within the first thirty minutes . . . his eyes began to tear up. He told me he felt that he had received increasing pressure to teach interrogation procedures and tactics that were a challenge to his ethics as a psychologist and moral fiber as a human being. . . . He witnessed many harsh and inhumane interrogation tactics, such as sexual humiliation, stress positions, detainees being stripped naked, and the use of K-9 dogs to terrorize detainees. He had no command authority, meaning he felt as though he had no legal right to tell anyone what to do or not to do. There were no guidelines or reference books he could refer to, nor old college professors he could consult. This young officer was dropped into this horrible situation without the training, informational background, senior military rank, or experience that would be necessary to derail this broken downhill train."[2]

Although apparently alarmed by what his colleague had witnessed, James chose to stay on at Guantánamo for a few months working with BSCT personnel and interrogators until early May 2003.[3] Many psychologists have strongly criticized the BSCT program and those practitioners who have participated in it.[4] A principal BSCT function was to engineer the camp experiences of "priority" detainees to make interrogation more productive. BSCT personnel coached interrogators on how to stress, coerce, and offer incentives to secure information from detainees. BSCT personnel "prepared psychological profiles [of detainees] for use by interrogators; they also sat in on some interrogations, observed others from behind one-way mirrors, and offered feedback to interrogators."[5] Army medical personnel also provided

[1] See M. Gregg Bloche and Jonathan H. Marks, "Doctors and Interrogators at Guantánamo Bay," *New England Journal of Medicine,* 353 (2005): 6-8.

[2] James, *Fixing Hell,* 39.

[3] Ibid., 72.

[4] Bloche and Marks, "Doctors and Interrogators at Guantánamo Bay."

[5] Ibid.

medical information to interrogators.[6] In a confidential report, the International Committee for the Red Cross called the participation of doctors in designing interrogation plans a "flagrant violation of medical ethics."[7] In 2006, in response to publicity about the clinical participation in coercive interrogations at Guantánamo, the American Medical Association and the American Psychiatric Association endorsed more stringent guidelines for military doctors and psychiatrists who are asked to participate in interrogations.[8] In 2008, after several years of often acrimonious debate, members of the American Psychological Association voted to prohibit consultation by its members in the interrogations of detainees held at Guantánamo or so-called "black sites" operated by the CIA overseas.[9]

[6]Ibid. Bloche and Marks note: "An internal, May 24, 2005, memo from the Army Medical Command, offering guidance to caregivers responsible for detainees, refers to the 'interpretation of relevant excerpts from medical records' for the purpose of 'assistance with the interrogation process.' The memo, provided to us by a military source, acknowledges this nontherapeutic role, urging health professionals who serve in this capacity to avoid involvement in detainee care, absent an emergency." According to Amnesty International, "Such practices are a gross violation of international standards which state that it is a breach of medical ethics for health personnel to be involved in any professional relationship with prisoners or detainees the purpose of which is not solely to evaluate, protect or improve their physical or mental health." Amnesty International, *Cruel and Inhuman*, 23. Also see *UN Principles of Medical Ethics relevant to the Role of Health Personnel, particularly Physicians, in the Protection of Prisoners and Detainees against Torture and Other Cruel, Inhuman or Degrading Treatment or Punishment* (adopted by General Assembly resolution 37/194 of 18 December 1982).

[7]Jane Mayer, *The Dark Side: The Inside Story of How the War on Terror Turned into a War on American Ideals* (New York: Doubleday, 2008), 210.

[8]See American Medical Association Council on Ethical and Judicial Affairs, *Statement on Interrogation of Prisoners* (July 7, 2006), available at http://pn.psychiatryonline.org/cgi/content/full/41/13/4-a (accessed July 30, 2008). The AMA statement provides: "Physicians must neither conduct nor directly participate in an interrogation, because a role as physician-interrogator undermines the physician's role as healer and thereby erodes trust in both the individual physician-interrogator and in the medical profession. Physicians should not monitor interrogations with the intention of intervening in the process, because this constitutes direct participation in interrogation. Physicians may participate in developing effective interrogation strategies that are not coercive but are humane and respect the rights of individuals." Also see American Psychiatric Association, *Psychiatric Participation in Interrogation of Detainees* (May 21, 2006), available at http://pn.psychiatryonline.org/cgi/content/full/41/12/1-b (accessed July 30, 2008). The APA resolution states: "No psychiatrist should participate directly in the interrogation of persons held in custody by military or civilian investigative or law enforcement authorities, whether in the United States or elsewhere. Direct participation includes being present in the interrogation room, asking or suggesting questions, or advising authorities on the use of specific techniques of interrogation with particular detainees. However, psychiatrists may provide training to military or civilian investigative or law enforcement personnel on recognizing and responding to persons with mental illnesses, on the possible medical and psychological effects of particular techniques and conditions of interrogation, and on other areas within their professional expertise."

[9]The referendum prohibits psychologists from working in settings where "persons are held outside of, or in violation of, either International Law (e.g. U.N. Convention Against Torture and the Geneva Conventions) or the U.S. Constitution, where appropriate," unless they represent a detainee or an independent third party. The association's bylaws require that it institute the policy at the next annual meeting in August 2009. See Benedict Carey, "Psychologists Vote to End Interrogation Consultations," *New York Times*, September 18, 2008. It should be noted that Col. Larry C. James was a member of an APA task force created in 2005 to evaluate the professional ethics of members' participation in interrogations.

Another respondent said interrogators told him and other detainees they would only receive family mail if they cooperated with interrogators: "They used letters against you. . . . They would say, 'You cooperate and we'll give you [your mail]. Look it's yours. It's got your name. It's your mom's handwriting'—or your dad's or your brother's. 'Talk to us and we'll give it to you.' They want something from you, but you can't give in because it's not you, it's not your story. And then they would walk away. And they would keep on coming back, saying, 'Here's the last chance, last chance.'"

ABUSIVE TREATMENT

Respondents reported widely varying treatment during interrogation sessions at Guantánamo. Of the 55 respondents who discussed their interrogation sessions at the prison, 24 said they did not experience any problems. A few said their interrogators were "very nice," and one commented that his interrogator "was a very nice and very good woman. . . . She provided me with shampoo, toothbrush, and oil for my hair." He did not elaborate whether or not he received these items because he cooperated with the interrogator. Over half (31) of the respondents who discussed their interrogation sessions at Guantánamo, however, characterized them as abusive.

Short Shackling and Stress Positions

Twelve of the former detainees said they were subjected on one or more occasions to painful shackling and stress positions during questioning. Nearly 15 percent of identified former detainees in the media database (32) reported that they had been shackled in painful positions for hours while at Guantánamo. As previously described, Secretary of Defense Rumsfeld specifically approved the use of shackling and stress positions in a December 2, 2002, memo;[55] the memo was rescinded on January 15, 2003.[56] While many of our respondents were in Guantánamo during that time period, our data suggest that short shackling and other stress positions were used both prior to and following that window, a conclusion that is supported by the media reports[57] and has been corroborated by the OIG/FBI Report and other military investigations.[58]

Many respondents said they were questioned by interrogators and then left sitting alone in a chair or on the floor for hours, hunched over with their hands and feet short shackled to a metal ring in the floor. Two respondents said this treatment occurred after they had repeatedly denied allegations by their interrogators that they were terrorists, which their interrogators deemed evidence that they were not "cooperating." One former detainee said he was left shackled and alone in the room, once for a full day, and his interrogator returned periodically to ask: "Are you ready to confess yet?" According to the OIG/DOG Report: "Over 30 FBI agents told investigators with the Department of Justice that they saw or heard about the use of prolonged shackling or stress positions on detainees at GTMO. . . . Several agents described detainees being short-shackled overnight or while being subjected to cold temperatures, loud music, and flashing lights."[59]

Environmental Manipulation

"Environmental manipulation" was an approved interrogation technique at Guantánamo from April 2003 until September 2006.[60] The procedures allowed interrogators to adjust the room temperature during interrogations but required that detainees be accompanied at all times to ensure they were not injured.[61] In issuing the directive permitting this technique, Secretary Rumsfeld stated that "interrogations must always be planned deliberate actions that take into account . . . a detainee's emotional and physical strengths and weaknesses. . . . [And] are designed to manipulate the detainees' emotions and weaknesses to gain his willing cooperation."[62] Several FBI agents at Guantánamo reported that "detainees were intentionally subjected to extreme temperatures by unknown interrogators in an apparent effort to break the detainee's resolve to resist cooperating."[63]

Nineteen respondents described prolonged exposure to cold temperatures; for all but five of these detainees exposure occurred during interrogations at Guantánamo and appear to have occurred throughout the period they were held on the base.[64] Some said they were left shackled alone in cold rooms for prolonged periods as part of their interrogation. One person said he spent nine hours alone in a room in shackles with the air conditioning on. "It was extremely cold, I wasn't allowed to use the toilet, and I was very ill with the flu," he said. Recalled another former detainee: "They interrogated us for about thirty minutes and then they locked the door, went away, and we usually stayed there on the chair for more than three hours . . . with the music and the air conditioner turned on in order to make the room cold."

Eight respondents singled out being held in isolation in cold rooms as the worst treatment they endured at Guantánamo. As one respondent explained:

> Just being put into isolation when going through interrogation all the time was really difficult. You've been there for hours and hours, being chained to the floor and not being able to move. The worst thing is you don't know what's going on. And you're just sitting in there, the AC is on and you're freezing and chained to the floor. . . . If you try to move, the shackles start digging into your wrists and your ankles and it's painful. . . . That was really the worst time for me, mentally and physically.

Isolation under these conditions was exacerbated by not knowing when it would end. Recalled a former detainee: "The most painful of all was having to wait for a very long time not knowing what was going to happen. We were cold, we'd hurt, and we just kept waiting there not knowing what would happen next." A former guard who escorted detainees to the isolation room confirmed that there was a "room in which detainees are shackled to the floor for periods of time, I've discovered, more than 10 hours pretty frequently. And they're shackled by their hands and feet to the floor so that they are in a constant crouching position without being able to really put their ass on the floor, like sit down or anything. And the room is incredibly cold."

The Schmidt-Furlow Report found that bright flashing lights and/or loud music were also used to manipulate a detainee's environment on "numerous occasions" between July 2002 and October 2004, as an "Incentive and Futility" interrogation technique authorized by the Army Field Manual.[65] In addition, approximately 50 FBI agents who had been stationed at Guantánamo told DOJ investigators that "they witnessed or heard about the use of bright lights on detainees, sometimes in conjunction with other harsh non-law enforcement techniques."[66] One FBI agent told DOJ investigators

> that approximately halfway through his tour at GTMO . . . he observed a detainee alone in a darkened interrogation room, apparently bolted to the floor in a kneeling position, with a strobe light close to his face and loud music blaring in the room. The agent described the music as hard rock music, similar to the music performed by the group Metallica, played at a volume equivalent to a rock concert. The agent stated that he and another agent reported this activity.[67]

Several respondents reported being short shackled and left alone in a room while being bombarded with loud music and strobe lights for hours on end. One former detainee described the experience this way:

> You lose track of time. . . . [A]fter a while—because you're confined to a really small room, you're tied down into this position, they've got the stereo banging out really loud with strobe lights flashing like ten times a second— it makes you hallucinate. At the beginning it doesn't really affect you. But after a while, after like 20 minutes, 10 minutes, you start getting cramps in your thighs, and your buttocks, and your calves, and slowly your legs, you know, just go numb. You're flimsy, and you've got no control. And when you move over, [the shackles] start cutting into you. . . . And even if you close your eyes you can still see the light and you start hallucinating. . . . Sometimes you'd get punched or kicked as well.

Sexual Humiliation

Three respondents in our study said that female interrogators humiliated them during interrogation sessions, mocking their devotion to Islamic teachings that prohibit any physical contact between unrelated men and women. One said he did not want to discuss the details of the incident.

"They were decreasing the temperature of the room, and that's when the woman began harassing me," he said. Another respondent recalled an interrogation session when a male interrogator kept asking him if he was a member of Al Qaeda. He replied repeatedly that he was not.

> Then a woman in civilian clothes entered the room and [the male interroga-
> tor] said, "Well, we'll leave you with her, maybe this will change your mind."
> I kept my head down, I did not know what was going on, I was trying not to
> talk to her, but she started to undress. And while she was talking to me in
> English, this lasted for a long time. I was still looking down, I was not look-
> ing at her, I did not know if she was completely naked or still in her under-
> wear. But she started to touch me and then after a while, after about an hour,
> a guard came in and said, "Okay, it's not working, that's enough." And I could
> hear the laughter of the people who were watching this from behind the
> mirror, the glass, the one-way window. I could hear the laughter, and this was
> just a very humiliating experience.

The authors of the Schmidt-Furlow Report confirmed that such techniques of humiliation by female interrogators, "designed to take advantage of their gender in relation to Muslim males,"[68] were practiced at Guantánamo but argued that they were authorized under military policies as "futility" and "mild non-injurious physical touching."[69] The OIG/DOJ Report notes that over 20 FBI agents reported "that they had seen or heard about female interrogators touching or acting toward a detainee in a sexual manner."[70] One FBI agent said that while he was at Guantánamo other "agents told him that they observed female military interrogators straddling detainees, whispering in their ears, and gener-ally invading the detainees' personal space."[71]

Do short shackling, stress positions, environmental manipulation, and sexual humiliation as described above constitute "torture" or "cruel and inhuman and degrading treatment"?

A legal perspective on this question is informed by several interna-tional and regional instruments. The 1984 UN Convention Against Torture defines torture as any act that consists of the intentional inflic-tion of "severe pain or suffering, whether physical or mental," involving a public official and carried out for a specific purpose.[72] Other legal instruments, including the International Covenant on Civil and Political Rights[73] and the European Convention on Human Rights[74] prohibit in absolute terms both torture and inhuman or degrading treatment. International humanitarian law equally forbids torture (whether physical or mental) and cruel, humiliating or degrading treatment, as well as any form of physical or moral coercion.[75]

What is key here—and often not amplified sufficiently in international human rights instruments, but widely recognized by health professionals who treat victims of torture and prisoner abuse[76]—is the psychological damage that can result not only from *individual acts of extreme cruelty* but from the cumulative nature of *seemingly less severe acts*, such as short shackling, stress positions, environmental manipulation, and sexual humiliation, over time. This suggests that such methods constitute cruel, humiliating, and degrading treatment and, in some cases, clearly rise to the level of torture. Indeed, as the International Criminal Tribunal for the former Yugoslavia ruled in 2002:

> [Torture] may be committed in one single act or can result from a combination or accumulation of several acts, which, taken individually and out of context, may seem harmless. . . . The period of time, the repetition and various forms of mistreatment and severity should be assessed as a whole.[77]

"The cumulative (or combined) use of these methods," writes Hernán Reyes of the International Committee of the Red Cross, "is not merely theoretical: the legality of such 'combined effects' has just recently come under renewed public scrutiny. . . . Finally, the stress and hence suffering produced by [these cumulative acts] will most certainly be compounded by any ongoing uncertainty as to the legal status [of a detainee]."[78]

Interrogation and Intimidation by Foreign Governments

Several respondents reported that they were interrogated by representatives from their home country and threatened with imprisonment and/or death upon their return home. Secretary of Defense Rumsfeld initially resisted visits from foreign governments to the facility, and then only agreed to visits for "intelligence" (rather than consular) purposes.[79] One former detainee said an official from his country told him: "When you come back to us, you know that we can make you talk." Another former detainee said he had fled his native land because of persecution and later was taken into U.S. custody in Afghanistan and sent to Guantánamo. Then one day at Guantánamo he was brought before a delegation of government officials from his home country. One member of the delegation, he said, threatened to harm him and his family: "I will take you by force . . . and you know what is going to happen to you and your family if you return, don't you?" Believing that he and his family would be killed, this respondent attempted suicide. When the delegation came to question him the next day at the hospital, he started to yell and tried to get out of his bed, but was prevented by restraints. The former detainee was later transferred to a special block for mentally unstable inmates, where he remained for a year and a half.[80]

Detainees brought to Guantánamo became the subjects of the Administration's new system for detention and interrogation for those it claimed to have captured in its war against Al Qaeda and the Taliban. Decisively breaking with the strict rules of the Geneva Conventions, the Administration created a detention facility, virtually sealed off from public view, designed to break the will of detainees and extract useful intelligence. This new system set out to maximize harsh living conditions, antagonize, if not inflame, the religious sensibilities of detainees, and expose detainees to newly sanctioned "harsh" interrogation practices. The impact of living in this system was profound. The next chapter examines some further elements of the detention system and their impacts, including how punishment was meted out, the health status of detainees, and their struggle for release.

Chapter 4

GUANTÁNAMO

No Exit

The U.S. detention facility at Guantánamo Bay is an institution of total confinement designed largely to serve the needs of interrogators and their superiors. Rules and regulations governing detention have given guards and interrogators total control over nearly every aspect of the lives of detainees. Most former detainees interviewed for this study experienced their detention in Guantánamo as arbitrary and humiliating, punctuated at times by excruciating mental or physical pain. Many responded to perceived injustices by camp personnel through collective and individual acts of resistance, ranging from refusal to respond to orders to hunger strikes and attempted suicide. Years of confinement took a toll on the physical and mental health of many detainees who were completely dependent on camp personnel for their care. Similarly, detainees struggled for years without judicial recourse to prove their claims of innocence. Release for respondents, when it came, seemed just as arbitrary as their transport to the island.

PUNISHMENT

Nineteen of the 62 detainees interviewed for this study stated they had been punished for various infractions at Guantánamo. This number is significant since it was not a topic about which each respondent was asked. It is likely that reported incidents would be even higher if each respondent had been specifically questioned about this topic. The most common types of punishment reported were the removal of what camp personnel called "comfort items," and solitary confinement, which typically ranged from a few days to 30 days, although regulations allowed additional days for infractions or because "military necessity justifies continued detention."[1]

Two respondents who were being given medication for mental health problems described being punished for behavior they could not control. One former detainee said he would shout uncontrollably at night: "When I didn't stop they would take me to the punishment cells." Guards reportedly taunted one detainee who was suffering from a mental illness: "I had a disorder where I would hit my head on the wall and the door. The soldiers would come and say I was crazy and make fun of me. Because this made me angry, I would spit or throw water at them. So they put me in these isolation cells for 20 to 25 days. I experienced that a couple of times."

One respondent said his isolation cell was "very cold, with just a metal bed. There was nothing else. No soap, nothing. Just a naked cell block." Another said his isolation room had some "comfort items," including a Quran, but no bed. He recalled that it was cold, and that he had to sleep on the metal floor. Each night around midnight a soldier would come by his cell and give him a small blanket and then return again at three in the morning and take it away.

Many types of behavior could result in physical isolation at Guantánamo. These ranged from engagement in collective protests to individual acts of defiance, including physically assaulting guards or failing to obey orders. One respondent described how he and fellow detainees became involved in a collective protest:

MPs were creating problems, searching for the Quran, and giving [detainees a] hard time, and they were taking [detainees] out. . . . And [the detainees] were yelling, and shouting, and knocking [on their cells] and stuff to resist. So when we heard this, we wanted to support them, so we also yelled and knocked on the cell doors.

Guards noted the identities of those participating in the disturbance and eventually moved them to isolation cells.

Another respondent described being put in isolation for making yogurt: "We were given milk, and I had an orange and I just squished the orange into the milk. The milk turned into yogurt so I was just breaking my fast with the yogurt. When the U.S. soldiers saw what I had done, they took me to a dark room and punished me there for 20 days and nights." Another respondent recalled how he was placed in an isolation cell after his pent-up frustration burst one day. He was one of a group of detainees who had been cleared for release from the base and moved to a special housing unit. Day after day, he and the others waited to be told they would leave. "What happened is, they were not giving me the things that I asked for," he recalled.

> [M]y back and nose were hurting. So I asked for a medical check-up. But they wouldn't call the doctor for me. I was so frustrated I asked [the guards] to bring the person in charge, the commander, so I could talk to him. But they wouldn't call him. So I grabbed the television, and brought it out [in to the yard], and [threw] it over, and broke it.

As a result, he spent 15 days in isolation. Another respondent said he was punished for spitting at a female guard who was shackling another detainee in what he perceived to be an abusive manner: "She was putting the shackles on badly and he was screaming. I spat at her so . . . she would release him." In response, the guard called for an Immediate Reaction Force (IRF) team, which subdued the detainee and took him to an isolation cell.

Isolation or solitary confinement[2]—whether used as a means to disorient, break, or punish detainees—has caused serious concern at Guantánamo over the years. In a meeting with Guantánamo authorities in October 2003, the ICRC reportedly brought its concerns about prolonged isolation to the attention of U.S. officials at Guantánamo,[3]

An IRF team is a group of five or more guards who collectively serve as "a forced cell extraction team, specializing in the extraction of a detainee who is combative, resistive," or appears to have a weapon.[1] Outfitted in protective gear and carrying polycarbonate shields, IRF teams are authorized to enter the cells of detainees who appear to be "resistant" and subdue them. Before the team enters the cell, a guard sprays the detainee across the bridge of the nose with a form of pepper spray[2] to incapacitate him. A former guard interviewed for this study described the spray as being "10 times stronger" than mace. He recalled an IRF training session where he was sprayed with this mace-like substance: "[I]t pretty much kicked my ass for three days. . . . I cried that whole night, and the next day I was in total agony." While IRFing is not supposed to be used for punishment,[3] several respondents said guards resorted to IRFing in response to minor offenses or confrontations. One respondent recalled how guards turned off the shower on several occasions in a manner that intimidated detainees: "In the middle of the shower when we had soap all over our faces, [the guards] would cut the water off . . . they would say, 'If you don't come out now, we will call the Extreme Reaction Force.'" If the detainees protested, an IRF team moved in to subdue the men, and then took them to a separate room and forcibly shaved their facial hair. The entire process was filmed. Afterwards, detainees were put in isolation cells.

[1] See Chapter 24 of the 2004 SOPs entitled "Immediate Reaction Force (IRF) Operations." Chapter 25 provides instructions for "Quick Response Force (QRF) Operations." This operation was designed "to deter all errant behavior from unruly detainees . . . and react to authorized instruction into the compound to protect U.S. forces and detainees."

[2] The reactive chemical in the spray is Oleoresin/Capsicum.

[3] 2004 SOP §24-6(b).

but the practice was still in evidence as of October 2008. Detainees in Camp 5 and Camp 6 reportedly are held in sparse solitary confinement cells in which the lights are never turned off.[4] In a 2006 report on the situation of Guantánamo detainees a group of UN experts stated that "the conditions of their confinement have had profound effects on the mental health of many of them. . . . These conditions [including long periods of solitary confinement] have led in some instances to serious mental illness, over 350 acts of self-harm in 2003 alone, individual and mass suicide attempts and widespread, prolonged hunger strikes."[5]

Stuart Grassian, a psychiatrist with extensive experience in evaluating the psychiatric effects of stringent conditions of confinement, has found that solitary confinement, especially when combined with severely restricted stimuli and activity, can have "a profoundly deleterious effect on mental functioning"[6] and can cause short- and long-term psychological and physical damage. Seventy-five experts in medicine and law meeting in Istanbul in 2007 concluded that solitary confinement can cause "serious health problems regardless of the specific conditions, regardless of time and place, and regardless of pre-existing personal factors."[7] Studies of the health aspects of solitary confinement suggest that symptoms can include perceptual distortions and hallucinations, extreme anxiety, hostility, confusion, difficulty with concentration, hyper-sensitivity to external stimuli, sleep disturbance, and psychosis.[8] "Negative health effects can occur after only a few days in solitary confinement, and the health risks rise with each additional day spent in such conditions."[9]

Twelve of the 18 attorneys interviewed for this study said that their clients' mental states had deteriorated as a result of their detention in Guantánamo. Of these, nine explicitly stated that prolonged periods of isolation and solitary confinement had particularly affected the mental condition of their clients. One attorney put it this way:

> You know, the principal problem now is that . . . they are in this new large Camp Six. . . . They're practically in isolation there. I mean, they used to be in these cage like things where you could see through the metal across to several different guys and could communicate to them and now they're in rooms that are fully enclosed and there's just a little window [and] they really can't see other people, they can [only] hear them under the door . . . they're essentially in isolation.

Another attorney recounted a harrowing incident that he believed was brought on by his client's isolation and feelings that he would never be released from Guantánamo:

> [My client] had been held for over a year in a solid wall cell that he couldn't see out of, from which he couldn't speak to any other detainees, and where

he stayed for 22–24 hours a day. He's a very social person and that isolation was just brutal for him. In fact, at the end of one meeting after he talked to me about living like that he looked at me and said, "How can I keep myself from going crazy?" Ultimately, he decided that he just couldn't continue. And so during a break in a meeting of ours he hung himself and cut his arm open. I came in a few minutes later and found him hanging and unconscious. We were able to get him down, he had surgery and he survived. That was in October of 2005. Subsequent to that, he made serious suicide attempts four more times, always driven by the fact of his isolation . . . the fact that he had been told that he would stay at Guantánamo living like that forever and so really in his mind he had no reason to be hopeful at all. In July of this year [2007], he was released and is now [home] where he is doing far, far better.

Hunger Strikes and Other Collective Actions

Individual and collective hunger strikes have been a common form of protest at Guantánamo since detainees began arriving there in early 2002. Criminologist Kieran McEvoy, writing on Republican prisoners in Northern Ireland, noted that hunger strikes may become rational options for prisoners in a "situation where actions within the prison are laden with political significance to the conflict on the outside, and options narrowed."[10] In the late 1970s, Irish prisoners initiated several protests against their lack of status as political prisoners, using their bodies as the "instrument of resistance." Prisoners refused to wear clothes, leave their cells to shower, and smeared their cells with their feces and urine as forms of protest.[11]

Half of the respondents who participated in our Guantánamo study undertook hunger strikes, ranging from a few days to 14 days. None said they were subjected to force feeding, a practice that was particularly prevalent during large hunger strikes in 2005. By September 2005, the largest hunger strike at Guantánamo had peaked with 131 detainees refusing meals for at least three straight days. As of April 2008, the number of detainees on hunger strikes was approximately 10, with strikers force fed twice a day through a feeding tube inserted through the nose.[12] None of the former detainees interviewed for this study had been held later than 2007.

Respondents in our survey said the primary reasons they had participated in hunger strikes were desecration of the Quran or interference with detainees' religious practice. Some detainees also went on hunger strikes to protest their personal confinement. Recalled a respondent: "It's always the same reason: I don't deserve to be here." When detainees organized a collective hunger strike, there was generally a call for all of them to participate. Many chose not to heed such calls. Several respondents who said they chose not to participate in a hunger strike declined because it was physically too difficult or because they wanted to avoid any collective action.

A respondent described a hunger strike triggered by the beating of a fellow detainee, a young man who refused to leave his cell to go to interrogation:

> He was a young Arab prisoner and he was with me in the same cellblock. He seemed to be 17 or 18 years old . . . and, one day, he refused to go to the interrogation room. . . . He told the [guard], "I have been arrested when I am innocent. They have arrested me illegally and why are they just asking me questions?" After that about 10 soldiers with armored clothes appeared. They went to his cell and they started beating that boy. And I saw myself that blood was . . . coming out of his cell. . . . So we saw that the boy was put on the stretcher and he was tied around his waist . . . he could not move, he was just chained and tied up. . . . Then he was taken to the hospital. And after that a lot of the prisoners went on a hunger strike. . . . I did not participate in the hunger strike, but I didn't eat anything because I was sad. . . . I never saw [that detainee] again, no one saw him again. And they were shouting through loud speakers that he was okay, eat your food, he's fine. All the prisoners were very angry and they were kicking the walls and they were shouting. And the soldiers would stand in the corner of the hall, they would not come in the middle of the hall.

Detainees engaged in other forms of collective action in addition to hunger strikes to protest their treatment at Guantánamo. Occasionally detainees would create mixtures of bodily excretions known on the blocks as "cocktails" and fling them at guards. Army psychologist Larry C. James, who was stationed at the base for several months in early 2003, recalled walking toward a cellblock one evening and finding detainees throwing bodily fluids at the guards:

> On this night, I had no idea what started the riot, but I could see the guards and other staff were trying to dodge urine, feces, and other bodily fluids. . . . I learned from talking to the MPs afterwards that . . . the methodology was the same: make the deposit in a cup, add some toilet paper for stability when throwing, douse liberally in urine, and hide the concoction in your cell for a while and let ferment. Then wait for an opportune moment when the guard let his attention wander and suddenly . . . fling [it] . . . through the "bean chute" used to pass in meals.[13]

What sparked collective resistance varied. Here is one account:

> I was left in interrogation for eight hours at a time, shackled, music playing, air conditioning blowing. This happened continuously for three months. This [type of treatment] would provoke a strike, it wouldn't be a hunger strike, it would be a non-cooperation strike. I mean the whole block . . . would not speak during interrogation sessions. Then they would . . . forcefully take you into interrogation. Your facial hair would be shaved off, your head hair would be all shaved off. And this would be filmed on camera. So depending on what kind of treatment you got, you would spark a different kind of strike.

Another described a collective strike in which detainees refused to take showers to protest searches for the Quran by female soldiers. The strike was successful, although the detainees were punished for their actions:

> Yeah, they accepted it, but we were punished for the strike. They used tear gas on us. And they shaved our beards and confined us in small cells like cages and when it was very cold; there were ACs on our head. The reason our strike was successful was because 60 to 70 prisoners tried to kill themselves. They wanted to hang themselves with their clothes on the ceiling, so that's why the high ranking officer admitted that the women would not search the Qurans anymore.

HEALTH

Since the first arrival of detainees in January 2002, the quality and consistency of health care provided detainees at Guantánamo have been mixed. Many respondents said that medical staff responded quickly to life-threatening illness and reported positive relationships with nurses and doctors. Eighteen respondents in our study reported that they were satisfied with the medical care they received at Guantánamo. However, some former detainees said medical personnel were inexperienced and intentionally withheld proper medications. Twenty-three respondents said that care was delayed, ineffective, or denied. Five also complained they were not informed about medical decisions or did not consent to procedures.[14] Several FBI agents reported that they had received complaints from detainees about lack of medical attention.[15]

Physical Health

Dental problems were particularly common at Guantánamo. One respondent blamed the "dirty and infected" drinking water for affecting two of his teeth to such an extent they had to be extracted. While most former detainees said they received dental attention, many complained they were told there was no treatment available and the only option was to pull a decayed tooth, or they had to wait to see a dentist, resulting in delays in treatment of up to a year. One former detainee complained that delayed treatment resulted in his losing several teeth.

A number of former detainees said prior medical conditions (which ranged from hypertension and stomach ailments to asthma and worsening eyesight) went untreated or were inadequately treated at Guantánamo. One former detainee described his futile attempts to convince skeptical guards that he needed to be treated for a prior condition that affected his veins. When he was finally taken to the hospital, it turned out he was right, and he was given medications that helped his condition. Some respondents said they were plagued by back, knee, or foot injuries initially sustained at Kandahar or Bagram. Recalled a former detainee:

When the soldiers were taking me down from the second floor in Bagram Air Base my eyes were blindfolded. When we came to the stairs the soldiers let go of me and I fell down and did something to my back. At Guantánamo, they took X-rays and found I had a space in my backbones. They gave painkillers. There was a sports doctor, and he took me two or three times to do exercise, but it didn't help.

Another respondent told of arriving in Guantánamo on a stretcher because of a gunshot wound in his leg. After eight days in isolation, authorities discovered that his wounds were infected and took him to the hospital where he underwent an operation for dead body tissue (necrosis) that had resulted from earlier inattention.[16]

Several respondents reported delays in receiving medications at Guantánamo. One former detainee explained that he had cut tendons and could not put weight on his right leg. He had to wait more than 20 days before he was given painkillers. Some respondents said they had undergone surgery or other invasive procedures and been prescribed pain medication only to find out from a guard that they were not on the list to receive medication.

Mental Health

Indefinite confinement clearly took an emotional toll on detainees at Guantánamo. A dozen of the 18 attorneys interviewed for this study explicitly mentioned that their clients had mentally deteriorated while in detention. Many respondents said some of the worst moments of their confinement were those when they felt a deep sense of injustice for being detained without just cause combined with not knowing if or when they would ever be released.

Many detainees with mental illnesses were segregated and housed in Delta Block, the mental ward within Camp Delta. A small group of mental health personnel staffed the unit, but none of them had extensive training, according to Dr. Daryl Matthews, a civilian forensic psychiatrist who assessed the facility shortly after it opened. He found that caregivers provided "pro forma" care which consisted primarily of diagnosis and medication. A former guard who worked at the camp in 2004 described the scene inside the mental unit as chaotic. "Walking on Delta Block," he said, "was like walking into a quintessential madhouse. . . . Some [detainees] were virtually catatonic. . . . Some would just babble to themselves. Some yelled all day long, all day, every day."

Respondents housed in the mental health unit generally described receiving some relief from their symptoms. One respondent said he developed a disorder in which he repeatedly hit his head against the wall and spat at guards. He was eventually moved to the mental health unit and reported that regular medication helped his condition. Another respondent said he preferred being housed in the unit because his diagnosis meant that he could act out without being punished.

Two respondents described being sent to the mental health unit in error. One of these said that a guard initially sent him to the mental ward for repeatedly requesting medical treatment for an injured leg. Once at the unit, he repeatedly protested that he was not "crazy" and refused medications. One day an IRF team appeared, and a guard entered his cell to subdue him with pepper spray. "They came in and beat me," he said. "Blood came on my face. There were six soldiers." A physician finally examined him in the detainee hospital and confirmed that his leg was injured. After 45 days in the unit, he was returned to the general population.

Matthews described in an interview for this study several factors that, in his words, made "it impossible to deliver mental health care services properly" to alleviate the emotional toll of detainment. First, he said, there were too few interpreters at Guantánamo: "To treat this population, you would have needed much more in the way of interpretation, much more interpreter staff. The doctors had to rely on the same interpreters as everyone else. . . . [T]hey didn't have their own so the first thing if a psychologist wanted to see a patient, he had to run around the place and make phone calls and maybe wait a day or two to get an interpreter." Several respondents said language barriers contributed to confusion or delays in their ability to receive mental or physical health care at Guantánamo. One released detainee explained how fortunate he was that the nurse treating his wounds spoke his native language: "If I asked for some kind of medical attention, someone would take notes, and then it would go up the channels—sometimes it would take days and weeks for a response. . . . But, finally, I was well cared for thanks to this nurse because I could communicate with her directly and explain what I needed. . . . So I was lucky."

Second, according to Matthews and other sources,[17] many detainees distrusted mental health professionals[18] at the camp because information shared with care providers was used by their interrogators. Finally, Matthews said, "the caregivers were extremely inexperienced," especially in providing care to this particular population. "These [were] the most inexperienced mental health people in the Army who were sent there," Matthews said.

> Going to Guantánamo gave me a special interest in certain aspects of Islamic culture and I tried to study up. The thing that was apparent to me when I got there was that there was nobody in that place knew anything about that that I ran into. . . . Certainly, the hospital director didn't. Certainly, the mental health people didn't. The guards I talked to, you know, nobody was really sensitive to what the cultural issues might be in any aspect of their illness or their care. So let me give you one big, big example. That is that people from traditional Islamic cultures would be disinclined to believe that mental symptoms are appropriately treated with medications and yet that was the only treatment that was offered. And so that's not a good fit. There would be . . . medication refusal. There would be checking medicine [pretending to take medicine]. There would be taking the medication and being very unhappy.

Sense of Futility

Many of the former detainees we interviewed went through periods when they believed they would spend the rest of their lives in Guantánamo, a view encouraged by some interrogators. "According to the U.S. court, I would be a prisoner for 95 years," one respondent said he had been told by his interrogators. Another former detainee expressed his sense of futility this way:

I think the worst was not knowing . . . not knowing you know why you're there, or when you can go home. Or when they're going to take you to court. You know, when's something going to happen? . . . If they told us like, next week you're going to court, you've got a lawyer and so forth, then you know, it gives your mind a rest.

An attorney explained how the boredom, uncertainty, and isolation of camp life took its toll on her detainee clients:

You ask a client what he does all day . . . it's the same thing, get up at 3:30 or 4 and pray, go back to sleep, wake up, pray, walk up and down my cell, they can all tell you it's 8 steps wide or 8 steps long and then they just stare at these blank walls. And once every however many days they are let out for "recreation" and in Camp 6 they're let out in a little cage that has two stories of cement wall surrounding it with a grate across the top, so if they look straight up into the air they can see a little bit of sky and that's quote "recreation time." So they're all going nuts, and some of them have, the part that's really difficult is some of them have a certain amount of awareness of it. They can remember what they used to be like, and they know they're having difficulty concentrating. . . . They're the ones that will want most desperately something to do besides sit in a cell all day.

Over months and then years, detainees' attorneys observed an increasing sense of isolation and hopelessness in their clients. One of the attorneys representing a number of detainees said:

Overall, the most painful thing is the interaction with my clients. Going down there and having them see no hope. One of my clients said, "Look, you can't help me. This is just inconvenient. I'd rather lie in my cell than pretend I have hope."

SUICIDES AND SUICIDE ATTEMPTS

Research on suicide rates among prisoners in high-security units in U.S. prisons suggests that the isolation, stark conditions, and lack of stimuli are contributing factors to the mental deterioration of inmates.[19] Some Guantánamo detainees, depressed and despairing about their future, broke under the strain of detention and tried to kill themselves. As of

October 2008, U.S. officials have confirmed three suicides, all of which occurred in June 2006. Investigators from the Naval Criminal Investigative Service (NCIS) found suicide notes in the pockets and cells of the three detainees.[20] A fourth unconfirmed suicide allegedly took place in May 2007, and another detainee died in December 2007, reportedly due to a treatable medical condition.[21] There is sharp controversy surrounding these deaths and there has been no independent investigation confirming their cause.[22]

Six of the former detainees we interviewed admitted to having attempted suicide on one or more occasions; several others witnessed suicide attempts by fellow detainees. This figure is significant given the strict prohibition against suicide in Islam—the number of attempts may thus be higher than reported.[23] A former guard reported that he was aware of at least 12 suicide attempts during his 10-month tour at the camp. The DOD does not isolate and report suicide attempts, which are included under a broader category called "manipulative self-injurious behavior." As of August 2006, however, there had been more than 460 such incidents. As many as 120 hanging "gestures" (a subset of such behavior) occurred in 2003 alone.[24] In August of that same year, 23 detainees attempted to hang themselves over an eight-day period, leaving one detainee permanently brain-damaged.[25] The lack of clear reporting data of suicide attempts makes it difficult to assess the scope and severity of mental health problems. However, the study data suggest the problems are serious and deserve full investigation.

Because of the visibility of the cells, suicide attempts and guard interventions were public events. Many guards and camp officials claim suicide attempts were part of a long campaign of protest. The camp commander Rear Admiral Harry Harris, for example, characterized the three suicides of June 2006 as acts of "asymmetrical warfare" by committed fighters.[26] However, several respondents said that fellow detainees frequently alerted the guards when a suicide attempt was in progress. Recalled one:

You know, you're sitting there . . . then all of a sudden you just hear noises like [makes a gasping noise] noises. And you're thinking what the hell is that? And you look, and the guy's hanging. And you can see his face going blue. So you start banging your cell. And you start calling for the emergency personnel, the MP [Military Police], and you shout. And they would come out, rescue, whatever. It's not the best thing to see in your life.

Suicide attempts at the camp are high stakes for both detainees and guards. Once notified, guards have to respond quickly, since deaths can occur within as few as three minutes.[27] According to a former guard who intervened in a suicide attempt, before entering the cell of a detainee attempting suicide, guards have to enter the neighboring cell, shackle that detainee, and then rush to the adjoining cell and cut down and remove the makeshift noose from the detainee's neck. The entire procedure takes the guards about two minutes. "I mean guards had to act really quickly because their careers were on the line," he said. "It is totally understood in that camp that if a detainee dies on your shift, you are done. I mean that's it! You are going to be so in trouble that you don't even want to have to deal with it."[28]

LACK OF DUE PROCESS AND INDETERMINATE LEGAL STATUS

During the initial months of operations in Afghanistan, the U.S. military captured thousands of Afghans and foreigners who claimed they were not soldiers or terrorists and had been picked up by mistake. If these men were unsuccessful in convincing U.S. authorities of their innocence shortly after their capture, they usually ended up in Guantánamo where it took years to secure their release.

As early as September 2002, high-level government officials were aware of concerns within military and intelligence circles about whether and how many detainees were actually dangerous Al Qaeda fighters. A senior CIA analyst with extensive Middle East experience assessed detainees at the base in summer 2002 and concluded in a top-secret report that approximately a third of the population—at that time 200 of 600 detainees—had no connection to terrorism.[29] Many had been "caught in the dragnet. They were not fighters, they were not doing jihad. They should not have been there."[30] Guantánamo's commander, Major General Dunlavey, agreed with him and later estimated that half the camp population was innocent.[31] An FBI counterterrorism expert went even further and told a committee of the National Security Council there were at most only 50 detainees worth holding at Guantánamo.[32] A few former detainees said their interrogators confessed they did not understand why they were being held. "When I asked my investigator why I was being held in Guantánamo, he told me that he was surprised as well after looking at my background file," one respondent said, but he continued to be held.

Nevertheless, the military moved cautiously in releasing detainees, for several reasons. First, in a meeting to discuss the CIA report in early fall 2002, hard-liners in the Administration, primarily David Addington, legal counsel to Vice President Cheney, rejected any proposal to review the detainees' status. To do so, Addington argued, would be tantamount to second-guessing the President and undercutting executive power. Second, the military was fearful of releasing the wrong men. Finally, top commanders at Guantánamo, including Dunlavey and his replacement, General Miller, felt many detainees did have information they had not disclosed and gave priority to trying new, harsher interrogation tactics to yield desired results.[33]

As a result, in the first years of operation, detainees had virtually no means to convince U.S. authorities they were wrongfully imprisoned and were not among "the worst of the worst." The International Committee of the Red Cross (ICRC) visited those held in Guantánamo, but they had no power, other than through written and verbal persuasion, to change the way detainees were treated, and no mandate to advocate for their release. Some former detainees said they viewed the ICRC's "powerlessness" as suspicious and thought they were working in collaboration with interrogators. This suspicion may have been reinforced by the fact that the military often "isolated [detainees] immediately before and after they met with the Red Cross," according to the OIC/DOJ Report.[34] Others thought the ICRC was simply ineffective; one respondent referred to the organization as nothing more than a "glorified postman."

Nor could detainees rely on their home governments to help secure their release. Virtually all respondents reported that they met with officials from their native countries while they were in the camp, many within weeks of arrival. Some respondents felt their governments were not interested in their claims of innocence or in exerting pressure to secure their release.

One former detainee described his feelings after meeting an intelligence officer sent by his government:

> He said to me that everything I had told him was a lie, and that I was going to spend the rest of my life in Guantánamo. And this was within 48 hours of my arrival there. . . . To hear it from American authorities, it's different. You still have some hope. But then to hear it from your own government, knowing that you've done nothing wrong, it was, it was really hard.

It was not until June 2004, over two years after Camp X-Ray had been opened, that the U.S. Supreme Court ruled in *Rasul v. Bush* that detainees in Guantánamo should have access to U.S. courts to contest the legal basis for their detention. The Center for Constitutional Rights (CCR), which had brought *Rasul*, along with several other lawyers, immediately set to work to locate families of dozens of detainees. In the first week after the decision, CCR rushed to file habeas corpus petitions on behalf of many detainees and organized dozens of law firms and law school clinics, whose members volunteered pro bono assistance.

In response to *Rasul*, rather than conduct habeas hearings in federal courts, the U.S. military established an internal system of military panels called Combatant Status Review Tribunals (CSRTs) to review the evidence on each detainee and assess whether he was an "enemy combatant."[35] These procedures became the only legal avenue detainees had to contest their classification. By January 2005, the military had reviewed the cases of 558 detainees and found all but 38 subject to continued detention as enemy combatants. Officially, the U.S. military had not determined these 38 men to be "innocent" of wrongdoing but rather designated each of them "No Longer an Enemy Combatant" and thus eligible for release.[36] Military Administrative Review Boards (ARBs) re-examined each detainee's case yearly to determine whether he should be held because he "represents a continuing threat to the U.S. or its allies" or has "continuing intelligence value." An ARB may recommend that detention be continued or that the detainee be transferred from U.S. custody.[37]

Many former detainees reported that the U.S. authorities never explained why they were being held in Guantánamo. Nor was it clear to some whether they had ever had a CSRT hearing. Others did not understand the difference between having a "lawyer" who would represent their interests (which was not allowed) and the "personal representative" that the military provided them for their CSRT. Many respondents spoke of their "lawyer" who, in their recollection, generally asked whether they wanted to address the tribunal or preferred the representative to do so. For many, the status review process was opaque. This common sentiment is illustrated by the remarks of a former detainee who recalled that the first he knew of his CSRT hearing was when guards brought him before the panel. Few former detainees could recall in any detail what the accusations against them were. "There was a piece of paper with all the charges written down . . . connection with Al Qaeda, connection with Taliban. I kept [the paper] but at one search they took it away, so I don't remember exactly what else was on that," recalled one.

One respondent summed up his two review hearings as follows: "On the first occasion they gave me a letter and I was told that I was enemy of Americans and my second court they gave me a paper and I was told that I was free." Others felt they had no opportunity to plead their case or to defend themselves because the charges were so vague. Many former detainees stated they were never told the evidence against them, despite their request to have it shown to them. One respondent said that he understood there were two types of charges against him, one was an alleged link to the Taliban, the other set of charges "was secret." He continued, "when I asked them about my secret crime, they didn't answer me and they usually told me that it was safe and sacred to them. It was a secret." Echoing the sentiments expressed by other respondents, one former detainee put it this way:

> It was a very simple court and I was told that I'd been a Taliban and a terrorist—but those names had different meanings for me. I told them: "I have been here for more than three years, so what is my [crime]? If I am guilty, just show me the proof and if I am a terrorist, or if I belong to the Taliban insurgency, show me the proof . . . explain it to me." But they couldn't explain it.

In June 2008 the Supreme Court decided *Boumediene v. Bush*[38] and found that Guantánamo detainees had a constitutional right to have a federal court adjudicate their petitions for habeas corpus, challenging the legality of their detention. There had been no habeas hearings since *Rasul*, because of subsequent legal challenges. In *Boumediene*, the Court ruled that the Congressionally created circuit court review of a CSRT decision was flawed and an "inadequate substitute" for habeas corpus proceedings.[39] In particular, the Court pointed to the limits placed on a detainee's ability to call witnesses or present evidence to rebut the government's allegations.[40]

In general, detainees did not believe they had the opportunity to call witnesses at their hearings when they occurred, while others were rebuffed in their attempts to do so. "We weren't allowed to show any witnesses," said one. Another had his request for two witnesses, whom he claimed could confirm he had no links to Al Qaeda or the Taliban, turned down. As a result, he refused to appear in a subsequent hearing. A later ARB board recommended he be released.

When asked what helped them to survive their stay in Guantánamo, many respondents said that because they were innocent they believed that eventually they would be released. This common sentiment was expressed by one former detainee: "I hadn't committed any crime. I knew I was innocent, and I knew that one day I would be free."

RELEASE

Guantánamo has held over 770 detainees from the war in Afghanistan since January 2002. Of these, over 65 percent have been released. The average length of confinement at the camp of those we interviewed was three years, the longest was six years and the shortest was five months. Approximately 255 detainees remain, some of whom have been held for six years or more.[41]

The vast majority of respondents said they were extremely surprised when they learned of their imminent release from Guantánamo. News of a detainee's release could come from a number of sources, including sympathetic guards, military officers, and interrogators. Yet many doubted the veracity of what they heard. Recalled one respondent: "[I]t was very difficult for me to trust an American. So when they told me, I still did not believe them."

Preparing detainees for release involved a number of procedures. First, they received a full medical exam and a new set of clothes, including a jacket and a pair of Levis jeans. Most respondents remembered feeling elated when they finally realized they would be returning home. But a few felt guilty or sad to be leaving while fellow detainees remained. One former detainee put it this way:

> On the one hand I was very happy I was going home. On the other hand I was very upset for those young prisoners who would remain in Guantánamo. . . . [S]ome were Arabs who were not linked to any groups, they were just like . . . Islamic preachers. . . . And there was a guy who was always saying, "Oh my God, I have my mom, my wife and son, and I was arrested from the street, from the bazaar." I knew another prisoner who was from Jalalabad. He was a butcher buying and selling cows, and he was arrested based on wrong information from the street. . . . So I was happy that I got released but also very sad for those people who stayed behind.

Figure 6 *(opposite).* Release agreement.

AGREEMENT

WHEREAS, as a result of certain terrorist attacks, the United States and its coalition partners are engaged in armed conflict with al Qaida, an international terrorist organization, and its Taliban supporters; and

WHEREAS, _____ was detained as an enemy combatant during such armed conflict;

_____ undertakes as conditions for no longer being detained the following:

- THAT he will not in any way affiliate himself with al Qaida or its Taliban supporters;

- THAT he will not engage in, assist, or conspire to commit any combatant activities, or act in preparation thereof against the United States or its citizens, or against allies of the United States or citizens of such allies;

- THAT he will not engage in, assist, or conspire to commit any acts of terrorism or knowingly harbor anyone who does;

FURTHERMORE, _____ agrees that if he does not fulfill any of the above stated conditions, he may be detained immediately consistent with the law of armed conflict;

IN CONSIDERATION of these conditions, it is agreed that _____ will not be further detained by the United States, but should he not fulfill any of these conditions he may again be detained consistent with the law of armed conflict.

The agreement has been read to me and I understand the contents.

Signed this ____ day of _____, 200__

_____   _____
Signature of Detainee to be released   Appropriate U.S. Official

_____   _____
Witness   ISN# and Printed Detainee Name

11/20/2003   Release Agreement.dc

Within a day of their departure, detainees were presented with a
letter from the U.S. Department of Defense and told they had to sign it
in order to be released (see page 89). The letter stated that because
"the United States and its coalition partners are engaged in armed
conflict with Al Qaeda, an international terrorist organization, and its
Taliban supporters; and . . . [the individual] was detained as an enemy
combatant during such armed conflict," the individual agrees to several conditions to his release including that the detainee will not affiliate with Al Qaeda "or its Taliban supporters" or otherwise act against
the United States or its citizens or allies. If the released detainee violated any of these conditions he agrees that he "may again be
detained."

Many respondents said they signed the letter because they felt they
had no other choice. "I was ready to sign absolutely anything to leave
that place," a former detainee recalled. "They told me you sign this or
you don't go. So, of course, I signed." Yet others refused to sign, concerned that to do so would constitute an admission of guilt:

> I couldn't read the letter. So I asked the translator if he would read it. After I
> heard what was written in the letter, I think it was something like I had links
> to the Taliban and Al Qaeda and there was mention that I had been a terror-
> ist. And it said if, in the future, I committed such and such a crime, or fault,
> or sin, they would capture and detain me again. After I heard these words, I
> refused to sign the letter. . . . I told them that I hadn't been involved in any
> terrorist activity, and I hadn't helped any terrorist or Al Qaeda member . . . I
> didn't want to sign the letter because after I signed it, then I'd be guilty. They
> told me if I didn't sign the letter, they would not send me back to Afghanistan
> and they would keep me in detention forever. . . . So, I told them that I would
> write down that I hadn't been involved in any terrorist activities and that I
> hadn't had any link with Al Qaeda or the Taliban. After that, I signed it, and
> they agreed to let me go.

Still others said they flatly refused to sign the letter but were still
released.

Most respondents said they left Guantánamo the same way they had arrived—on U.S. military transport planes. Some home governments sent planes to the base to transport detainees home. While some detainees boarded the planes still fettered in shackles and hoods, others had them removed. One respondent described his feelings after U.S. soldiers removed his shackles and he walked toward the plane his government had sent to transport him home:

> I was thinking, "Wait, I haven't got my shackles on. This is wrong. I have to be shackled. . . . This is wrong what they are doing to me." [Then the policeman from my country] said, "Just walk straight, don't look back." I wanted to swear, I wanted to do something, stick my fingers up at the Americans. But I just kept walking toward the plane. When I sat down in my seat, they said, "When you want to get up just tell us, and you can get up and walk on this spot." And I still didn't understand. I should have shackles on me right? Because it was normal to be shackled, but then off they went, and that was it.

One former detainee even found a touch of irony in his long-awaited departure:

> We were all loaded onto these buses that had blacked out windows and taken to the airfield. The coaches had a capacity for about fifty people each and they were full, but not with detainees. There were only four detainees on my bus and I was one of them. Everybody else was a soldier. And again it was overkill: my detention began with overkill, and now my release was ending with overkill. . . . I was placed again in the so-called "three-piece suit," only this time there was no hood or goggles. There was a padlock, a big thick padlock, on the shackles, too, for good measure, just in case, you know, I tried to escape on the way to freedom.

Chapter 5

RETURN

The Legacy of Guantánamo

As of October 2008, the United States had transferred approximately 520 detainees from the detention facility in Guantánamo Bay to the custody of governments in 30 countries.[1] Many respondents in our study said they were elated when they learned about their impending departure from Guantánamo. In their minds, "release" from U.S. custody meant vindication of their claims of innocence and an opportunity to resume their lives. None of these detainees had been charged with a crime by the United States. What few understood at the time was that U.S. policy was not to "release" detainees but rather to "transfer" their custody to another state. In the weeks and months ahead, many former detainees would discover that the "Guantánamo" chapter of their lives was not entirely over: it had simply moved into a "post-Guantánamo phase" in a different land.

Over time, the U.S. government has negotiated the conditions of detainee transfer with foreign governments. Its stated chief consideration in Guantánamo releases is assurance that the detainee will not "increase the risk of further attacks on the United States and its allies."[2] Determinations that a detainee was "no longer a risk" or was "no longer of intelligence value" were made in some cases through annual status reviews.[3] However, as a U.S. official interviewed for this study explained, the government negotiates detainee transfers regardless of the outcome of the annual status reviews and detainees may be transferred regardless of whether they have been "cleared" for transfer or release by the review procedures.[4]

As part of its negotiations, the U.S. government obtains guarantees that the receiving government will "establish . . . measures . . . that will ensure that the detainee will not pose a continuing threat."[5] Such measures often include subsequent detention or prosecution, although the U.S. never makes these determinations public.[6] Thus, detainees are not aware of their fate as they leave Guantánamo. They can be immediately freed, placed "in confinement or subject to other restrictions,"[7] or prosecuted under the domestic law of their home country. A detainee cleared by the review boards nonetheless may continue to be held if the Department of Defense does not obtain sufficient security guarantees, a U.S. government official also explained. In addition, detainees cleared for release may continue to be held if the U.S. government recognizes they are at risk of being tortured or persecuted in their native country and the U.S. has not been able to reach agreement for resettlement with a third country. As of October 2008, the U.S. was holding more than 60 detainees in Guantánamo who it acknowledged were eligible for transfer or release to their own or a third country.[8]

DETENTION AND PROSECUTION

Of the more than 500 detainees the United States has transferred from Guantánamo to the custody of other governments, scores have been destined for further "detention, investigation and/or prosecution."[9] The U.S. states it seeks "diplomatic assurances" from receiving states that all detainees will be treated humanely.[10] While no official, comprehensive data exist on the circumstances and outcomes of subsequent national proceedings against released Guantánamo detainees, human rights organizations have reported cases of their abuse in detention, arbitrary and prolonged detention without trial, and irregular criminal prosecutions.

Of our sample, ten respondents were arrested upon arrival in their home countries and incarcerated for periods ranging from three months to two years. Some were held in security prisons on domestic anti-terrorism charges and later released. Others were released without trial. One respondent who was detained for a year and a half in his home country after he left Guantánamo explained: "it was like leaving one nightmare to go into another one." Still, he was grateful for the counseling he received while incarcerated by his government, and his confinement gave him a period to adjust. He noted that the prison psychologists in his home country were not like those in Guantánamo. A therapeutic relationship of trust developed, from which he benefited: "I think it's a good thing that I went to jail after I returned because I could not have been just released into the outside world after what I had been through in Guantánamo."

A few of our respondents reported they had been abused in detention at home. One described being beaten by domestic security agents in prison and forced to take drugs that made him hallucinate so badly he saw "snakes coming from beneath the floor." Held without charge, he was accused of being a spy for the Americans. Another respondent was beaten during his initial interrogation while authorities demanded he confess that he was a member of a terrorist organization. He was released eight months later, without trial.

There have been several reports of abuse of former detainees upon their transfer to home countries.[11] Human Rights Watch, for example, has documented the abuse of Russian[12] and Tunisian former detainees by their governments. In the Tunisian case, courts had convicted at least ten Guantánamo detainees in absentia.[13] In June 2007, two of the convicted were transferred from U.S. custody to a Tunisian prison. One was interrogated for two days, during which authorities reportedly slapped him, threatened to rape his wife and daughters, and deprived him of sleep;[14] the other was reportedly threatened with torture during his initial interrogation. According to Human Rights Watch, both men told visitors their conditions at the new facility were so bad they preferred to return to Guantánamo.[15]

In late 2006 and 2007, the U.S. government transferred two detainees to Libyan custody reportedly after receiving assurances of humane treatment. Both men have been in custody for over a year, without known charges or access to lawyers or representatives of human rights groups.[16]

Several respondents interviewed for this study who had been formally charged upon their arrival or had been detained by home governments for several months reported that their governments placed them under surveillance when they were freed. Some had their passports confiscated; others had strict reporting requirements to follow for domestic travel or were required to report regularly to authorities.

RELEASE UPON ARRIVAL

According to the Department of Defense, most Guantánamo detainees who have been transferred into detention in their home countries were subsequently quickly released.[17] This is consistent with our findings. The vast majority of respondents in our study, 45 of 62, were released from the custody of their governments within 72 hours of arriving home. Several were initially arrested under domestic anti-terrorism laws, for example, but quickly sent home after questioning.

RESETTLEMENT AND COMMUNITY RECEPTION

With one exception, who was not among our respondents,[18] none of those yet released from Guantánamo has been convicted or punished for a crime by the U.S. government. Nor have they received any official acknowledgement of their innocence. The U.S. government has repeatedly stated that its decision to release detainees is not an admission that they are cleared of wrongdoing or that U.S. forces committed an error in capturing them or later detaining them in Guantánamo. Without a formal exoneration, people in some communities to which former detainees have returned have regarded them as suspect, even a threat to public safety.

Most respondents interviewed for this study said they received a mixed reception in the communities in which they settled. Although their families generally embraced them, some were shunned by some other community members after learning they had been at Guantánamo.

Some respondents who returned to Western European countries reported that they received death threats over the phone, saw signs denouncing them in their neighborhood, and encountered people hurling profanities in their direction on the street. One interviewee remarked that even some of his old friends were now afraid of him, believing that he was an Al Qaeda terrorist. Another reported that non-Muslims were often more understanding than some in the Muslim community. One said that he no longer felt comfortable walking alone in certain neighborhoods. "[It is] just the way that people look at me," he confessed. "I don't feel comfortable."

Of the 221 Afghans detained in Guantánamo (the largest single group), 192 have been returned home.[19] Some returnees to Afghanistan reported being threatened, mostly by old enemies, they said. Others from impoverished backgrounds reported being neglected after their return, just as they had been before their arrest. "There is no change in my relation with other people in my community because I am a poor guy so no one cares about me," remarked one respondent. Two Afghan respondents said that rumors of sexual abuse at Guantánamo had stigmatized them and made it difficult to find a marriage partner. One of these was also accused of being an American spy and as a result was fearful of becoming a Taliban target.

However, several Afghan respondents experienced a remarkably different reception: village-wide celebrations of their return. The neighbors of one family even invited the local police to join the festivities. In these tight-knit communities, respondents explained that their innocence was never in doubt. "My reputation has not been damaged in the community among my people. People still feel that I am not a traitor," one said.

Another former detainee, a teacher to over 200 local students before his detention, reported that he was "well respected" before *and after* his arrest. Another released detainee, who was a shepherd, received an outpouring of sympathy from his community. "[W]hen I'm walking on the streets and I meet some people, they usually say to me, 'We're sorry for you . . .' Everyone [in my tribe knows] that I'm innocent, that I'm not involved in any political activities."

In 2006, eight former detainees who were unable to return to their country of origin because of fears they would be abused were transferred to Albania.[20] These former detainees faced difference challenges than those returning home. U.S. authorities, the Albanian government, local UN officials, and some lawyers for respondents told these former detainees that they would be reunited with their families and provided homes and jobs in Albania but the reality turned out to be quite different. Continued and indefinite familial separation weighed heavily on the refugees. "I will never be able to go back. I cannot bring them here. I cannot see my family for the rest of my life," said one respondent. Most of their families had been visited by officials in their home country who knew that the individual had been in Guantánamo and was now living abroad, and several refugees were concerned about the safety of their families. A family member of one had been threatened with termination of the pension which was the sole support for the family.

None of the refugees spoke Albanian, and language instruction was halting, making social integration particularly difficult. The new arrivals struggled to learn the language, but twice the language course offered at the refugee center was discontinued. At the time of the interviews, none of the refugees was employed and their job prospects were bleak, especially since some potential employers did not want to hire anyone who had been held in Guantánamo.

The Guantánamo refugees lived initially in single rooms at a state-run refugee center on the outskirts of the capital, though in early spring 2008 they were relocated into apartments with a promise that the Albanian government would subsidize the rents for two years. Still,

Saudi Arabia is unique among countries receiving its nationals from Guantánamo. In late 2006 and early 2007, the Saudi government expanded its existing rehabilitation and reintegration program for identified Islamic extremists to include former Guantánamo detainees. As part of an unpublished agreement with the United States, the Saudi government reportedly agreed to enroll returning detainees in the program as a condition of their release from U.S. custody.[2] The Saudi government program is based on the premise that extremists "were tricked" into false beliefs of Islam and could be re-educated and reformed.[3] Former Guantánamo detainees undergo a six-week program taught by clerics.[4] After completing the program, former detainees are moved to a half-way house on the outskirts of Riyadh. At the "Care Rehabilitation Center" compound, former Guantánamo detainees are housed separately from Saudis who have been jailed for their extremist views. Returned detainees, called "beneficiaries," live for several months in a guarded compound but have substantial privileges. They receive religious and psychological counseling, including art therapy, and can swim, play soccer, and relax with PlayStations.[5] After release, the Saudi government encourages the former detainees to marry and settle into Saudi society and provides them with financial support and jobs.[6] The government claims that of the more than 100 released detainees, none have been rearrested.[7]

[1]Researchers were unable to obtain permission from Saudi authorities to travel to the country and therefore did not interview any former detainees in Saudi Arabia.

[2]Josh White and Robin Wright, "After Guantánamo, 'Reintegration' for Saudis," *Washington Post*, December 10, 2007.

[3]Christopher Boucek, "Extremist Reeducation and Rehabilitation in Saudi Arabia," *Terrorism Monitor* 16 (2007): 2; Caryle Murphy, "Saudis use cash and counseling to fight terrorism," *The Christian Science Monitor*, August 20, 2008.

[4]In the program, they are taught that only the Saudi state can declare a holy war, thereby breaking any allegiance to Al Qaeda or groups who call for jihad. Shiraz Maher, "Perks of Penance for Saudi Jihadis," *BBC News*, July 9, 2008, available at http://news.bbc.co.uk/1/hi/world/middle_east/7496375.stm (accessed August 28, 2008).

[5]Shiraz Maher, "A Betty Ford Clinic for Jihadis," *Times Online*, July 6, 2008.

[6]Murphy, "Saudis use cash and counseling to fight terrorism."

[7]Farah Stockman, "Nationality Plays Role in Detainee Release: More Saudis Are Freed from Guantánamo," *The Boston Globe*, November 22, 2007.

without jobs, their ability to sustain themselves remained uncertain. And, as one former detainee noted, the stigma of Guantánamo remained: "It doesn't matter I was found innocent. It doesn't matter that they cleared my name by releasing me. We still have this big hat on our heads that we were terrorists."

FAMILY

Prior to their detention, over half of the respondents were married with at least one child. Some had kept abreast of family news through correspondence, while others found it difficult to maintain meaningful contact with their families during their detention in Afghanistan and Guantánamo. Some families believed their loved one was dead and learned what had befallen him only at the time of his release.

Reestablishing primary family relationships was difficult for many former Guantánamo detainees and because of deaths, or estrangements, impossible for others. One former detainee likened his experience to that of the lead character in the film *Cast Away*, played by Tom Hanks, who returned home after years of being stranded on an island to find his fiancée married and with a young child. This former detainee returned home to find his wife had divorced him, while another returned home to learn that his father had been murdered and his estranged wife had taken their children to another part of the country. "I was living in hell in Guantánamo. And when I returned home, it was another hell," he said. Of the Afghan respondents, eight came home to discover that an immediate family member had "developed a mental problem," which they attributed to the stress caused by their detention. Others attributed the physical ailments of family members to the anxiety caused by their absence.

Several released detainees spoke of the impact of their absence on their children. Several reported their children had dropped out of school for lack of funds or had fallen behind academically because of their time away. One respondent lamented that his sons "quit their education because of me, and now they're going to be illiterate." There were other difficulties too. As one former detainee remarked, it was particularly difficult for his children to explain that their father was in Guantánamo, so they simply said "my Dad's in jail." He recalled: "You can't express to a child that there is something in this world called 'detention without trial' where the rule of law doesn't exist." He believed that his children only understood that "if you're in jail you must be bad, because that's what society does."

Many of their families made great sacrifices in seeking their release, some former detainees said. Several families undertook extensive efforts to obtain their loved one's liberty, often with the support of local groups or international organizations like Amnesty International. "I know that my parents' life stopped when I was away," explained one respondent. His family did not want to discuss this topic now, he said, because they did not want him to feel badly for the disruption to their lives. Eleven Afghan respondents reported their families were forced to sell property, borrow money, and/or quit jobs in order to finance efforts to secure their freedom. One former detainee said his brothers quit their jobs to devote themselves full-time to lobbying officials in their country and the United States for his return.

Five Afghan respondents complained that their relatives even paid bribes to corrupt officials who promised to help but ultimately did nothing. Government officers approached one of his brothers and promised to secure his release if the brother bought them a vehicle, one respondent said. The brother complied and was told to meet the officials at a hotel in three days to pick up the former detainee. However, when he arrived, he was beaten by "several police" who threatened to arrest him. Subsequently, another group approached the brother, again promising to return the former detainee to his family if he paid them U.S. $4,000 and accompanied them to another city. The brother sold his car to pay the fee and went to the agreed location to retrieve his brother. The men then admitted they did not know where the brother was. Now broke, the brother had to borrow cash to get home.

For many other Afghan families, the financial toll of trying to secure the release of a family member was even higher, but with no happier results. Some lost their family's assets. "[My father] sold our land in order to seek my release," one respondent reported. And another said: "[T]hey spent all the money I had at home just looking for me. . . . And at the moment, there isn't anything I have to survive on or to make a better life." And a third told of a brother who had returned to Afghanistan to care for their ailing mother and undertake a search for him. He said the family spent approximately U.S. $60,000 trying to secure his release.

SUPPORT AND LIVELIHOODS

Most respondents said economic hardship was one of the primary after-effects of Guantánamo incarceration. As one respondent put it: "The greatest need is financial because as a man, a son, and a father, I should support my family." The economic impact of their detention varied among respondents. Most of the former detainees from Europe were young, unmarried men, and they said their absence did not deprive their families of needed income. Several non-European respondents struggled to make ends meet, but were able to rely on their families for support. Virtually all of the released Afghan detainees, however, reported that their family's wealth had been substantially diminished by their incarceration.

A few respondents reported that they had received some assistance from non-state sources such as community groups, religious institutions, or nongovernmental organizations such as Amnesty International and the Red Cross. But 45 of our 62 respondents said they received little or no support from *any* group—government or private—upon their arrival in their country of origin or a third country. One respondent in Europe noted that convicted criminals in his country receive more assistance than he did. In Afghanistan, national security forces quickly processed the respondents who appeared before the Peace and Reconciliation Commission in a public ceremony in Kabul. The ICRC gave the new arrivals a nominal amount of money (reportedly 500 to 2,000 Afghanis, approximately U.S. $10 to $40) to travel home from the capital. Two Afghan respondents reported that the government had not provided anything beyond these modest handouts. Others said they received nothing.[21] Many respondents said the government was unresponsive to their efforts to recover their illegally seized property or reclaim lost government jobs. In two cases, former detainees said that corrupt government officials seized their property after they were accused of being members of the Taliban. Both said they had to pay bribes to regain their lands.

Many Afghan former detainees in particular said they were destitute and had little hope of recouping lost capital. They had lost wealth in a variety of ways, as we have seen: their property was destroyed or confiscated during capture or seized in their absence, sold by their families, or expended by family members to pay bribes or search for them. Several also remarked they were struggling to buy medicines prescribed in Guantánamo for their mental health. Recalled one Afghan respondent: "I am now needy and destitute . . . I even have to ask people to lend me money to buy medicines." For some, physical impairments compounded difficulties in paying off debt and supporting their families. One former detainee lost not only his business and built up debts to his family while he was in U.S. custody, he also lost the use of his leg from an untreated injury sustained when he was arrested.

Four Afghan respondents said their property was confiscated after their arrests. One said his pharmacy was looted because U.S. and Afghan forces left the doors open "so all of the property, the drugs, and even the notepads from the drugstores had gone missing." Others said their homes were bombed or destroyed during their arrest. One reported that U.S. and Afghan national security forces "snatched almost everything" during a raid of his house, including some $45,000 in cash. His brother complained to authorities about the seizure, to no avail: "[N]obody has scratched their heads about it," he said. A few respondents reported that the arresting authorities—Pakistani, Afghan, or U.S.—confiscated cash, watches, or other personal property from them. Their property typically was not returned: one respondent, however, said that U.S. authorities had returned the watch, flashlight, and U.S. $20 in cash that had been taken from him at the time of his capture over four years earlier. Several Afghan respondents said their families had to sell assets to survive.

"[W]hen I got arrested," one recalled, "there was no [one] responsible for my children and wives and they had to sell my land and property." Another former detainee learned that his family sold his agricultural land to pay for needed medical treatment for family members. He cannot afford to buy land now or pay for the prescriptions his mother needs for an emotional condition she developed while he was in U.S. custody.

Many families assumed significant loans. The families of at least thirteen former detainees reportedly borrowed money, debts that participants said they were struggling to pay off. "I owe money," one said. "They're coming to our house every day." Another remarked: "I have a family of five. So it was difficult for my family while I was in Guantánamo. And now there is a loan. They were borrowing to buy food and flour." Another respondent said: "I don't have any job. There's no land now. There's no house now. And I've got such a big family, and there is no [one] responsible for my family. I don't know what to do. That's all."[22]

EMPLOYMENT

Thirty-four of our respondents said they were unemployed, while only six reported they had permanent employment (the remaining did not specify their employment status). Only one respondent, from Western Europe, expressed optimism about his economic future. Several younger respondents from Western Europe were enrolled in training programs with the hope of obtaining jobs at the conclusion of their courses. Seven former detainees reported they had tried unsuccessfully to find a job. One reported that prospective employers always noticed the three-year gap in his employment history. When he disclosed he had spent time in U.S. custody, he never heard from them again.

The stigma of Guantánamo interfered with the ability of several Afghan former detainees to regain their former positions. Those who were government employees found they could not reclaim their jobs. "The government authorities think we are terrorists," said one respondent.

"I want my job back," exclaimed another. "I want my rights, like the salaries that I was supposed to receive, and I want [a] promotion." Another respondent, a highly educated man, expressed frustration that his time in Guantánamo indelibly marred his reputation and career. He was a practicing physician, who had operated a clinic before his arrest. Now he had to "start again from a drugstore so that people can trust me."

PHYSICAL IMPAIRMENT AND TRAUMA

We asked respondents to describe how they felt physically and psychologically since their release from Guantánamo to gauge how their incarceration may have affected them. As noted earlier, researchers did not conduct medical examinations or evaluate the medical records of the former detainees interviewed for this study. Nor did they conduct psychological evaluations of former detainees. Their responses nevertheless indicate a range of difficulties suffered by detainees after their release. According to Harvard psychiatrist Judith Herman, "[c]hronically traumatized" individuals may lose their "baseline state" of physical comfort and complain "not only of insomnia and agitation," but "numerous types" of physical symptoms, including "tension headaches, gastrointestinal disturbances, and abdominal, back, or pelvic pain."[23]

Many respondents complained of a range of physical impairments, which they attributed to their incarceration by U.S. forces. The most common ailment was pain in the wrists, knees, back, and ankles as a result of prolonged short shackling, hanging, or stress positions. Another complaint was deteriorating eyesight. Some reported chronic pain, fatigue, or a generalized deterioration that interfered with their ability to perform physical labor for extended periods. One respondent, comparing his current state of health to his condition before Guantánamo, said, "I was a strong man. But at the moment, I am nothing." Despite their ailments, few former detainees had been treated for their symptoms following their release, which in some cases had been several years prior to their interview.

Almost two-thirds of the respondents reported having emotional difficulties since leaving Guantánamo.[24] Memories of being short shackled, exposed to extreme temperatures, and exposed to violence by guards remained vivid for many. One former detainee said he had been diagnosed by a psychiatrist with Post-Traumatic Stress Disorder (PTSD).[25] Another explained that he was depressed and became frustrated easily: "I think if I don't leave the room, that I will die and I will burst . . . like a bomb." Images of Guantánamo still haunted him years later, another man said, and he found he had developed a quick temper. "I realized that I didn't return to this life as intact as I thought I had." Many respondents reported suffering memory loss. Others reported disturbing dreams. "I still do get nightmares. I think I'm still back there, with chains and people swearing at me," said one respondent who had been released several years earlier.

Another respondent explained that he had developed an obsession with cleanliness in Guantánamo. "I used to always clean myself, clean myself, clean myself. 'Cause I had nothing to do. Just clean." Throughout the interview, he said, his mind drifted to the bathtub ring that he had not yet had the opportunity to clean and he had to control his impulse to go and clean it. Another released detainee described how his detention experience continued to separate him from those around him. Words like "isolation" and "detention" had acquired whole new meanings for him. He described feeling as though he was "in a world where people just don't understand." A few respondents reported an intense need at times to withdraw from their surroundings and be by themselves.

Whether former detainees who reported mental health problems developed or will develop PTSD or other disorders remains an open question.[26]

CHANGES IN RELIGIOUS BELIEF

No respondent reported becoming less faithful as a result of his detention. One of the doctrines of Islam is *qismah*, which holds that God is omnipotent, that one's overall fate has been predetermined but the individual has agency to determine appropriate courses of action.[27] Guantánamo, according to one respondent, was a "test of faith." Twenty-two former detainees reported no change in their religiosity, and 21 reported their faith had strengthened as a result of their detention. As one respondent put it: "I'm in the same position and the same condition, and I'm a Muslim, and I will be Muslim forever." A few Afghan detainees reported they had learned to read the Quran while· in Guantánamo. Although raised in Muslim families, two European interviewees reported they had not practiced Islam until they were taken into custody. For others, even though their attitude had not changed, their religious practice was a source of strength as they struggled to reestablish their lives.[28] One respondent said: "Right now, actually, the only thing keeping us going is our faith, faith in God because we understand God is the only one who can help us with our current situation."

BELIEFS ABOUT ACCOUNTABILITY

"Who do you feel is responsible for your detention and treatment at Guantánamo?" we asked, along with "What should happen, if anything, to those responsible?" A few respondents wanted criminal trials for those responsible for their detention. One noted that only a few low-level soldiers had been held accountable for detainee abuses. He traced responsibility for their actions to "the attitude of people like Donald Rumsfeld," and statements by U.S. officials that those held in Guantánamo were "terrorists" and "killers."[29] Some respondents said such labels sent a permissive signal to guards and others to abuse them and that those who had abused them should be punished. None of the respondents was aware that those who had allegedly abused them had been held accountable.

Many Afghan former detainees stressed they wanted the authorities to find and punish the individuals in Afghanistan who had reported them. As one respondent explained:

I'm introduced to you and you are told that I'm a criminal, so this is your job to find out whether I'm a criminal or not. If you find me guilty, punish me. If you find me innocent, I should be released and then it's your job to target the person who had introduced me to you and it's your right to punish him for mistakenly or wrongly introducing me to you.

One respondent explicitly called for vengeance. He wanted those responsible for his initial arrest and detention to be put in jail in his home country to "taste the torture and the sufferings." Another wanted those responsible to be put in Guantánamo to "see how it is," but then added that he did not want anyone tortured.

REPARATIONS AND RESTORATIVE MEASURES

Thirty-eight respondents said they believed they should receive financial compensation for what they saw as wrongful imprisonment, for their losses, and for their treatment in Guantánamo.[30] Three said they did not want compensation. Although most respondents said they deserved compensation, few were actively pursuing it. A few living in Europe were aware of legal actions pending against U.S. officials, although they did not hold out much hope of success. In 2008, a U.S. federal appeals court affirmed the dismissal of a suit former Guantánamo detainees had brought against military officials for torture and abuses suffered during their detention.[31] None of the respondents had received any compensation for their treatment. Several Afghan respondents did not think they could seek compensation or that officials would be responsive. A few asked researchers if they would assist them in their efforts. Two former detainees indicated they had approached Afghan or U.S. officials in Afghanistan to take action to satisfy their demands, but had been rebuffed.

With only a few exceptions, respondents wanted compensation from U.S. authorities rather than their own governments. "[I]f they found me guilty . . . they should've killed me. [I]f they have any proof regarding my case, and even if they find me guilty now, I'm ready to be punished; otherwise, they should compensate me," said one former detainee.

Several respondents underscored the reasonableness of their request by pointing to their abject conditions. "I have lost everything as a result of being detained in Guantánamo. I've lost my property. I've lost my job. I've lost my will. . . . There isn't any work for me in Afghanistan," said one. He was prescribed medications in Guantánamo but cannot afford them. "So what to do?" he wondered aloud. The family of another destitute and unemployed respondent forced him to leave home, and his wife returned to her family for support. "I have a plastic bag holding my belongings that I carry with me all the time," he explained. "And I sleep every night in a different mosque. And that is my situation."

Several respondents said the United States should publicly acknowledge their innocence. "If they came and said: 'These guys were innocent. It was all our fault,' I think that would help," remarked one. Another put it this way:

> The four and a half years of my life that's wasted, and which nobody can do anything to bring back, what's done is done, and I can't bring back my life. But, until this point, the American government has not even recognized that it's responsible for this, and has not given any kind of apology or care or concern for me.

Another respondent said, "I just want to prove to the world people that I was innocent, and I want compensation from the Americans." Many felt the U.S. had admitted they were innocent by releasing them and therefore owed them compensation: "As they found us innocent, so now it is their liability to compensate, to pay for us."

Released detainees, in general, wanted compensation sufficient to resume a "normal life." Most Afghan interviewees wanted compensation for their lost property and economic losses. Others felt the U.S. ought to enable them to have a sustainable future. Many felt compensation was needed so that former detainees could move forward with their lives without rancor toward the United States.

Several respondents, however, felt it was impossible for any authority to compensate them for what they lost. In particular, time was something many felt could not be replaced. As one former detainee expressed it:

> Years of my life were wasted over there. I lost the chance of living as a human being, my family lost the chance of being with their father and husband, I lost the chance of being with my children and my wife, a person's life passing by, you never can get that back.

Another respondent said, "I was 19 years old at that time, so . . . they, they took a part of my life, and one of the most important times of my life, like between 19 and 24. Nobody can give me that back, of course."

OPINIONS AND ATTITUDES OF FORMER DETAINEES

Former detainees were asked their opinions on a number of topics, including their views about their own government as well as the United States; what they would like to tell the American public; and what meaning, if any, they derive from the experience of detention, custody, and return. Their responses indicate a range of attitudes and suggest complexity and variation. The range of responses, including declining to provide a response, suggests former detainees were mostly candid in their views.

Home Government

Respondents expressed a range of opinions toward their governments. Many felt their government at best failed to advocate for them while they were incarcerated at Guantánamo. One respondent said he felt "betrayed" by his government. He expected his government to protect him, but believed they only secured his release because of the public campaign his family conducted with the support of Amnesty International. Another was disappointed that his government had not gathered evidence to help demonstrate his innocence to his American captors: "The Americans didn't know anything about me, and my government could [have] collected information from people in my community. Why didn't it try?" At the same time, a few European former detainees were grateful their governments secured their release, even those who were imprisoned upon release. "Well, it may seem strange because I've spent [time] in jail here after I returned, but I'm extremely grateful to [my] government," said one.

Former Afghan detainees had mixed opinions about their government. One remarked that he had supported the transitional government, which he believed should have intervened on his behalf. Others excused the failure of the Afghan government to do more because their leaders were powerless against the United States. "[T]hey didn't have the power to tell the Americans not to take me to Guantánamo," said one. Several believed U.S. forces did not know enough about local politics to avoid being manipulated by unscrupulous members of the community who saw an opportunity to settle old scores. On the other hand, some Afghan former detainees expressed general support for their government and felt their country was heading for better times after decades of civil war.

The United States

Of those who responded to the question, 31 said their opinion of the United States changed from positive to negative as a result of their experiences in U.S. custody. Fifteen respondents reported that their attitude had not changed and remained generally positive. Five of those we interviewed declined to answer the question or stated they had no opinion.

Many respondents expressed feelings of bitterness that, in their view, the United States had disregarded the rule of law and humanitarian principles. "We never imagined Americans, the country that was the defender of democracy, would treat anybody like this," remarked one. An Afghan respondent noted that the U.S. supported Afghan forces when they were fighting the Russians, but had turned on these same fighters after 9/11. He now was boycotting American products, he said. "It's very good for humankind and the world to get rid of terrorism and bad people. I think there are many other ways to beat terrorism rather than fighting, battling, destroying the roads, schools, killing our children, killing our families," he remarked. Others also held strong views, but affirmed their desire to address their concerns peacefully. One respondent said that despite his mistreatment in U.S. custody, "I'm not going to plan an attack. . . . We know that within the States you also have organizations and courts and you have the legal system that works quite well, and that is how I will try to get my problem solved and try to claim compensation."

Several respondents wanted to assure Americans that they harbored no ill will toward them. Two in particular said they wanted to thank those U.S. citizens who had protested against U.S. Guantánamo policy. One former detainee, whose attitude toward the U.S. had not changed, recalled candid conversations with Guantánamo guards. He said, "[They] tried to understand why I was there and what had brought me there. And as they tried to understand me, I also tried to understand them." As a result, he concluded: "I realized that the situation is extremely complicated, and that responsibilities are shared." Others said they only wanted the American public to recognize that they were innocent. "I just want to tell them that I am not this savage beast, what they were told I am," explained one respondent.

Other respondents offered more muted criticism, believing a misinformed American public was unable to correct the mistaken policies of its government. Several respondents expressed the opinion that Guantánamo damaged America's reputation as a leading democracy. Nine respondents made clear they distinguished between U.S. citizens and their political leaders and reserved their ire for the U.S. authorities. In the words of one: "I would still love to go to America. . . . I've got nothing against the American public, nothing at all. . . . [T]he country hasn't done anything to me. Individuals have. So you can't just go and blame the whole country."

The Department of Defense has claimed that as many as 37 former detainees (of more than 500) have returned to "the battlefield," a recidivism rate of approximately 6 percent.[32] This figure has been

What should happen to detainees still held in Guantánamo? Almost half of those who responded to this question (13 of 29) said the remaining detainees should be charged and prosecuted or, if there was no evidence, they should be freed. As one respondent put it: "I feel that the United States should follow its own laws and constitution. If these detainees are guilty, try them, sentence them to many years in jail or life in jail or something. If they are not, if they are innocent, then they should be released." A few respondents said trials for the remaining detainees should be conducted by an international court because they believed U.S. courts lacked credibility.

While a few respondents felt that the detainees who remained in Guantánamo were innocent and should be released, others focused only on nationals of their own country. Explained one respondent: "I know the Afghan prisoners completely because I was a teacher, and they were my students [in Guantánamo]. Most of them have been arrested based on personal feuds." A few respondents said the detainees still held in Guantánamo should be tried by their home governments. "[H]olding [detainees] in Guantánamo is unjust and unfair," one respondent said. "They shouldn't be there in the first place, especially since it's not proven legally that they've committed any crime."

strongly disputed. The government-released information was not sufficient to enable independent verification of these cases and critics have pointed out that the government list of those who returned to fight against the U.S. included "those who have publicized anti-American opinions," namely the "Tipton 3" (British former detainees whose experiences were depicted in the film *The Road to Guantánamo*), and Uighur refugees who gave interviews to international press and against whom no other evidence has been introduced.[33] While published interviews with a few former detainees have suggested they became radicalized during their time in Guantánamo,[34] none of the respondents in our study expressed such opinions.

REFLECTION

Recovering from trauma inflicted in captivity typically comes in stages: first comes the establishment of safety, then remembrance and mourning, and finally reconnection with ordinary life, according to Judith

Herman. Progression through these stages is not always linear and is influenced by a number of factors.

A few, mostly younger men, expressed anger or bitterness about their years in U.S. custody. For them, Guantánamo was a dark coming-of-age experience which gave them a sober perspective on the abuse of power. One young respondent said: "I stayed in Guantánamo so I know about . . . [the] torture done by Americans." He said he wanted to forget the past, but found it hard to do so: "I was detained for only two years. I left Guantánamo at age 23. But it has put me in distress for the rest of my life."

Many former detainees painted if not an angry picture, a bleak one of their time at Guantánamo and how it colored their present. "What happened to me is the worst memory I have ever had," said one respondent. Looking back, another said he lost his capacity to be human at Guantánamo. Others described their time in U.S. custody as a dark dream. "When I remember Guantánamo," said a respondent, "I feel as if I have just woken up from the grave or a tomb."

Some talked about learning the virtue of patience during detention. As one respondent put it: "We learned how to become really patient and that is something that I did not expect." Another remarked: "All those times when we didn't have enough to eat, all those freezing cold temperatures, and months and months without showers. All the things that we have experienced there, when I look back at it now I'm surprised by my patience, actually." Still, another: "Allah, our God, has wished me such a period in my life. I don't condemn anybody at all." Others spoke about their desire to forget the past and move forward with their lives. As one put it: "Guantánamo was this big nightmare. Now I just want to close that page and open a new page with my family and my children." Another former detainee simply reported that his Guantánamo chapter was not over: "I am still looking for my path in my life."

Herman notes that at the final stage of recovery a minority of trauma survivors may become engaged in social action as a way to give meaning and worth to their past suffering.[35] Reflecting on their time at

Guantánamo, a number of former detainees commented that the experience had given them a new sense of determination and resolve. A few former detainees left Guantánamo determined to speak out against unjust imprisonment and treatment anywhere in the world. Others said they had become more principled because of the hardships they had endured. "I wouldn't be who I am today," one said. "And I wouldn't care about the world. . . . And in some degree I thank America for that."

The positive sentiments of a few, however, can never mask the feelings of despair and uncertainty shared by most of the former detainees we interviewed. Some arrived home to find that their families had suffered in their absence and without their support. Family assets had diminished or been lost altogether. Years of separation made family reunifications difficult. For many the "stigma of Guantánamo" hindered their ability to find meaningful employment. Some had tried to move on with their lives but were plagued by intrusive memories of the abuses they had suffered in U.S. custody. Common to most—if not all—was the sense that the legacy of Guantánamo remained.

Chapter 6

CONCLUSIONS AND RECOMMENDATIONS

CONCLUSIONS

Our research reveals serious flaws in the system created by the Bush Administration for the apprehension, detention, interrogation, and release of suspected members of the Taliban and Al Qaeda taken into U.S. custody since the attacks of September 11, 2001. One of the most egregious aspects of this system was a series of high-level directives issued between September 2001 and April 2003 authorizing the use of "enhanced interrogation techniques."[1] Many of these interrogation methods—whether used individually or simultaneously over prolonged periods of time—appear to have violated international and domestic prohibitions on torture or other cruel, inhuman, or degrading treatment.

By adopting a "take the gloves off" approach,[2] top U.S. civilian and military leaders established unprecedented parameters for the treatment of detainees at U.S. detention facilities in Afghanistan, Guantánamo Bay, and other locations. This permissive environment allowed—if not encouraged—guards and interrogators to dehumanize and, in some cases, torture detainees in their custody.[3] The totality of this experience deeply affected the lives of former detainees—many of whom government officials believe were imprisoned in error. Stigmatized by their imprisonment, a significant number of these detainees now face difficulties finding employment, and some report lasting emotional and psychological scars.

Our research raises troubling questions about the process by which the U.S. military apprehended and screened suspected Al Qaeda and Taliban fighters and their ostensible supporters. In particular, the U.S. government's payment of cash bounties created an indiscriminate and unscrupulous dragnet in Afghanistan and elsewhere that resulted in the detention of thousands of people, many of whom it appears had no connection to Al Qaeda or the Taliban and/or posed no threat to U.S. security. Once in U.S. custody, the screening procedures of detainees often failed to distinguish civilians from combatants. Instead of holding battlefield hearings mandated by the Geneva Conventions to determine the combat status of detainees,[4] President Bush determined unilaterally that all prisoners captured in the "war on terror" were "unlawful enemy combatants" and could be held indefinitely.[5] Yet the Administration failed to employ sufficient procedural safeguards to minimize errors in determining who fell into that category. Ultimately, the incentive to capture suspected members of Al Qaeda and the Taliban became a higher priority than the diligence and investigation necessary to discern accurately whose detention was justified.

As early as September 2002, high-level U.S. officials were aware of concerns within military and intelligence circles about how many of those held at the U.S. naval base in Guantánamo Bay were actually dangerous Al Qaeda or Taliban fighters. A senior Central Intelligence Agency (CIA) analyst with extensive Middle East experience assessed detainees at the base in summer 2002 and concluded in a top-secret report that approximately a third of the population—at that time 200 of the 600 detainees—had no connection to terrorism.[6] Many, he said, had been "caught in the dragnet. They were not fighters, they were not doing jihad. They should not have been there."[7] Guantánamo's commander, Major General Dunlavey, agreed with him and later estimated that half the camp population was mistakenly detained.[8] A Federal Bureau of Investigation (FBI) counterterrorism expert went even further and told a committee of the National Security Council that there were at most only 50 detainees worth holding at Guantánamo.[9]

The consequences of false identification were dire. Detainees faced years of confinement in Guantánamo without any meaningful opportunity to show they had been wrongly detained. In June 2008, more than six years after the first detainees arrived at Guantánamo, the Supreme Court ruled in *Boumediene v. Bush* that detainees held there had the right to access U.S. courts to review the legal basis of their continued confinement, and as of the date of this writing, no full habeas hearing has been held.[10]

As of October 2008, the Department of Defense states that approximately 255 detainees remain at Guantánamo.[11] Meanwhile, over 520 detainees have been released from the camp, while approximately 60 detainees continue to be held even though military status boards have recommended their release.[12] Of the more than 770 individuals known to have been incarcerated for some period at Guantánamo, the U.S. government has charged only 23 with war crimes as of October 2008.[13] These figures argue in favor of a full investigation to determine how and why the U.S. has held so many men for so long without adequate legal safeguards.

Our qualitative data and secondary sources indicate that many detainees held in U.S. custody in Kandahar and Bagram, Afghanistan, repeatedly experienced physical abuse, deprivations, humiliation, and degradation. The conditions in which detainees were held, as well as their treatment at these facilities, contravened international guidelines for the humane treatment of detainees, violated fundamental cultural and religious taboos against public nudity, interfered with religious practice, and created an environment that maximized physical and psychological discomfort and uncertainty. Respondents held at Bagram in particular reported abuses that included beatings, stress positions, prolonged hanging by the arms, sleep deprivation, intimidation, and being terrorized with dogs.

In Guantánamo, military commanders explicitly subordinated camp administration and procedures to the priorities of interrogation and thus created an atmosphere of constant surveillance and intrusion in the cellblocks that dehumanized detainees. The operating assumption was that camp conditions should serve to weaken the defenses of detainees and enable interrogators to break them down psychologically. Indeed, each component of the camp system—from the use of numbers to identify detainees to solitary confinement—was designed to increase the authority and power of camp interrogators while compounding the detainees' sense of isolation, powerlessness, and uncertainty.

Camp procedures were designed to support the work of interrogators; however, they also fostered hostility and conflict between detainees and camp personnel. With detainees' autonomy and control greatly reduced, one of the few ways they could protest the conditions under which they were held was through collective resistance. Respondents said they felt particularly humiliated and outraged when guards mishandled, dropped, or threw the Quran to the floor. Such incidents frequently sparked acts of collective resistance, including hunger strikes. Detainee resistance often exacted retribution by camp personnel, which generated a further response from detainees, fueling a vicious cycle in which the use of physical force by guards and the imposition of solitary confinement became predictable consequences.

Uncertainty over their fate, often encouraged by their interrogators, haunted Guantánamo detainees, who had no effective avenue to challenge the legality of their confinement. From January 2002 until June 2004, Guantánamo detainees had no access to courts or lawyers. This did not change in any meaningful way even after the 2004 Supreme Court ruling in *Rasul v. Bush*, which required that detainees be permitted access to the federal courts for the purpose of challenging the legality of their detention through habeas corpus review.[14] Moreover, procedures established in the wake of the *Rasul* decision to review whether detainees were "enemy combatants" and therefore could be detained indefinitely were ineffective and fundamentally flawed. Many respondents said they did not understand the Combatant Status Review Tribunals and annual Administrative Review Boards. Other respondents understood only too well that these procedures did not provide a meaningful opportunity to prove their claims of innocence. Without access to an attorney, unable to obtain witnesses, and generally denied access to all evidence against them, detainees remained effectively outside of the rule of law.

In interviews former detainees used words like "futile," "desperate," "helpless," and "hopeless" to describe their feelings as they reflected on their incarceration at Guantánamo. As months turned into years, the *cumulative effect* of indefinite detention, environmental stressors, and other forms of abuse began to exact an increasing psychological toll on many detainees. The International Committee of the Red Cross (ICRC) raised concerns over several years about the deleterious effects of confinement on the psychological health of detainees at Guantánamo.[15] For example, when the ICRC visited Guantánamo in June 2004, it found a high incidence of mental illness produced by stress, much of it triggered by prolonged solitary confinement.[16] Indeed, the number of attempted suicides reported and witnessed by former detainees interviewed for this study was considerable.

Over half of the study respondents (31) of the 55 who discussed their interrogation sessions at Guantánamo characterized them as "abusive," while the remainder (24) said they did not experience any problems. Abuses reported by these detainees who were ultimately released included being subjected to short shackling, stress positions, prolonged isolation, and exposure to extreme temperatures for extended periods—often simultaneously. On some occasions, these tactics were used in conjunction with sensory bombardment, including extremely loud rock music and strobe lights.

Camp officials attempted to integrate medical personnel into the process of interrogation at Guantánamo, prompting both the American Medical Association and the American Psychiatric Association to issue statements in 2006 restricting participation of members in interrogations.[17] In September 2008, members of the American Psychological Association voted to prohibit psychologists from consulting or participating in the interrogation of detainees held at Guantánamo or so-called black sites operated by the CIA.[18] Former medical personnel at the base have said that through 2003 (and possibly later) interrogators had access to detainee medical records and used that knowledge to extract information from detainees. Furthermore, since late 2002, military psychologists and psychiatrists serving on Behavioral Science Consultation Teams (BSCTs) have played an active role in developing and implementing interrogation strategies at Guantánamo.[19]

Interrogation policies and standards at Guantánamo changed over time, but the data demonstrate that some practices remained consistent throughout the period when the study respondents were held there (January 2002 to January 2007). While more needs to be revealed about the specific interrogation techniques used at Guantánamo, it appears that many of the methods which detainees complained about most bitterly—cold rooms and short shackling, in conjunction with prolonged isolation—were permitted under the U.S. military's interrogation guidelines in force from April 2003 to September 2006.[20] These practices contravene the Geneva Conventions of 1949, which the United States ratified in 1955. However, President Bush sidestepped these prohibitions in January 2002, when he determined that the Third Geneva Convention, also known as the Geneva Convention Relative to the Treatment of Prisoners of War (POWs), did not apply to suspected members of the Taliban and Al Qaeda taken into detention in Afghanistan.[21]

To date, no independent, comprehensive investigation has been conducted to determine the role that camp personnel as well as officials farther up the civilian and military chains of command played in the design and implementation of interrogation techniques at Guantánamo. No broad investigation has yet addressed whether or not these officials should be held accountable for any crimes they or their subordinates may have committed.

After release from Guantánamo, many respondents said they confronted a host of challenges upon arrival in their country of origin or a third country. Only a handful of former detainees said they received any meaningful or effective assistance. Labeled the "worst of the worst," they left Guantánamo shrouded in "guilt by association," particularly as their innocence or guilt had never been determined by a court of law. Some respondents referred to this state of affairs as their "Guantánamo stigma" and said it contributed to their difficulties finding employment and reintegrating into their communities. Upon arriving home, some detainees found their families had extinguished their assets and assumed significant debt. Some respondents returned home with compromised physical and mental health, and were unable to afford or access rehabilitative care and services. To date, there has been no official acknowledgment of any mistake or wrongdoing by the United States as a result of its detention or treatment of any Guantánamo detainee. No former detainees have been compensated for their losses or harm suffered as a result of their confinement.

RECOMMENDATIONS

This book provides the first *systematic* glimpse into the world of former detainees once held in U.S. custody in Afghanistan and Guantánamo Bay.[22] But it is only a glimpse, albeit a very troubling one. There is more to be learned, and our hope is that further investigations and studies will follow with the aim of removing the shroud of official secrecy that has hidden what has been taking place at Guantánamo and other detention facilities from full public scrutiny.

As a first step, we recommend the establishment of an independent, non-partisan commission to investigate and publicly report on the detention and treatment of detainees held in U.S. custody in Afghanistan, Iraq, Guantánamo Bay, and other locations since the attacks of September 11, 2001. The mandate of the commission should be sufficiently broad to include a probe of how the policies and practices of these detention facilities have affected the return and reintegration of former detainees in their countries of origin or third countries.

The commission should be composed of individuals of the highest caliber, known for their integrity, credibility, and independence. Commission members should include former members of the U.S. military and specialists in U.S. constitutional and military law, international humanitarian and human rights law, public health, psychology, and medicine. To leverage the expertise of its members, the commission should be divided into working groups to focus on discrete areas.

The commission should have subpoena power to compel witnesses and gain access to all classified materials concerning apprehension, detention, interrogation, and release of detainees taken into U.S. custody. The commission should be allocated adequate funding and expert staff to fulfill its mandate. Commission members and staff should undergo expedited review to ensure prompt receipt of the necessary security clearances to gain access to all relevant materials. Most important, the commission should have authority to recommend criminal investigations at all levels of the civilian and military command of those allegedly responsible for abuses or having allowed such abuses to take place. The work of this commission must not be undercut by the issuance of pardons, amnesties, or other measures that would protect those culpable from accountability.

The mandate of the commission should include—but not be limited to—the following areas of inquiry:

- **Apprehension and Screening.** What were the procedures used in the screening of suspected "unlawful enemy combatants" and were they lawful, appropriate, and effective? If not, what should be the proper screening procedures for suspected enemy fighters? Did the U.S. military detain and transfer individuals to Guantánamo who had no connection to Al Qaeda or the Taliban or otherwise posed no threat to U.S. security? Did the use of monetary bounties contribute to the detention and interrogation of individuals who should never have been taken into U.S. custody? How did the decision not to apply the Geneva

Conventions affect the apprehension and screening of detainees?

- **Conditions and Treatment of Detention.** Did the conditions in U.S. detention facilities in Afghanistan and Guantánamo meet humane standards of treatment? Did the decision not to apply the Geneva Conventions affect the conditions and treatment of detainees? How did the U.S. deviate from the "golden rule" standard articulated in the Army Field Manual which states that no interrogator should use a technique that the interrogator would not want used on a U.S. soldier?[23] What role did medical and psychological personnel play in the treatment of detainees? Did they contravene professional codes of conduct or violate any laws?

- **Interrogations.** Did U.S. interrogation practices subject detainees to abusive treatment including torture and cruel, inhuman, or degrading treatment? How did interrogation policies and practices evolve since President Bush's declaration of a "war on terror" on September 20, 2001? And what was the role of civilian and military officials in designing and implementing these polices?

- **Reintegration and Rehabilitation.** What has been the *cumulative effect* of indefinite detention on those released from Guantánamo? What was the process to determine whether it was safe to transfer a detainee to the custody of a foreign government? What protections were used, and were they sufficient? Have any former detainees been subjected to cruel and inhumane treatment since their transfer to the custody of other governments? How successful are former detainees in reintegrating and resettling in their countries of origin or third countries? What impediments do they face? If any returnees pose a security threat, what steps and agreements with receiving governments have been taken to minimize such a threat?

If appropriate, the commission should recommend institutional reforms and other measures to (1) improve the apprehension and screening of suspected enemy fighters, (2) prevent abusive detention and interrogation practices, and (3) monitor the treatment of former detainees upon their release from U.S. custody.

If the commission concludes the U.S. government has violated the rights of individuals held in its custody, it should recommend corrective measures, including issuing an apology, providing compensation, and providing a fair means for clearing that person's name. If applicable, the commission should make recommendations for further criminal investigation of those responsible for any crimes at all levels of the chains of command.

With the advent of a new U.S. administration, it is an opportune time to review and correct policies and, if necessary, make institutional reforms to ensure the means used to protect U.S. security are consistent with American values and U.S. obligations under domestic and international law.

APPENDIXES

Appendixes A through C are selected documents provided to the Senate Armed Services Committee in conjunction with the Committee's June 2008 hearings on the origins of aggressive interrogation techniques used on detainees in U.S. custody.

APPENDIX A

Counter Resistance Strategy Meeting Minutes

TAB 7

Counter Resistance Strategy Meeting Minutes   Page 2 of 5

Counter Resistance Strategy Meeting Minutes

Persons in Attendance:

COL Cummings, LTC Phifer, CDR Bridges, LTC Beaver, MAJ Burney, MAJ Leso, Dave Becker, John Fredman, 1LT Seek, SPC Pimentel

The following notes were taken during the aforementioned meeting at 1340 on October 2, 2002. All questions and comments have been paraphrased:

BSCT Description of SERE Psych Training (MAJ Burney and MAJ Leso)

- Identify trained resisters
    - Al Qaeda Training
- Methods to overcome resistance
    - Rapport building (approach proven to yield positive results)
    - Friendly approach (approach proven to yield positive results)
    - Fear Based Approaches are unreliable, ineffective in almost all cases
- What's more effective than fear based strategies are camp-wide, environmental strategies designed to disrupt cohesion and communication among detainees.
    - Environment should foster dependence and compliance

LTC Phifer	Harsh techniques used on our service members have worked and will work on some, what about those?
MAJ Leso	Force is risky, and may be ineffective due to the detainees' frame of reference. They are used to seeing much more barbaric treatment.
Becker	Agreed

→ At this point a discussion about ISN 63 ensued, recalling how he has responded to certain types of deprivation and psychological stressors. After short discussion the BSCT continued to address the overall manipulation of the detainees' environment.

BSCT continued:

- Psychological stressors are extremely effective (ie, sleep deprivation, withholding food, isolation, loss of time)

COL Cummings   We can't do sleep deprivation
LTC Beaver   Yes, we can - with approval.

- Disrupting the normal camp operations is vital. We need to create an environment of "controlled chaos"

LTC Beaver   We may need to curb the harsher operations while ICRC is around. It is better not to expose them to any controversial techniques. We must have the support of the DOD.

Becker   We have had many reports from Bagram about sleep deprivation being used.

LTC Beaver   True, but officially it is not happening. It is not being reported officially. The ICRC is a serious concern. They will be in and out, scrutinizing our operations, unless they are displeased and decide to protest and leave. This would draw a lot of negative attention.

COL Cummings   The new PSYOP plan has been passed up the chain
LTC Beaver   It's at J3 at SOUTHCOM.
Fredman   The DOJ has provided much guidance on this issue. The CIA is not held to the same rules as the military. In the past when the ICRC has made a big deal about certain detainees, the DOD has "moved" them away from the attention of ICRC. Upon questioning from the ICRC about their whereabouts, the DOD's response has repeatedly been that the detainee merited no status under the Geneva Convention. The CIA has employed aggressive techniques on less than a handful of suspects since 9/11.
Under the Torture Convention, torture has been prohibited by international law, but the language of the statutes is written vaguely. Severe mental and physical pain is prohibited. The mental part is explained as poorly as the physical. Severe physical pain described as anything causing permanent damage to major organs or body parts. Mental torture described as anything leading to permanent, profound damage to the senses or personality. It is basically subject to perception. If the detainee dies you're doing it wrong. So far, the techniques we have addressed have not proven to produce these types of results, which in a way challenges what the BSCT paper says about not being able to prove whether these techniques will lead to permanent damage. Everything on the BSCT white paper is legal from a civilian standpoint.[Any questions of severe weather or temperature conditions should be deferred to medical staff.] Any of the techniques that lie on the harshest end of the spectrum must be performed by a highly trained individual. Medical personnel should be present to treat any possible accidents. The CIA operates without military intervention. When the CIA has wanted to use more aggressive techniques in the past, the FBI has pulled their personnel from theatre. In those rare instances, aggressive techniques have proven very helpful.

LTC Beaver   We will need documentation to protect us

Fredman   Yes, if someone dies while aggressive techniques are being used, regardless of cause of death, the backlash of attention would be severely detrimental. Everything must be approved and documented.

Becker   LEA personnel will not participate in harsh techniques

LTC Beaver   There is no legal reason why LEA personnel cannot participate in these operations

→At this point a discussion about whether or not to video tape the aggressive sessions, or interrogations at all ensued.

Becker   Videotapes are subject to too much scrutiny in court. We don't want the LEA people in aggressive sessions anyway.

LTC Beaver   LEA choice not to participate in these types of interrogations is more ethical and moral as opposed to legal.

Fredman   The videotaping of even totally legal techniques will look "ugly".

Becker   (Agreed)

Fredman   The Torture Convention prohibits torture and cruel, inhumane and degrading treatment. The US did not sign up on the second part, because of the 8th amendment (cruel and unusual punishment), but we did sign the part about torture. This gives us more license to use more controversial techniques.

LTC Beaver   Does SERE employ the "wet towel" technique?

Fredman   If a well-trained individual is used to perform this technique it can feel like you're drowning. The lymphatic system will react as if you're suffocating, but your body will not cease to function. It is very effective to identify phobias and use them (ie, insects, snakes, claustrophobia). The level of resistance is directly related to person's experience.

MAJ Burney   Whether or not significant stress occurs lies in the eye of the beholder. The burden of proof is the big issue. It is very difficult to disprove someone else's PTSD.

Fredman   These techniques need involvement from interrogators, psych, medical, legal, etc.

Becker   Would we get blanket approval or would it be case by case?

Fredman   The CIA makes the call internally on most of the types of techniques found in the BSCT paper, and this discussion. Significantly harsh techniques are approved through the DOJ.

LTC Phifer   Who approves ours? The CG? SOUTHCOM CG?

Fredman   Does the Geneva Convention apply? The CIA rallied for it not to.

LTC Phifer   Can we get DOJ opinion about these topics on paper?

LTC Beaver   Will it go from DOJ to DOD?

LTC Phifer   Can we get to see a CIA request to use advanced aggressive techniques?

Fredman   Yes, but we can't provide you with a copy. You will probably be able to look at it. An example of a different perspective on torture is Turkey. In Turkey they say that interrogation at all, or anything you do to that results in the subject betraying his comrades is torture.

LTC Beaver   In the BSCT paper it says something about "imminent threat of death", ...

Fredman   The threat of death is also subject to scrutiny, and should be handled on a case by case basis. Mock executions don't work as well as friendly approaches, like letting someone write a letter home, or providing them with an extra book.

Becker   I like the part about ambient noise.

→ At this point a discussion about ways to manipulate the environment ensued, and the following ideas were offered:

- Medical visits should be scheduled randomly, rather than on a set system
- Let detainee rest just long enough to fall asleep and wake him up about every thirty minutes and tell him it's time to pray again
- More meals per day induce loss of time
- Truth serum; even though it may not actually work, it does have a placebo effect.

Meeting ended at 1450.

APPENDIX B

Physical Pressures Used in Resistance Training and Against American Prisoners and Detainees

INTRODUCTION

(FOUO) Physical pressures used in resistance training are not designed to elicit compliance, to produce enduring or damaging consequences, or to render the student so incapacitated by physical or emotional duress that learning does not take place. The purpose of applying physical pressures is to project the students' focus into the resistance scenario and realistically simulate conditions associated with captivity and resistance efforts. The pressures used in training are minor in comparison to that which American prisoners have experienced in the past. The tactics are used in lieu of pressures used historically.

(FOUO) The application of physical pressures in training is necessary to produce the correct emotion and physiological projection a student requires for stress inoculation and stress resolution to be accomplished. This "Controlled Realism" must exist for the correct learning to take place. If too little physical pressure is applied, the student will fail to acquire the necessary inoculation effect and run the risk of underestimating the demands real captivity can produce. If too much physical pressure is applied, the student is made vulnerable to the effects of learned helplessness, which will render him/her less prepared for captivity than s/he was prior to training.

(FOUO) Applying physical pressures in an intense, simulated captivity role-play requires considerable skill and composure on the part of the resistance-training instructor. This is an acquired skill which demands considerable knowledge, experience, and grounding in human behavior and resistance theory. Not all resistance-training role-players are necessarily suited to perform this particular element of instruction. Careful training and monitoring of the instructor of qualified individuals are necessary to maintain the desired application of this critical education tool. The instructor who uses these physical pressures in training must:

- Remember physical pressure must be uniquely applied to each individual student depending on his/her physical size and resilience.
- Constantly monitor the student's resistance behavior and appropriately applied physical pressure in a manner that is consistent with controlled realism, but also facilitates the desired learning outcome.

(FOUO) APPROVED PHYSICAL PRESSURES USED IN JPRA RESISTANCE TRAINING INCLUDE:

1. (FOUO) FACIAL SLAP: Slap the subject's face midway between the chin and the bottom of the corresponding ear lobe. The arm swing follows an ark no greater than approximately 18 inches. "Pull" the force of the slap to generate the appropriate effect. Use no more than 2 slaps with any singular application-- typically, the training effectiveness of slapping has become negligible after 3 to 4 applications. (Typical conditions for application: to instill fear and despair, to punish selective behavior, to instill humiliation or cause insult).

2. (FOUO) WALLING: With a hood, towel or similar aide, roll or fold the hood the long way, place it around the subject's neck. Grasp each side firmly and roll your fist inwardly till a relatively flat surface is created by the first joint of your fingers or the back of your hand. Quickly and firmly push, numerous times, the student into the wall in a manner, which eliminates a 'whip lash' effect of the head - push with

your arms only. Do not use 'leg force' to push the student--ensure the wall you are using will accommodate the student without injury and adjust your 'push' accordingly. (Typical conditions for application: to instill fear and despair, to punish selective behavior, to instill humiliation or cause insult).

3. (FOUO) SILENCING FACIAL HOLD: This tactic is used when the subject is talking too much or about inappropriate subjects. The interrogator attempts to physically intimidate the subject into silence by placing their hand over the subject's mount and violating their personal space. (Typical conditions for application: to threaten or intimidate via invasion of personal space, to instill fear and apprehension without using direct physical force, to punish illogical, defiant, or repetitive responses).

4. (FOUO) FACIAL HOLD: This tactic is used when the subject fails to maintain eye contact with the interrogator. The interrogator grasps the subject's head with both hands holding the head immobile. Again, the interrogator moves into and violates the subject's personal space (Typical conditions for application: to threaten or intimidate via invasion of personal space, to instill fear and apprehension without using direct physical force, to punish illogical, defiant, or repetitive responses).

5. (FOUO) ABDOMEN SLAP: This tactic is used when the subject is illogical, defiant, arrogant and generally uncooperative. It is designed to gain the subject's attention (Typical conditions for application: to instill fear and despair, to punish selective behavior, to instill humiliation or cause insult).

6. (FOUO) FINGER PRESS: This tactic is using the forefinger to forcefully, repeatedly jab the chest of the subject. The motion should be firm but not forceful enough to cause injury. (Typical conditions for application: to instill apprehension and insult).

7. (FOUO) WATER: When using this tactic, water is poured, flicked, or tossed on the subject. The water is used as a distracter, to disturb the subject's focus on the line of interrogation. When pouring, the subject is usually on their knees and the water is poured slowly over their head. Flicking water is generally directed to the face and again used to distract the subject's attention and focus. Tossing water is more forceful and should come as a surprise. The water is usually directed to the mouth and chin area of the face and care is used to avoid the subject's eyes. (Typical conditions for application: to create a distracting pressure, to startle, to instill humiliation or cause insult).

8. (FOUO) BLOCK HOLD: The subject can be sitting, kneeling or standing with their arms extended out straight with the palms up. The interrogator puts a weighted block, 10-15 lbs., on their hands. The subject is required to keep their arms straight, told not to drop the block at risk of additional punishment (typical conditions for application: to create a distracting pressure, to demonstrate self-imposed pressure, to instill apprehension, humiliation or cause insult).

9. (FOUO) BLOCK SIT: Using a block with a pointed end that is pointed to the floor, the subject is told sit on the flat top with feet and knees together. The knees are bent 90 degrees, and the subject is not allowed to spread their legs to form a tripod. The process of trying to balance on this very unstable seat and concentrate on the interrogator's questions at the same time is very difficult (typical conditions for application: to create a distracting pressure, to demonstrate self-imposed pressure, to instill apprehension, humiliation or cause insult).

10. (FOUO) ATTENTION GRASP: In a controlled, quick motion the subject is grabbed with two hands, one on each side of the collar. In the same motion, the interrogator draws the subject into his or her own space. (Typical conditions for application: to startle, to instill fear, apprehension, and humiliation or cause insult).

11. (FOUO) STRESS POSITION: The subject is placed on their knees, told to extend their arms either straight up or straight to the front. The subject is not allowed to lean back on their heels, arch their back or relieve the pressure off the point of the knee. Note: there are any number of uncomfortable physical positions that can be used and considered in this category (typical conditions for application: to create a distracting pressure, to demonstrate self-imposed pressure, to instill apprehension, humiliation or cause insult).

(FOUO) APPROVED PHYSICAL PRESSURES USED IN OTHER SERVICE SCHOOL RESISTANCE TRAINING PROGRAMS INCLUDE:

NOTE: In addition to the tactics listed below, the individual service school programs include many of the same pressures used in JPRA training. It is important to remember that as with any physical pressure, these tactics are closely monitored, strict time limits are applied and training safety is always paramount.

1. (FOUO) SMOKE: Pipe tobacco smoke is blown into the subject's face while in a standing, sitting or kneeling position. This is used during interrogation to produce discomfort. A smoking pipe is filled with dry tobacco, the pipe is lit and the bit of the pipe has a hose attached. The interrogator blows back through the pipe bowl creating an extraordinary amount of thick, sickening smoke. Maximum duration is five minutes (typical conditions for application: to instill fear and despair, to punish selective behavior, to instill humiliation or cause insult).

2. (FOUO) WATERBOARD: Subject is interrogated while strapped to a wooden board, approximately 4'x7'. Often the subject's feet are elevated after being strapped down and having their torso stripped. Up to 1.5 gallons of water is slowly poured directly onto the subject's face from a height of 12-24 inches. In some cases, a wet cloth is placed over the subject's face. It will remain in place for a short period of time. Trained supervisory and medial staff monitors the subject's physical condition. Student may be threatened or strapped back onto the board at a later time. However, no student will have water applied a second time. This tactic instills a feeling of drowning and quickly compels cooperation (typical conditions for application: to instill fear and despair, to punish selective behavior).

3. (FOUO) SHAKING AND MANHANDLING: Subject is grasped with a rolled cloth hood or towel around their neck (provides stability to the head and neck). The subject's clothing is grasped firmly and then a side-to-side motion is used to shake the subject. Care is used to not create a whipping effect to the neck. (Typical conditions for application: to instill fear and despair, to punish selective behavior, to instill humiliation or cause insult).

4. (FOUO) GROUNDING: This tactic is using the manhandling pressure and forcefully guiding the subject to the ground, never letting go (typical conditions for application: to instill fear and despair, to punish selective behavior).

5. (FOUO) CRAMPED CONFINEMENT ("the little box"): This is administered by placing a subject into a small box in a kneeling position with legs crossed at the ankle and having him learn [sic]forward to allow the door to be closed without exerting pressure on the back. Time and temperature is closely monitored (typical conditions for application: to instill fear and despair, to punish selective behavior, to instill humiliation or cause insult).

6. (FOUO) IMMERSION IN WATER / WETTING DOWN: Wetting the subject consists of spraying with a hose, hand pressure water cans, or immersing in a shallow pool of water. Depending on wind and temperature, the subject may be either fully clothed or stripped. Immersion of the head or back of head is prohibited for safety reasons (typical conditions for application: to instill fear and despair, to punish selective behavior, instill humiliation or cause insult).

OTHER TACTICS TO INDUCE CONTROL, DEPENDENCY, COMPLIACE, AND COOPERATION

1. (FOUO) Isolation / Solitary confinement: See JPRA Instructor Guide Module 6.0 *I* Lesson 6.1; para. 5.3.1

2. (FOUO) Induced Physical Weakness and Exhaustion: See JPRA Instructor Guide Module *6.0* / Lesson 6.1; para. 5.3.2

3. (FOUO) Degradation: See JPRA Instructor Guide Module 6.0 / Lesson 6.1; para. 5.3.3

4. (FOUO) Conditioning: See JPRA Instructor Guide Module 6.0 / Lesson 6.1; para. 5.3.4

5. (FOUO) Sensory Deprivation: When a subject is deprived of sensory input for an interrupted period, for approximately 6-8 hours, it is not uncommon for them to experience visual, auditory and/or tactile hallucinations. If deprived of input, the brain will make it up. This tactic is used in conjunction with other methods to promote dislocation of expectations and induce emotions.

6. (FOUO) Sensory overload: This includes being continually exposed to bright, flashing lights, loud music, annoying / irritating sounds, etc. This tactic elevates the agitation level of a person and increases their emotionality, as well as enhances the effects of isolation.

7. (FOUO) Disruption of sleep and biorhythms: Sleep patterns are purposefully disrupted to make it more difficult for the subject to think clearly, concentrate, and make rational decisions.

8. (FOUO) Manipulation of diet: Purposeful manipulation of diet, nutrients, and vitamins can have a negative impact on the subject's general health and emotional state. Medical personnel in the POW camps in North Korea believe that a B vitamin compound was responsible, in large part, to the phenomena called "give-up-itis." Recent studies suggest the removal of certain amino acids from a diet can induce heightened levels of emotional agitation.

APPENDIX C

*Assessment of JTF-170 Counter-Resistance Strategies
and the Potential Impact on CITF Mission and Personnel*

The Criminal Investigative Task Force (CITF) operated under a separate chain of command from the military interrogators stationed at Guantánamo. It also interrogated detainees but focused on gathering evidence for legal proceedings rather than information about current threats, and raised concerns about interrogation techniques.

TAB 11

~~SECRET//NOFORN~~
DEPARTMENT OF DEFENSE
CRIMINAL INVESTIGATION TASK FORCE
6010 6ᵗʰ Street
FORT BELVOIR, VA 22060-5506

REPLY TO
ATTENTION OF:

CITF   4 November 2002

MEMORANDUM THRU

Division Chief, Plans, Policy and Integration, DoD CITF, Bldg. 714, Fort Belvoir,
Virginia 22060-5506

FOR COMMANDER, CITF

SUBJECT: Assessment of JTF-170 Counter-Resistance Strategies and the Potential
Impact on CITF Mission and Personnel.

1. Pursuant to your directive I have reviewed the following documents in order to
provide an assessment of potential impacts on the CITF mission:

· DOD JTF 170 Memorandum from LTC Beaver, dated 11 October 2002,
SUBJECT: Legal Review of Aggressive Interrogation Techniques, with attached Legal
Brief of the same date.

· DOD JTF 170 Memorandum from LTC Jerald Phifer, dated 11 October 2002,
SUBJECT: Request for Approval of Counter-Resistance Strategies

· DOD JTF 170 Memorandum from MG Michael E. Dunlavey dated 11 October 2002,
SUBJECT: Counter-Resistance Strategies

'USSOCOM Memorandum from General James T. Hill, dated 25 October 2002,
SUBJECT: Counter-Resistance Techniques

2. The following represents my assessment of the adverse impacts on the CITF mission
if certain counter-resistant techniques are used at GTMO:

a. Liability. CITF personnel who are aware of the use or abuse of certain
techniques may be exposed to liability under the UCMJ for failing to intercede or report
incidents, if an inquiry later determines the conduct to be in violation of either the Eighth
Amendment to the U.S. Constitution, the Uniform Code of Military Justice or
18 U.S.C. §2340.

(1) The legal memorandum cited above opines that certain treatment,
although not amounting to torture, has been determined to constitute cruel and unusual,
or inhumane treatment or punishment insofar as it is defined in the Convention Against
Torture. ("CAT"). Although the United States has not ratified the entire CAT, it has

*Remarked Unclassified to far as
Source Documents Declassified
By OSD 2004*

ratified the definition of cruel, inhuman, and degrading treatment insofar as the Eighth Amendment to the U.S. Constitution defines it. Therefore, any conduct that would constitute cruel and unusual punishment would be prohibited by the Constitution and would be illegal.

(2) The suggested Tier III and certain Tier II techniques may subject service members to punitive articles of the UCMJ. The following are the most likely provisions to be violated if service members participated in the described techniques: Article 93 (Cruelty and Maltreatment), Article 124 (Maiming), Article 128 (assault) and Article 134 (Communicating a Threat). Should the detainee die in the process or as a result of the techniques, then Article 118 (Murder) and Article 134 (Negligent Homicide) could apply. CITF members who are aware of or participate in the conduct could be held responsible under the inchoate offenses of Article 80 (Attempt), Article 81 (Conspiracy) or Article 82 (Accessory After the Fact).

prob. value to reasonable person

b. Evidentiary Issues. Under Military Commission Order Number 1, if the Presiding Officer determines that the information is probative to a reasonable person, then it will be admitted. This would apply to confessions as well as statements about other defendants. The voluntary nature of any statement, however, will affect the weight accorded that evidence. Consequently, any information derived from the aggressive techniques, although admissible, will be of diminished value during any subsequent proceedings. The taint concerning the diminished weight accorded the statements would apply not only to the detainee making the statements, but also against those individuals about whom the detainee has provided incriminating information.

Additionally, the adverse impact may have consequences on all Commission actions. The al Qaeda training manual instructs members to assert that they have been tortured. The assertion is designed to mitigate the value of any incriminating statements the al Qaeda member may have made during the course of the interrogation. One detainee subjected to these techniques could taint the voluntary nature of all other confessions and information derived from detainees not subjected to the aggressive techniques.

3. Recommendations: Both the utility and legality of applying certain techniques identified in the memorandum listed above are, in my opinion, questionable. Any policy decision to use the Tier III techniques, or any technique inconsistent with the analysis herein, will be contrary to my recommendation. Nonetheless, if the application of the requested measures is approved, I recommend the following actions to mitigate the adverse impact on the CITF:

a. The aggressive techniques should not occur at GTMO where both CITF and the intelligence community are conducting interviews and interrogations. By not using these techniques in a co-located setting, other detainees not subjected to these techniques are less likely to be under the impression that they will be subjected to similar treatment if they do not provide the answers the government is seeking. It is unlikely that a detainee who has been exposed to Tier III techniques will distinguish between CITF and

Intelligence Interrogators. His impression will be that he will be punished for any responses that differ from what the interrogator determines to be acceptable.

b. A decision should be made prior to applying the aggressive procedures that the detainee subject to the treatment would not be a considered for referral to the Military Commission. This will reduce the risk that the more aggressive techniques used against a few detainees would be revealed resulting in assumption that these techniques had been used on all the detainees.

c. CITF personnel should not participate in the aggressive techniques, either in their administration, observation or designation of who will be subjected to the strategies. A firm nonporous wall should be erected between CITF personnel and those planning and engaging in the aggressive techniques. This measure will help preserve the integrity of our investigations, any Commission case and will insulate CITF personnel from potential administrative or criminal liability.

4. Conclusion. While some of the techniques identified in Tier I and II pose no threat to either the integrity of the investigation or to subsequent liability of the CITF personnel, i.e. using a ruse, raising one's voice, for the most part they are inconsistent with well-established law enforcement techniques. Any of the Tier III techniques could expose persons involved to administrative and criminal liability as well as negatively impact on subsequent Military Commission proceedings.

In legal analysis conducted by the SJA for JTF-170, there are two common themes running throughout the document justifying the use of the procedures, 1) There is no civil liability that will flow to the U.S. Government by using the asserted techniques, and 2) because the purpose of inflicting pain and treating detainees in a degrading manner is not in and of itself to cause pain or harm but to elicit information, it does not conflict with the well established authority under the U.S. Constitution.

There is no Constitutional case law related to the infliction of pain on prisoners, other than that related to causing pain for pain's sake, because it is not the prison official's objective to elicit information from those in their custody. Conversely, our objective is specifically to elicit information from the detainees. The intended use of Tier III techniques, if detected, will establish new case law in this area, much to the detriment of the U.S. foreign and domestic interests. I cannot advocate any action, interrogation or otherwise, that is predicated upon the principal that all is well if the ends justify the means and others are not aware of how we conduct our business.

4 Encls

SAM W. MCCAHON
MAJ, JA
Chief Legal Advisor

APPENDIX D

Executive Orders of January 22, 2009

THE WHITE HOUSE
Office of the Press Secretary

For Immediate Release   JANUARY 22, 2009

EXECUTIVE ORDER

REVIEW AND DISPOSITION OF INDIVIDUALS DETAINED AT THE GUANTÁNAMO BAY NAVAL BASE AND CLOSURE OF DETENTION FACILITIES

By the authority vested in me as President by the Constitution and the laws of the United States of America, in order to effect the appropriate disposition of individuals currently detained by the Department of Defense at the Guantánamo Bay Naval Base (Guantánamo) and promptly to close detention facilities at Guantánamo, consistent with the national security and foreign policy interests of the United States and the interests of justice, I hereby order as follows:

SECTION 1. DEFINITIONS. AS USED IN THIS ORDER:

(A) "Common Article 3" means Article 3 of each of the Geneva Conventions.

(B) "Geneva Conventions" means:

    (i).   the Convention for the Amelioration of the Condition of the Wounded and Sick in Armed Forces in the Field, August 12, 1949 (6 UST 3114);

    (ii).   the Convention for the Amelioration of the Condition of Wounded, Sick and Shipwrecked Members of Armed Forces at Sea, August 12, 1949 (6 UST 3217);

    (iii).   the Convention Relative to the Treatment of Prisoners of War, August 12, 1949 (6 UST 3316); and

    (iv).   the Convention Relative to the Protection of Civilian Persons in Time of War, August 12, 1949 (6 UST 3516).

(c) "Individuals currently detained at Guantánamo" and "individuals covered by this order" mean individuals currently detained by the Department of Defense in facilities at the Guantánamo Bay Naval Base whom the Department of Defense has ever determined to be, or treated as, enemy combatants.

SEC. 2. FINDINGS.

(A) Over the past 7 years, approximately 800 individuals whom the Department of Defense has ever determined to be, or treated as, enemy combatants have been detained at Guantánamo. The Federal Government has moved more than 500 such detainees from Guantánamo, either by returning them to their home country or by releasing or transferring them to a third country. The Department of Defense has determined that a number of the individuals currently detained at Guantánamo are eligible for such transfer or release.

(B) Some individuals currently detained at Guantánamo have been there for more than 6 years, and most have been detained for at least 4 years. In view of the significant concerns raised by these detentions, both within the United States and internationally, prompt and appropriate disposition of the individuals currently detained at Guantánamo and closure of the facilities in which they are detained would further the national security and foreign policy interests of the United States and the interests of justice. Merely closing the facilities without promptly determining the appropriate disposition of the individuals detained would not adequately serve those interests. To the extent practicable, the prompt and appropriate disposition of the individuals detained at Guantánamo should precede the closure of the detention facilities at Guantánamo.

(c) The individuals currently detained at Guantánamo have the constitutional privilege of the writ of habeas corpus. Most of those individuals have filed petitions for a writ of habeas corpus in Federal court challenging the lawfulness of their detention.

(D) It is in the interests of the United States that the executive branch undertake a prompt and thorough review of the factual and legal bases for the continued detention of all individuals currently held at Guantánamo, and of whether their continued detention is in the national security and foreign policy interests of the United States and in the interests of justice. The unusual circumstances associated with detentions at Guantánamo require a comprehensive interagency review.

(E) New diplomatic efforts may result in an appropriate disposition of a substantial number of individuals currently detained at Guantánamo.

(F) Some individuals currently detained at Guantánamo may have committed offenses for which they should be prosecuted. It is in the interests of the United States to review whether and how any such individuals can and should be prosecuted.

(G) It is in the interests of the United States that the executive branch conduct a prompt and thorough review of the circumstances of the individuals currently detained at Guantánamo who have been charged with offenses before military commissions pursuant to the Military Commissions Act of 2006, Public Law 109-366, as well as of the military commission process more generally.

SEC. 3. CLOSURE OF DETENTION FACILITIES AT GUANTÁNAMO.

The detention facilities at Guantánamo for individuals covered by this order shall be closed as soon as practicable, and no later than 1 year from the date of this order. If any individuals covered by this order remain in detention at Guantánamo at the time of closure of those detention facilities, they shall be returned to their home country, released, transferred to a third country, or transferred to another United States detention facility in a manner consistent with law and the national security and foreign policy interests of the United States.

SEC. 4. IMMEDIATE REVIEW OF ALL GUANTÁNAMO DETENTIONS.

(A) Scope and Timing of Review. A review of the status of each individual currently detained at Guantánamo (Review) shall commence immediately.

(B) Review Participants. The Review shall be conducted with the full cooperation and participation of the following officials:

(i). the Attorney General, who shall coordinate the Review;

(ii). the Secretary of Defense;

(iii). the Secretary of State;

(iv). the Secretary of Homeland Security;

(v). the Director of National Intelligence;

(vi). the Chairman of the Joint Chiefs of Staff; and

(vii). other officers or full-time or permanent part-time employees of the United States, including employees with intelligence, counterterrorism, military, and legal expertise, as determined by the Attorney General, with the concurrence of the head of the department or agency concerned.

(c) Operation of Review. The duties of the Review participants shall include the following:

(i). Consolidation of Detainee Information. The Attorney General shall, to the extent reasonably practicable, and in coordination with the other Review participants, assemble all information in the possession of the Federal Government that pertains to any individual currently detained at Guantánamo and that is relevant to determining the proper disposition of any such individual. All executive branch departments and agencies shall promptly comply with any request of the Attorney General to provide information in their possession or control pertaining to any such individual. The Attorney General may seek further information relevant to the Review from any source.

(ii). <u>Determination of Transfer</u>. The Review shall determine, on a rolling basis and as promptly as possible with respect to the individuals currently detained at Guantánamo, whether it is possible to transfer or release the individuals consistent with the national security and foreign policy interests of the United States and, if so, whether and how the Secretary of Defense may effect their transfer or release. The Secretary of Defense, the Secretary of State, and, as appropriate, other Review participants shall work to effect promptly the release or transfer of all individuals for whom release or transfer is possible.

(iii). <u>Determination of Prosecution</u>. In accordance with United States law, the cases of individuals detained at Guantánamo not approved for release or transfer shall be evaluated to determine whether the Federal Government should seek to prosecute the detained individuals for any offenses they may have committed, including whether it is feasible to prosecute such individuals before a court established pursuant to Article III of the United States Constitution, and the Review participants shall in turn take the necessary and appropriate steps based on such determinations.

(iv). <u>Determination of Other Disposition</u>. With respect to any individuals currently detained at Guantánamo whose disposition is not achieved under paragraphs (2) or (3) of this subsection, the Review shall select lawful means, consistent with the national security and foreign policy interests of the United States and the interests of justice, for the disposition of such individuals. The appropriate authorities shall promptly implement such dispositions.

(v). <u>Consideration of Issues Relating to Transfer to the United States</u>. The Review shall identify and consider legal, logistical, and security issues relating to the potential transfer of individuals currently detained at Guantánamo to facilities within the United States, and the Review participants shall work with the Congress on any legislation that may be appropriate.

SEC. 5. DIPLOMATIC EFFORTS.

The Secretary of State shall expeditiously pursue and direct such negotiations and diplomatic efforts with foreign governments as are necessary and appropriate to implement this order.

SEC. 6. HUMANE STANDARDS OF CONFINEMENT.

No individual currently detained at Guantánamo shall be held in the custody or under the effective control of any officer, employee, or other agent of the United States Government, or at a facility owned, operated, or controlled by a department or agency of the United States, except in conformity with all applicable laws governing the conditions of such confinement, including Common Article 3 of the Geneva Conventions. The Secretary of Defense shall immediately undertake a review of the conditions of detention at Guantánamo to ensure full compliance with this directive. Such review shall be completed within 30 days and any necessary corrections shall be implemented immediately thereafter.

SEC. 7. MILITARY COMMISSIONS.

The Secretary of Defense shall immediately take steps sufficient to ensure that during the pendency of the Review described in section 4 of this order, no charges are sworn, or referred to a military commission under the Military Commissions Act of 2006 and the Rules for Military Commissions, and that all proceedings of such military commissions to which charges have been referred but in which no judgment has been rendered, and all proceedings pending in the United States Court of Military Commission Review, are halted.

SEC. 8. GENERAL PROVISIONS.

(A) Nothing in this order shall prejudice the authority of the Secretary of Defense to determine the disposition of any detainees not covered by this order.

(B) This order shall be implemented consistent with applicable law and subject to the availability of appropriations.

(c) This order is not intended to, and does not, create any right or benefit, substantive or procedural, enforceable at law or in equity by any party against the United States, its departments, agencies, or entities, its officers, employees, or agents, or any other person.

BARACK OBAMA

THE WHITE HOUSE,
January 22, 2009.

THE WHITE HOUSE

Office of the Press Secretary

For Immediate Release   JANUARY 22, 2009

EXECUTIVE ORDER

ENSURING LAWFUL INTERROGATIONS

By the authority vested in me by the Constitution and the laws of the United States of America, in order to improve the effectiveness of human intelligence-gathering, to promote the safe, lawful, and humane treatment of individuals in United States custody and of United States personnel who are detained in armed conflicts, to ensure compliance with the treaty obligations of the United States, including the Geneva Conventions, and to take care that the laws of the United States are faithfully executed, I hereby order as follows:

SECTION 1. REVOCATION.

Executive Order 13440 of July 20, 2007, is revoked. All executive directives, orders, and regulations inconsistent with this order, including but not limited to those issued to or by the Central Intelligence Agency (CIA) from September 11, 2001, to January 20, 2009, concerning detention or the interrogation of detained individuals, are revoked to the extent of their inconsistency with this order. Heads of departments and agencies shall take all necessary steps to ensure that all directives, orders, and regulations of their respective departments or agencies are consistent with this order. Upon request, the Attorney General shall provide guidance about which directives, orders, and regulations are inconsistent with this order.

SEC. 2. DEFINITIONS. AS USED IN THIS ORDER:

(A) "Army Field Manual 2-22.3" means FM 2-22.3, Human Intelligence Collector Operations, issued by the Department of the Army on September 6, 2006.

(B) "Army Field Manual 34-52" means FM 34–52, Intelligence Interrogation, issued by the Department of the Army on May 8, 1987.

(c) "Common Article 3" means Article 3 of each of the Geneva Conventions.

(D) "Convention Against Torture" means the Convention Against Torture and Other Cruel, Inhuman or Degrading Treatment or Punishment, December 10, 1984, 1465 U.N.T.S. 85, S. Treaty Doc. No. 100–20 (1988).

(E) "Geneva Conventions" means:

  (i). the Convention for the Amelioration of the Condition of the Wounded and Sick in Armed Forces in the Field, August 12, 1949 (6 UST 3114);

  (ii). the Convention for the Amelioration of the Condition of Wounded, Sick and Shipwrecked Members of Armed Forces at Sea, August 12, 1949 (6 UST 3217);

  (iii). the Convention Relative to the Treatment of Prisoners of War, August 12, 1949 (6 UST 3316); and

  (iv). the Convention Relative to the Protection of Civilian Persons in Time of War, August 12, 1949 (6 UST 3516).

(F) "Treated humanely," "violence to life and person," "murder of all kinds," "mutilation," "cruel treatment," "torture," "outrages upon personal dignity," and "humiliating and degrading treatment" refer to, and have the same meaning as, those same terms in Common Article 3.

(G) The terms "detention facilities" and "detention facility" in section 4(a) of this order do not refer to facilities used only to hold people on a short-term, transitory basis.

SEC. 3. STANDARDS AND PRACTICES FOR INTERROGATION OF INDIVIDUALS IN THE CUSTODY OR CONTROL OF THE UNITED STATES IN ARMED CONFLICTS.

(A) Common Article 3 Standards as a Minimum Baseline. Consistent with the requirements of the Federal torture statute, 18 U.S.C. 2340–2340A, section 1003 of the Detainee Treatment Act of 2005, 42 U.S.C. 2000dd, the Convention Against Torture, Common Article 3, and other laws regulating the treatment and interrogation of individuals detained in any armed conflict, such persons shall in all circumstances be treated humanely and shall not be subjected to violence to life and person (including murder of all kinds, mutilation, cruel treatment, and torture), nor to outrages upon personal dignity (including humiliating and degrading treatment), whenever such individuals are in the custody or under the effective control of an officer, employee, or other agent of the United States Government or detained within a facility owned, operated, or controlled by a department or agency of the United States.

(B) Interrogation Techniques and Interrogation-Related Treatment. Effective immediately, an individual in the custody or under the effective control of an officer, employee, or other agent of the United States Government, or detained within a facility owned, operated, or controlled by a department or agency of the United States, in any armed conflict, shall not be subjected to any interrogation technique or approach, or any treatment related to interrogation, that is not authorized by and listed in Army Field Manual 2-22.3 (Manual). Interrogation techniques, approaches, and treatments described in the Manual shall be implemented strictly in accord with the principles, processes, conditions, and limitations the Manual prescribes. Where processes required by the Manual, such as a requirement of approval by specified Department of Defense officials, are inapposite to a department or an agency other than the Department of Defense, such a department or agency shall use processes that are substantially equivalent to the processes the Manual prescribes for the Department of Defense. Nothing in this section shall preclude the Federal Bureau of Investigation, or other Federal law enforcement agencies, from continuing to use authorized, non-coercive techniques of interrogation that are designed to elicit voluntary statements and do not involve the use of force, threats, or promises.

(c) Interpretations of Common Article 3 and the Army Field Manual. From this day forward, unless the Attorney General with appropriate consultation provides further guidance, officers, employees, and other agents of the United States Government may, in conducting interrogations, act in reliance upon Army Field Manual 2-22.3, but may not, in conducting interrogations, rely upon any interpretation of the law governing interrogation—including interpretations of Federal criminal laws, the Convention Against Torture, Common Article 3, Army Field Manual 2-22.3, and its predecessor document, Army Field Manual 34-52—issued by the Department of Justice between September 11, 2001, and January 20, 2009.

SEC. 4. PROHIBITION OF CERTAIN DETENTION FACILITIES, AND RED CROSS ACCESS TO DETAINED INDIVIDUALS.

(a) CIA Detention. The CIA shall close as expeditiously as possible any detention facilities that it currently operates and shall not operate any such detention facility in the future.

(b) International Committee of the Red Cross Access to Detained Individuals. All departments and agencies of the Federal Government shall provide the International Committee of the Red Cross with notification of, and timely access to, any individual detained in any armed conflict in the custody or under the effective control of an officer, employee, or other agent of the United

States Government or detained within a facility owned, operated, or controlled by a department or agency of the United States Government, consistent with Department of Defense regulations and policies.

SEC. 5. SPECIAL INTERAGENCY TASK FORCE ON INTERROGATION AND TRANSFER POLICIES.

(A) <u>Establishment of Special Interagency Task Force</u>. There shall be established a Special Task Force on Interrogation and Transfer Policies (Special Task Force) to review interrogation and transfer policies.

(B) <u>Membership</u>. The Special Task Force shall consist of the following members, or their designees:

  (i). the Attorney General, who shall serve as Chair;

  (ii). the Director of National Intelligence, who shall serve as Co-Vice-Chair;

  (iii). the Secretary of Defense, who shall serve as Co-Vice-Chair;

  (iv). the Secretary of State;

  (v). the Secretary of Homeland Security;

  (vi). the Director of the Central Intelligence Agency;

  (vii). the Chairman of the Joint Chiefs of Staff; and

  (viii). other officers or full-time or permanent part-time employees of the United States, as determined by the Chair, with the concurrence of the head of the department or agency concerned.

(C) <u>Staff</u>. The Chair may designate officers and employees within the Department of Justice to serve as staff to support the Special Task Force. At the request of the Chair, officers and employees from other departments or agencies may serve on the Special Task Force with the concurrence of the head of the department or agency that employ such individuals. Such staff must be officers or full-time or permanent part-time employees of the United States. The Chair shall designate an officer or employee of the Department of Justice to serve as the Executive Secretary of the Special Task Force.

(D) <u>Operation</u>. The Chair shall convene meetings of the Special Task Force, determine its agenda, and direct its work. The Chair may establish and direct subgroups of the Special Task Force, consisting exclusively of members of the Special Task Force, to deal with particular subjects.

(E) <u>Mission</u>. The mission of the Special Task Force shall be:

  (i). to study and evaluate whether the interrogation practices and techniques in Army Field Manual 2-22.3, when employed by departments or agencies outside the military, provide an appropriate means of acquiring the intelligence necessary to protect the Nation, and, if warranted, to recommend any additional or different guidance for other departments or agencies; and

(ii). to study and evaluate the practices of transferring individuals to other nations in order to ensure that such practices comply with the domestic laws, international obligations, and policies of the United States and do not result in the transfer of individuals to other nations to face torture or otherwise for the purpose, or with the effect, of undermining or circumventing the commitments or obligations of the United States to ensure the humane treatment of individuals in its custody or control.

(f) <u>Administration</u>. The Special Task Force shall be established for administrative purposes within the Department of Justice and the Department of Justice shall, to the extent permitted by law and subject to the availability of appropriations, provide administrative support and funding for the Special Task Force.

(g) <u>Recommendations</u>. The Special Task Force shall provide a report to the President, through the Assistant to the President for National Security Affairs and the Counsel to the President, on the matters set forth in subsection (d) within 180 days of the date of this order, unless the Chair determines that an extension is necessary.

(h) <u>Termination</u>. The Chair shall terminate the Special Task Force upon the completion of its duties.

SEC. 6. CONSTRUCTION WITH OTHER LAWS.

Nothing in this order shall be construed to affect the obligations of officers, employees, and other agents of the United States Government to comply with all pertinent laws and treaties of the United States governing detention and interrogation, including but not limited to: the Fifth and Eighth Amendments to the United States Constitution; the Federal torture statute, 18 U.S.C. 2340-2340A; the War Crimes Act, 18 U.S.C. 2441; the Federal assault statute, 18 U.S.C. 113; the Federal maiming statute, 18 U.S.C. 114; the Federal "stalking" statute, 18 U.S.C. 2261A; articles 93, 124, 128, and 134 of the Uniform Code of Military Justice, 10 U.S.C. 893, 924, 928, and 934; section 1003 of the Detainee Treatment Act of 2005, 42 U.S.C. 2000dd; section 6(c) of the Military Commissions Act of 2006, Public Law 109-366; the Geneva Conventions; and the Convention Against Torture. Nothing in this order shall be construed to diminish any rights that any individual may have under these or other laws and treaties. This order is not intended to, and does not, create any right or benefit, substantive or procedural, enforceable at law or in equity against the United States, its departments, agencies, or other entities, its officers or employees, or any other person.

BARACK OBAMA

THE WHITE HOUSE,
January 22, 2009.

THE WHITE HOUSE
Office of the Press Secretary

For Immediate Release   JANUARY 22, 2009

EXECUTIVE ORDER

REVIEW OF DETENTION POLICY OPTIONS

By the authority vested in me as President by the Constitution and the laws of the United States of America, in order to develop policies for the detention, trial, transfer, release, or other disposition of individuals captured or apprehended in connection with armed conflicts and counterterrorism operations that are consistent with the national security and foreign policy interests of the United States and the interests of justice, I hereby order as follows:

SECTION 1. SPECIAL INTERAGENCY TASK FORCE ON DETAINEE DISPOSITION.

(A) <u>Establishment of Special Interagency Task Force</u>. There shall be established a Special Task Force on Detainee Disposition (Special Task Force) to identify lawful options for the disposition of individuals captured or apprehended in connection with armed conflicts and counterterrorism operations.

(B) <u>Membership</u>. The Special Task Force shall consist of the following members, or their designees:

    (i).   the Attorney General, who shall serve as Co-Chair;

    (ii).   the Secretary of Defense, who shall serve as Co-Chair;

    (iii).   the Secretary of State;

    (iv).   the Secretary of Homeland Security;

    (v).   the Director of National Intelligence;

    (vi).   the Director of the Central Intelligence Agency;

    (vii).   the Chairman of the Joint Chiefs of Staff; and

    (viii).   other officers or full-time or permanent part-time employees of the United States, as determined by either of the Co-Chairs, with the concurrence of the head of the department or agency concerned.

(c) <u>Staff</u>. Either Co-Chair may designate officers and employees within their respective departments to serve as staff to support the Special Task Force. At the request of the Co-Chairs, officers and employees from other departments or agencies may serve on the Special Task Force with the concurrence of the heads of the departments or agencies that employ such individuals. Such staff must be officers or full-time or permanent part-time employees of the United States. The Co-Chairs shall jointly select an officer or employee of the Department of Justice or Department of Defense to serve as the Executive Secretary of the Special Task Force.

(D) <u>Operation</u>. The Co-Chairs shall convene meetings of the Special Task Force, determine its agenda, and direct its work. The Co-Chairs may establish and direct subgroups of the Special Task Force, consisting exclusively of members of the Special Task Force, to deal with particular subjects.

(E) <u>Mission</u>. The mission of the Special Task Force shall be to conduct a comprehensive review of the lawful options available to the Federal Government with respect to the apprehension, detention, trial, transfer, release, or other disposition of individuals captured or apprehended in connection with armed conflicts and counterterrorism operations, and to identify such options as are consistent with the national security and foreign policy interests of the United States and the interests of justice.

(F) <u>Administration</u>. The Special Task Force shall be established for administrative purposes within the Department of Justice, and the Department of Justice shall, to the extent permitted by law and subject to the availability of appropriations, provide administrative support and funding for the Special Task Force.

(G) <u>Report</u>. The Special Task Force shall provide a report to the President, through the Assistant to the President for National Security Affairs and the Counsel to the President, on the matters set forth in subsection (d) within 180 days of the date of this order unless the Co-Chairs determine that an extension is necessary, and shall provide periodic preliminary reports during those 180 days.

(H) <u>Termination</u>. The Co-Chairs shall terminate the Special Task Force upon the completion of its duties.

SEC. 2. GENERAL PROVISIONS.

(A) This order shall be implemented consistent with applicable law and subject to the availability of appropriations.

(B) This order is not intended to, and does not, create any right or benefit, substantive or procedural, enforceable at law or in equity by any party against the United States, its departments, agencies, or entities, its officers, employees, or agents, or any other person.

BARACK OBAMA

THE WHITE HOUSE,
January 22, 2009.

NOTES

PREFACE

1. Jane Mayer, "The Hard Cases," *The New Yorker*, February 23, 2009, p. 41.

2. Barack Obama, "Remarks Following a Meeting with Retired Military Officers," January 22, 2009, available at http://fdsys.gpo.gov/fdsys/delivery/getcontent.action?filePath=http%3A%2F%2Fwww.gpo.gov%2Ffdsys%2Fpkg%2FDCPD200900013%2Fpdf%2FDCPD200900013.pdf.

3. See Appendix D.

4. See Bob Woodward, "Detainee Tortured, Says U.S. Official—Trial Overseer Cites 'Abusive' Methods Against 9/11 Suspect," *Washington Post*, January 14, 2009, p. A1.

5. Statement of Alberto J. Mora, "Hearing on the Treatment of Detainees in U.S. Custody," Senate Committee on Armed Services, June 17, 2008, pp. 2–3, available at http://www.armed-services.senate.gov/statemnt/2008/June/Mora%2006-17-08.pdf (accessed March 17, 2009).

6. Quoted in Mark Benjamin, "You Can't Sweep Unlawful Activities under the Table," Salon.com, February 20, 2009, available at http://www.salon.com/news/feature/2009/02/20/taguba (accessed March 17, 2009).

7. See B.H. Obama, *Statement of President Barack Obama on Release of OLC Memos*. Washington, DC: Office of the Press Secretary, 2009. Available at http://www.whitehouse.gov/the_press_office/Statement-of-President-Barack-Obama-on-Release-of-OLC-Memos.

CHAPTER 1. INTRODUCTION: "THE NEW PARADIGM"

1. President Bush first described this "new war" in his September 20, 2001, "Address to a Joint Session of Congress and the American People," available at http://www.whitehouse.gov/news/releases/2001/09/print/20010920-8.html (accessed July 18, 2008).

2. Vice President Dick Cheney's discussion of the attack on America and the United States' response to terrorism is documented in *NBC News Transcripts* (September 16, 2001): 5, available at http://www.whitehouse.gov/vicepresident/news-speeches/speeches/vp20010916.html (accessed August 30, 2008).

3. Jane Mayer, *The Dark Side: The Inside Story of How the War on Terror Turned into a War on American Ideals* (New York: Doubleday, 2008), 51–52.

4. Ibid., 52.

5. See Bill Gertz, *Breakdown: How America's Intelligence Failure Led to September 11* (Dover, United Kingdom: Regency Press, 2002).

6. Quoted in Philippe Sands, *Torture Team: Rumsfeld's Memo and the Betrayal of American Values* (New York: Palgrave Macmillan, 2008), 188.

7. President Bush first publicly revealed the existence of the directive only years later, during a speech on September 6, 2006: "Many specifics of this program, including where the detainees have been held and the details of their confinement, cannot be divulged. . . . And so the CIA used an alternative set of procedures. . . . I cannot describe the specific methods used—I think you understand why—if I did, it would help the terrorists learn how to resist questioning and to keep information from us that we need to prevent new attacks on our country." George W. Bush, "President Discusses Creation of Military Commissions to Try Suspected Terrorists," *The White House*, available at http://www.whitehouse.gov/news/releases/2006/09/20060906-3.html (accessed September 12, 2008).

8. Bob Woodward, "CIA Told to Do 'Whatever Necessary' to Kill Bin Laden," *Washington Post*, October 21, 2001.

9. Geneva Convention Relative to the Treatment of Prisoners of War, art. 3, August 12, 1949, 6 U.S.T. 3316, 75 U.N.T.S. 135 [hereinafter Geneva Conventions III], available at http://www.unhchr.ch/html/menu3/b/91.htm (accessed September 12, 2008).

10. Ibid.

11. See *Memorandum from Deputy Assistant Attorney General John Yoo to General Counsel of Department of Defense*, January 9, 2002, reprinted in Karen J. Greenberg and Joshua L. Dratel, *The Torture Papers: The Road to Abu Ghraib* (Cambridge: Cambridge University Press, 2005), 38–79; and *Memorandum from Assistant Attorney General Jay S. Bybee to White House Counsel Alberto Gonzalez*, January 22, 2002, reprinted in Greenberg and Dratel, *The Torture Papers*, 81–117.

12. *Memorandum from White House Counsel Alberto Gonzalez to President George W. Bush*, January 25, 2002, reprinted in Jameel Jaffer and Amrit Singh,

Administration of Torture: A Documentary Record from Washington to Abu Ghraib and Beyond (New York: Columbia University Press, 2006), A-1–3.

13. Ibid. Also see *Memorandum from President George W. Bush,* February 7, 2002, reprinted in Jaffer and Singh, *Administration of Torture,* A-6, also available at http://www.pegc.us/archive/White_House/bush_memo_20020207_ed.pdf (accessed September 30, 2008).

14. Mayer, *The Dark Side,* 8. Mayer is paraphrasing a statement made by Arthur Schlesinger, Jr., the Pulitzer Prize–winning historian and social critic, during an interview. Mayer goes on to ask Schlesinger what he thinks of "President Bush's policy on torture," to which Schlesinger replies, "No position taken has done more damage to the American reputation in the world—ever."

15. *Memorandum from President George W. Bush,* February 7, 2002, reprinted in Jaffer and Singh, *Administration of Torture,* A-6.

16. Fact Sheet, *Status of Detainees at Guantánamo,* February 7, 2002, available at http://www.whitehouse.gov/news/releases/2002/02/20020207-13.html (accessed September 12, 2008).

17. The Administration first referred to the suspected Al Qaeda and Taliban fighters as "enemy combatants" in a Pentagon briefing on March 21, 2002, during which William J. Haynes II, the DOD's General Counsel, declared that "we may hold enemy combatants for the duration of the conflict" regardless of whether acquitted in a military tribunal. See Peter Jan Honigsberg, "Chasing Enemy Combatants and Circumventing International Law: A License for Sanctioned Abuse," *UCLA J. Int'l L. & Foreign Aff.* 12 (2007). However, the term was not formally defined until the 2004 memorandum establishing the creation of Combatant Status Review Tribunals, designed to allow detainees to challenge their classification as enemy combatants. *Memorandum from Paul Wolfowitz, Deputy Sec'y of Def., on an Order Establishing Combatant Status Review Tribunal to the Sec'y of the Navy,* July 7, 2004, available at http://www.defenselink.mil/news/Jul2004/d20040707review.pdf (accessed September 12, 2008).

18. John Yoo, *War by Other Means: An Insider's Account of the War on Terror* (New York: Atlantic Monthly Press, 2006), 142.

19. Yoo, *War by Other Means,* 142. Also see *Memorandum from Deputy Assistant Attorney General Patrick Philbin and Deputy Assistant Attorney General John Yoo to Department of Defense General Counsel William J. Haynes, II,* December 28, 2001, reprinted in Greenberg and Dratel, *The Torture Papers,* 28–37.

20. For more details about the U.S. naval base at Guantánamo Bay, Cuba, see http://www.globalsecurity.org/military/facility/guantanamo-bay.htm (accessed September 23, 2008).

21. Many additional entities have conducted interrogations at Guantánamo, including representatives of foreign governments and a wide range of military institutions.

22. U.S. Dept. of Justice, Office of the Inspector General, *A Review of the FBI's Involvement in and Observations of Detainee Interrogations in Guantánamo Bay, Afghanistan, and Iraq*, May 2008, 63–64 [hereinafter OIG/DOJ Report], available at http://www.dodig.osd.mil/fo/Foia/ERR/06-INTEL-10-Public Release.pdf (accessed August 22, 2008).

23. Ibid., 64.

24. Ibid., vi.

25. By court order, in May 2008 the Central Intelligence Agency made public documents regarding the agency's interrogation and detention program. American Civil Liberties Union, "Press Release: ACLU Obtains Heavily Redacted CIA Documents Regarding Waterboarding," May 27, 2008, available at http://www.aclu.org/safefree/torture/35454prs20080527.html (accessed October 8, 2008). Heavily censored documents include statements that CIA interrogators subjected Al Qaeda suspect Khalid Shaykh Muhammad to waterboarding. See Other Document #7, available at http://www.aclu.org/safefree/torture/35454prs20080527.html (accessed October 8, 2008). See also Dana Priest and Scott Higham, "At Guantánamo, a Prison within a Prison: CIA Has Run a Secret Facility for Some Al Qaeda Detainees, Officials Say," *Washington Post*, December 17, 2004.

26. See "Counter Resistance Strategy Meeting Minutes," 3, attached to an email from Mark Fallon, Deputy Commander, Criminal Investigation Task Force (CITF), U.S. Department of Defense, which was sent to CITF chief legal adviser Sam McCahon on October 28, 2002, noting Fallon's concerns with the military's proposed interrogation techniques and the Counter Resistance Strategy Meeting.

27. Office of the Inspector General of the Department of Defense, *Review of DOD-Directed Investigations of Detainee Abuse*, August 25, 2006, 25, available at http://www.dodig.osd.mil/fo/Foia/ERR/06-INTEL-10-PublicRelease.pdf (accessed August 22, 2008) [hereinafter DOD IG Report].

28. Ibid., 23–24.

29. Appendix C is a document from Daniel J. Baumgartner, Jr., JPRA Chief of Staff for Office of the Secretary of Defense General Counsel, *Physical Pressures Used in Resistance Training and Against American Prisoners and Detainees*, July 25, 2002. The document, which provides an overview of SERE tactics, was attached to a July 26, 2002, memorandum from Baumgartner titled "Exploitation and

Physical Pressures," drafted to answer questions regarding SERE training that had arisen during a meeting between JPRA and the Secretary of Defense General Counsel. Examples of SERE techniques were also provided in a chart originally publicized by Albert D. Biderman in 1957, which details Communist interrogation techniques used against American soldiers during the Korean War. The techniques had been successful in eliciting confessions, many of them false, from American prisoners. The use of such tactics has been denounced by Senator Carl Levin: "What makes this document doubly stunning is that these were techniques to get false confessions. . . . People say we need intelligence, and we do. But we don't need false intelligence." Scott Shane, "China Inspired Interrogations at Guantánamo," *New York Times,* July 2, 2008. These documents collectively demonstrate the DOD's early involvement in the reverse-engineering of SERE tactics for use on Guantánamo detainees, and the techniques' origins in Communist interrogation methods.

30. DOD IG Report, 25.

31. See Mayer, *The Dark Side,* 198–99.

32. See sworn statement of General James Hill, October 7, 2005, available at http://images.salon.com/ent/col/fix/2006/04/14/fri/HILL.pdf (accessed August 30, 2008).

33. See "Counter Resistance Strategy Meeting Minutes," 3.

34. See memorandum from Jay S. Bybee, Assistant Attorney General, to Alberto R. Gonzales, White House counsel, regarding standards of conduct for interrogation under 18 U.S.C. §§ 2340-2340A, August 1, 2002, available at http://news.findlaw.com/hdocs/docs/doj/bybee80102ltr6.html (accessed August 30, 2008) [hereinafter Torture Memo]. The Bush Administration withdrew the memo in December 2004.

35. Ibid.

36. Ibid. For a definition of PTSD as provided for in the *Diagnostic and Statistical Manual of Mental Disorders (DSM-IV),* see http://www.mental-health-today.com/ptsd/dsm.htm (accessed October 6, 2008). For a discussion on the diagnosis and impact of PTSD see, for example, Richard J. McNally, *Remembering Trauma* (Cambridge, MA: Harvard University Press, 2003); Judith Herman, *Trauma and Recovery: The Aftermath of Violence—from Domestic Abuse to Political Terror* (New York: Basic Books, 1992); and Eric Stover and Elena O. Nightingale, *Breaking of Bodies and Minds: Torture, Psychiatric Abuse, and the Health Professions* (New York: W.H. Freeman and Company, 1985).

37. Torture Memo.

38. Ibid.

39. See Senator Carl Levin's opening statement at the June 2008 Senate Armed Services Committee hearings on the origins of aggressive interrogation techniques used on detainees at Guantánamo and other U.S. detention facilities. His opening statement provides a link to several U.S. government memoranda and documents that discuss the use of interrogation methods. Carl Levin, U.S. Senator, "Press Release: Senate Armed Services Committee Hearing: The Origins of Aggressive Interrogation Techniques," June 17, 2008 [hereinafter Levin Opening Statement], available at http://levin.senate.gov/newsroom/release.cfm?id=299242 (accessed July 17, 2008). Also see Sands, *Torture Team*, 210–32.

40. See Levin Opening Statement.

41. This document is an example of such concern within the military; DOD CITF chief legal adviser Sam McCahon issued a November 4, 2002, memo critically evaluating the proposed "enhanced" interrogation methods, in which he questioned the "legality and utility" of such techniques.

42. See *Action Memorandum* endorsed by Secretary of Defense Donald Rumsfeld, November 27, 2002, available in Jaffer and Singh, *Administration of Torture*, A-83. See also Admiral Albert T. Church III, *Review of Department of Defense Detention Operations and Detainee Interrogation Techniques: Executive Summary*, March 11, 2005, 201 [hereinafter Church Report]; DOD IG Report, 15–16, 27.

43. See *Action Memorandum*, A-83. See also Church Report, 201; DOD IG Report, 15–16, 27.

44. Email from Brittain Mallow, Commander, Criminal Investigation Task Force, Department of Defense, "Re: CITF Participation in discussions of interrogations strategies, techniques, etc.," reprinted in Jaffer and Singh, *Administration of Torture*, A-145.

45. See Jaffer and Singh, *Administration of Torture*, 12–13. See also Alberto J. Mora, *Memorandum for Inspector General, Department of the Navy*, July 7, 2004, 3 [hereinafter Mora Memorandum], available at http://www.aclu.org/pdfs/safefree/mora_memo_july_2004.pdf (accessed August 30, 2008); Jane Mayer, "The Memo," *The New Yorker*, February 27, 2006.

46. Mora Memorandum, 7.

47. Donald Rumsfeld, *Memorandum from Defense Secretary Donald Rumsfeld to U.S. Southern Command re Counter-Resistance Techniques*, January 15, 2003, available in Jaffer and Singh, *Administration of Torture*, A-146.

48. See Sands, *Torture Team*, 150–51.

49. *Memorandum from Secretary of Defense Donald Rumsfeld to Commander of U.S. Southern Command James T. Hill*, April 16, 2003, reprinted in Greenberg and Dratel, *The Torture Papers*, 360–63.

50. Principal among these reports are: (1) *Final Report of the Independent Panel to Review DoD Detention Operations,* August 2004 [hereinafter DOD Report]. The DOD Report sets out the findings of a panel appointed by the Secretary of Defense to review DOD detention operations in Afghanistan, Guantánamo Bay, and Iraq. Dr. James R. Schlesinger chaired the panel. The report states: "Interrogation techniques intended only for Guantánamo came to be used in Afghanistan and Iraq. Techniques employed at Guantánamo included the use of stress positions, isolation for up to 30 days and removal of clothing." DOD Report, 68. (2) The Church Report reviewed DOD investigations of 187 closed cases of alleged detainee abuses in Afghanistan, Guantánamo Bay, and Iraq. "Eight of the 71 cases occurred at GTMO, all of which were relatively minor in their physical nature, although two of these involved unauthorized, sexually suggestive behavior by interrogators, which raises problematic issues concerning cultural and religious sensitivities." Church Report, 13. (3) Army Regulation 15-6: *Final Report, Investigation into FBI Allegations of Detainee Abuse at Guantánamo Bay, Cuba Detention Facility,* April 1, 2005, amended June 9, 2005 [hereinafter Schmidt-Furlow Report]. The Schmidt-Furlow Report presents the findings of Lt. General Randall Schmidt and Brig. General John Furlow for the Department of Defense. It covers a three-year time frame (September 2001 to July 2004) and approximately 24,000 interrogations at Guantánamo. The authors "found no evidence of torture or inhumane treatment," but did find that three interrogation acts violated Army Field Manual 34-52 and DOD guidance; that the interrogation of one high value detainee in late 2002 rose to the level of degrading and abusive treatment; and that threats communicated to another detainee violated the Uniform Code of Military Justice.

51. Church Report, 13.

52. One example of a permissible tactic was an FBI accusation that a female interrogator "told a detainee that red ink on her hand was menstrual blood and then wiped her hand on the detainee's arm." The authors found this to be authorized as an example of the "futility" tactic (an "act used to highlight the futility of the detainee's situation"). Schmidt-Furlow Report, 8.

53. OIG/DOJ Report.

54. Ibid., 171. Table 8.1 on pages 172–73 summarizes the survey responses to questions regarding the use of particular interrogation techniques in Guantánamo.

55. Ibid., 307. In addition, FBI agents at Guantánamo created a "war crimes file" to document the abuses they were witnessing. Sometime in 2002, however, the agents were ordered to shut the file because "investigating detainee abuses

was not the FBI's mission." See Eric Lichtblau and Scott Shane, "Report Details Dissent on Guantánamo Tactics," *New York Times*, May 21, 2008; OIG/DOJ Report, xxii.

56. For example, while the authors of the Schmidt-Furlow Report recognized that some alleged abuses did take place at Guantánamo, they also concluded that the Army Field Manual on interrogations authorized most of these actions, despite their offensiveness. Schmidt-Furlow Report, 8.

57. U.S. Department of Defense, *News Release: Detainee Transfer Announced*, October 8, 2008, available at http://www.defenselink.mil/releases/release. aspx?releaseid=12275 (accessed October 8, 2008).

58. The average length of time respondents spent in U.S. custody in Afghanistan before being sent to Guantánamo was 12 weeks. The minimum reported time was three days, the longest was 28 weeks.

59. The project retains no record of the interviewees' identities. Researchers working with vulnerable populations, such as rape victims, battered children, psychiatric patients, court witnesses, or prisoners often keep the names of their interviewees anonymous to protect them from further harm.

60. The employment of both closed and open coding procedures allowed researchers to test hypotheses and generate new theories about the experiences of former detainees.

61. The database included articles from *Agence France Presse*, the *Associated Press*, the *British Broadcasting Company (BBC)* (online articles), the *New York Times*, *Reuters*, the *Washington Post*, and the Chinese news agency *Xinhua*. All articles were published between January 1, 2002, and December 31, 2006.

62. See Human Rights Data Analysis Group, *Core Concepts*, available at http://www.hrdag.org/resources/core_concepts.shtml (accessed August 18, 2008).

63. The team of research assistants underwent one month of training to ensure coding consistency, only coding articles once an appropriate level of inter-rater reliability was reached. The project reached an inter-rater reliability (IRR) coefficient of 70 percent. There are no clear standards for IRR coefficients because they can be measured in many different ways. Given the size and structure of the database (a single article normally generated over 200 fields), the length of time spent training the coders, and the complexity of interpreting vague language in media reports, 70 percent IRR was determined sufficient. See Romesh Silva, "On the Maintenance and Measurement of Inter-Rater Reliability when Documenting Large-Scale Human Rights Violations," Proceedings of the Joint Statistical Meetings of the American Statistical Association and Associated Societies, August 2002.

64. Wirtschaftsuniversität Wien: Vienna University of Economics and Business Administration, Department of Statistics and Mathematics, *The R Project for Statistical Computing*, available at http://www.r-project.org (accessed August 30, 2008). To avoid duplicate reporting, detainees mentioned in media reports were matched by name, nationality, and year of birth, when available. Because Arabic names have many English variants and traditionally reflect a lengthy genealogical chain, detainee names were often spelled differently or incompletely in various news reports. See A.F.L. Beeston, *Arabic Nomenclature* (Oxford: University Press, 1971), available at http://www.lib.umich.edu/area/ Near.East/cmenas520/BeestonNomen.pdf (accessed August 30, 2008). In consultation with a native Arabic speaker, a Soundex algorithm was used to match detainee names in articles to the list of released detainees (U.S. Department of Defense, "List of Individuals Detained by the Department of Defense at Guantánamo Bay, Cuba," as updated by the Center for Constitutional Rights).

65. As identified through data provided by the U.S. Department of Defense in their "List of Individuals Detained by the Department of Defense at Guantánamo Bay, Cuba," as updated by the Center for Constitutional Rights.

66. While the age structure of interviewees was remarkably similar to that of current and former detainees (the average age of interviewees was 29 at the time of capture), the interview sample was weighted toward Afghans and Western Europeans.

67. Interviewers gave respondents contact information for local nongovernmental organizations that could provide support on human rights issues and, if needed, psychosocial support.

68. Unlike media interviews, where time pressure, space constraints, and diverse interests mean that articles capture only a small portion of a detainee's full experience, the interview study was able to ask similar questions of each detainee. For this reason, we would expect the interview study to provide a fuller picture of detainee experiences than even comprehensive journalistic accounts.

CHAPTER 2. AFGHANISTAN: THE LONG JOURNEY BEGINS

1. Mark Denbeaux et al., *Report on Guantánamo Detainees: A Profile of 517 Detainees Through Analysis of Department of Defense Data*, Seton Hall Law School, 2006, 25, available at http://law.shu.edu/news/Guantánamo_report_final_ 2_08_06.pdf (accessed August 20, 2008). Also see Andy Worthington, *The Guantánamo Files: The Stories of the 774 Detainees in America's Illegal Prison* (Ann Arbor: Pluto Press, 2007); Herbert A. Friedman, "Psychological Operations in Afghanistan," http://www.psywarrior.com/Herbafghan02.html (accessed

July 25, 2008). The authors of the Seton Hall report cited above analyzed publicly available information on 518 Guantánamo detainee cases reviewed by the military. The report's authors found that "only 5% of the detainees were captured by United States forces," and that "86% of detainees were arrested by either Pakistan or the Northern Alliance and turned over to the United States." Denbeaux, *Report on Guantánamo Detainees*, 1. However, a report from the U.S. Military Academy at West Point examined the same data and concluded that there was no information on the location of capture for the majority of detainees. LTC Joseph Felter and Jarret Brachman, *CTC Report: An Assessment of 516 Combatant Status Review Tribunal (CSRT) Unclassified Summaries*, July 25, 2007, 13.

2. See Pervez Musharraf, *In the Line of Fire: A Memoir* (New York: Free Press, 2006), 237. Musharraf writes, "We have earned bounties totaling millions of dollars. Those who habitually accuse us of 'not doing enough' in the war on terror should simply ask the CIA how much prize money it has paid to the government of Pakistan." In the Urdu edition of the book, Musharraf reportedly dropped the references to "prize money" and having "earned bounties totaling millions of dollars." Qudssia Akhlaque, "Musharraf amends 'bounty' portion: Urdu translation of autobiography," *DAWN The Internet Edition*, October 23, 2006.

3. Some were detained in both Kandahar and Bagram. See, for example, Moazzam Begg (with Victoria Brittain), *Enemy Combatant: My Imprisonment at Guantánamo, Bagram, and Kandahar* (New York: The New Press, 2006). See also Physicians for Human Rights, *Broken Laws, Broken Lives: Medical Evidence of Torture by US Personnel and Its Impact*, June 2008, 62.

4. See Chris Mackey and Greg Miller, *The Interrogators: Task Force 500 and America's Secret War against Al Qaeda* (New York: Back Bay Books, 2005).

5. Eric Schmitt and Tim Golden, "U.S. Planning Big New Prison in Afghanistan," *New York Times*, May 17, 2008.

6. Katherine Shrader, "U.S. Has Detained 83,000 in War on Terror," *Associated Press*, November 16, 2005.

7. Mackey and Miller, *The Interrogators*, 3.

8. Ibid., 4.

9. See Alex Gibney (director), *Taxi to the Dark Side* (2006), documentary film (transcript on file with the Human Rights Center, University of California, Berkeley and the International Human Rights Law Clinic, University of California, Berkeley). Basic information about the documentary is available online at http://www.taxitothedarksidefilm.com (accessed August 7, 2008).

10. Mackey and Miller, *The Interrogators*, 4.

11. Ibid.

12. Ibid., 5.

13. See Human Rights Watch, *U.S. Operated Secret 'Dark Prison' in Kabul*, December 19, 2005; Craig Smith and Souad Mekhennet, "Algerian Tells of Dark Term in U.S Hands," *New York Times*, July 2, 2006.

14. Human Rights Watch documented the existence of the "Dark Prison." See Human Rights Watch, *U.S. Operated Secret 'Dark Prison' in Kabul*, December 19, 2005.

15. Murat Kurnaz, *Five Years of My Life, An Innocent Man in Guantánamo* (New York: Palgrave Macmillan, 2008), 54.

16. See International Committee of the Red Cross, *Visiting detainees: "The results don't happen overnight. . . ,"* August 13, 2004, available at http://www.icrc.org/web/eng/siteengo.nsf/html/63AGHE (accessed August 7, 2008).

17. In 2004, U.S. Defense Secretary Donald Rumsfeld appointed a panel to review U.S. detention procedures in Afghanistan and Iraq. The panel, chaired by former Defense Secretary James R. Schlesinger, linked forced nudity to the detainees' dehumanization: "The wearing of clothes is an inherently social practice, and therefore the stripping away of clothing may have the unintended consequence of dehumanizing detainees in the eyes of those who [interact] with them. . . . The process of dehumanization lowers the moral and cultural barriers that usually preclude the abusive treatment of others." See Hon. James R. Schlesinger et al., *Final Report of the Independent Panel to Review DoD Detention Operations*, submitted August 24, 2004, Appendix G: Psychological Stresses, 7 [hereinafter Schlesinger Report], available at http://www.defenselink.mil/news/Aug2004/d20040824finalreport.pdf (accessed August 20, 2008).

18. Quran, 24:30.

19. Abdelwahab Bouhdiba, *Sexuality in Islam* (London: Routledge and Kegan, 1985).

20. Begg, *Enemy Combatant*, 112.

21. John L. Esposito, *What Everyone Needs to Know about Islam* (New York: Oxford University Press, 2002).

22. See Philip Zimbardo, *The Lucifer Effect: Understanding How Good People Turn Evil* (New York: Random House, 2007); Stanley Milgram, *Obedience to Authority: An Experimental View* (London: Pinter & Martin Ltd, 2004). Also see A. Bandura, B. Underwood, and M.E. Fromson, "Disinhibition of Aggression Through Diffusion of Responsibility and Dehumanization of Victims," *Journal of Research in Personality* 9 (1975): 253–69.

23. Alberto J. Mora, *Memorandum for Inspector General, Department of the Navy: Statement for the Record: Office of the General Counsel Involvement in Interrogation Issues*, submitted on July 7, 2004, 4 [hereinafter Mora Memorandum]. The Mora Memorandum was submitted to Vice Admiral Albert Church, who led a Pentagon investigation in 2004 into abuses at Guantánamo.

24. See Tim Golden, "U.S. Report, Brutal Details of 2 Afghan Inmates' Deaths," *New York Times*, May 20, 2005, available at http://www.nytimes.com/2005/05/20/international/asia/20abuse.html?pagewanted=all (accessed September 23, 2008).

25. See *Taxi to the Dark Side*.

26. See Tom Lasseter, "U.S. Abuse of Detainees was Routine in Afghanistan Bases," *McClatchy Newspapers*, June 17, 2008.

27. U.S. Army investigators interviewed a Saudi detainee in June 2004 at Guantánamo who said an interrogator at Bagram named Damien M. Corsetti "had pulled out his penis during an interrogation [at the facility], held it against the prisoner's face and threatened to rape him." See Golden, "U.S. Report, Brutal Details of 2 Afghan Inmates' Deaths." Corsetti was charged in the incident but found not guilty of all charges.

28. See *Taxi to the Dark Side*. Habibullah's autopsy report is available online at http://action.aclu.org/torturefoia/released/102405/3146.pdf (accessed September 23, 2008). Also see Steven H. Miles, "Medical Investigations of Homicides of Prisoners of War in Iraq and Afghanistan," in the online medical journal *Medscape General Medicine*, at http://www.pubmedcentral.nih.gov/articlerender.fcgi?artid=1681676 (accessed September 23, 2008).

29. See CBS, "The Court-Martial of Willie Brand," *60 Minutes*, March 5, 2006, available at http://www.cbsnews.com/stories/2006/03/02/60minutes/main1364163_page3.shtml (accessed September 23, 2008). On the program, Bagram guards and interrogators interviewed by Alex Gibney for his documentary *Taxi to the Dark Side* describe how prison personnel shackled detainees with their arms extended above their heads. Also see Golden, "U.S. Report, Brutal Details of 2 Afghan Inmates' Deaths." The article contains a sketch by Thomas V. Curtis, a Reserve M.P. sergeant at Bagram, depicting how Dilawar and other detainees were chained to the ceiling of their cells.

30. For example, Murat Kurnaz, on pages 73–77 of his book *Five Years of My Life, An Innocent Man in Guantánamo*, describes being suspended by his arms for approximately five days.

31. Alex Gibney, in his documentary *Taxi to the Dark Side*, shows images of the chalkboard at the entrance to a cellblock at Bagram.

32. See *Taxi to the Dark Side.*

33. A former Kandahar detainee told Physicians for Human Rights that he was "subjected to electric shocks once by purposely being pushed into a generator." He described feeling "'as if my veins were being pulled out.' He was threatened with electric shock on other occasions, but was shocked only that one time." See Physicians for Human Rights, *Broken Laws, Broken Lives,* 56–57.

34. Headquarters, Dept. of the Army, *FM 34-52: Intelligence Interrogation* (Sept. 1992) [hereinafter FM 34-52]; *FM 2-22.3: Human Intelligence Collector Operations* replaced FM 34-52 on September 6, 2006. FM 34-52 was revised in the wake of the Abu Ghraib scandal to conform to proscriptions banning the use of cruel, inhuman, and degrading treatment in the *Detainee Treatment Act of 2005* (DTA), Pub. L. No. 109-148, §§ 1001–1006 (2005).

35. FM 34-52, 8.

36. Ibid., 9.

37. Mackey and Miller, *The Interrogators,* 85.

38. Damien M. Corsetti, quoted in *Taxi to the Dark Side.*

39. Mackey and Miller, *The Interrogators,* 85.

40. Jane Mayer, *The Dark Side: The Inside Story of How the War on Terror Turned into a War on American Ideals* (New York: Doubleday, 2008), 183.

41. Mackey and Miller, *The Interrogators,* 86.

42. Ibid., 194–95.

43. Begg, *Enemy Combatant,* 190.

CHAPTER 3. GUANTÁNAMO: PUSHED TO THE BREAKING POINT

1. A Department of Defense list available online includes information for a total of 759 detainees detained between January 2002 and May 12, 2006. U.S. Dept. of Defense, "List of Individuals Detained by the Department of Defense at Guantánamo Bay, Cuba, from January 2002 through May 12, 2006," available at http://www.defenselink.mil/pubs/foi/detainees (accessed October 8, 2008). However, a more recent version of the list, updated by the Center for Constitutional Rights through October 9, 2008, includes information for 778 detainees.

2. U.S. Dept. of Defense, "List of Individuals Detained by the Department of Defense at Guantánamo Bay, Cuba," as updated by the Center for Constitutional Rights.

3. U.S. Dept. of Defense, "News Release: Transfer of Detainees Completed," July 18, 2003.

4. U.S. Dept. of Defense, "News Release: Detainee Transfer Announced," October 8, 2008, available at http://www.defenselink.mil/releases/release. aspx?releaseid=12275 (accessed October 8, 2008).

5. Human Rights Watch, *Locked Up Alone: Detention Conditions and Mental Health at Guantánamo,* June 10, 2008, 14.

6. Global Security.org, "Joint Task Force GTMO," http://www.globalsecurity.org/military/agency/dod/jtf-gtmo.htm (accessed August 24, 2008); Philippe Sands, *Torture Team: Rumsfeld's Memo and the Betrayal of American Values* (New York: Palgrave Macmillan, 2008), 37.

7. James Yee, *For God and Country: Faith and Patriotism Under Fire* (New York: PublicAffairs, 2005), 55.

8. Philip Zimbardo, *The Lucifer Effect: Understanding How Good People Turn Evil* (New York: Random House, 2007), 414.

9. Jane Mayer, a correspondent with *The New Yorker,* quoted on PBS, "A Question of Torture," *Frontline,* October 18, 2005.

10. See Alex Gibney (director), *Taxi to the Dark Side* (2006), documentary film (transcript on file with the Human Rights Center and the International Human Rights Law Clinic at the University of California, Berkeley).

11. Department of the Army, *Article 15-6 Investigation of the 800th Military Police Brigade,* May 2, 2004, 8–9.

12. Kathleen T. Rhem, "Detainees Living in Varied Conditions at Guantánamo," *American Forces Press Service,* Feb. 16, 2005; Camp Delta Standard Operating Procedures (March 1, 2004) §8-7(a) [hereinafter 2004 SOP].

13. Rhem, "Detainees Living in Varied Conditions at Guantánamo;" 2004 SOP §8-7(a)(4).

14. 2004 SOP §8-7.

15. In May 2004, General Lance L. Smith, then Commander of U.S. Joint Forces Command, explained at a Senate hearing that some of the 20 interrogation techniques Miller authorized in Guantánamo Bay were subsequently banned in Iraq, because there, unlike Guantánamo, prisoners were protected by the Geneva conventions. See David Rose, "They Tied Me Up Like a Beast and Began Kicking Me," *The Observer,* May 17, 2004.

16. Camp Delta Standard Operating Procedures (March 28, 2003); 2004 SOP. Additional SOPs have been released by the military, but are heavily censored. One example is the SOP that governs the operation of medical facilities on base. See Detainee Hospital Guantánamo Bay Cuba Standard Operating Procedures (SOPs), available at http://www.dod.mil/pubs/foi/detainees/GITMO_MedicalSOPs.pdf (accessed September 13, 2008).

17. 2004 SOP §4-20.

18. William Glaberson, "Red Cross Monitors Barred from Guantánamo," *New York Times*, November 16, 2007, available at http://www.nytimes.com/2007/11/16/washington/16gitmo.html?_r=1&oref=slogin&ref=world&adxnnlx=11953 30242-K/tH1ClxRqCZd%20GtREMw%20A&pagewanted=print (accessed August 1, 2008).

19. GlobalSecurity.org, "Guantánamo Bay—Camp X-Ray," http://www.globalsecurity.org/military/facility/Guantánamo-bay_x-ray.htm (accessed August 25, 2008).

20. Omar el Akkad, "We don't have prisoners here," *Globe and Mail*, April 19, 2008.

21. "Guantánamo's New Jail," *BBC News*, April 30, 2002, available at http://news.bbc.co.uk/2/hi/americas/1960154.stm (accessed August 25, 2008).

22. In Camp Echo, detainees reportedly spent 23 to 24 hours a day confined to individual cells, exposed continuously to fluorescent lighting. Camp Echo closed in 2004, but then reopened reportedly to house detainees considered "unsuitable for the communal living structure of Camp 4." Human Rights Watch, *Locked Up Alone: Detention Conditions and Mental Health at Guantánamo*, June 10, 2008, 14. The doors of Camp Echo were replaced with bars that allow in some natural light. See Amnesty International, *Cruel and Inhuman: Conditions of Isolation for Detainees at Guantánamo Bay*, April 5, 2007, 8. Approximately 25 detainees were housed in Camp Echo in May 2008. Human Rights Watch, *Locked Up Alone*, 14.

23. Human Rights Watch reported that in May 2008, approximately six detainees were housed in Camp 3. Human Rights Watch, *Locked Up Alone*, 9.

24. Camp 2 appears to have been closed. See Human Rights Watch, *Locked Up Alone*.

25. Carol J. Williams, "Guantánamo Dangles New Incentives for Detainees," *Los Angeles Times*, August 3, 2008; "Inside Guantánamo Bay," *BBC News*, available at http://news.bbc.co.uk/2/shared/spl/hi/guides/457000/457023/html/nn2page1.stm (accessed August 25, 2008).

26. GlobalSecurity.org, "Guantánamo Bay, Camp Delta," http://www.globalsecurity.org/military/facility/Guantánamo-bay_delta.htm (accessed August 25, 2008); "Inside Guantánamo Bay," *BBC News*. Detainees are provided with nightshades to block out the lights that burn at all hours of the day and night. They have access to a classroom in which each desk has leg shackles bolted to the floor where some instruction is offered. Outside there is a basketball

net and a makeshift soccer field in the dirt. El Akkad, "We Don't Have Prisoners Here."

27. See Human Rights Watch, *Locked Up Alone,* 17–23. As of May 2008, approximately 60 percent of detainees at Guantánamo were living in Camp 5 or Camp 6. Completed in late 2004, Camp 5 has over 100 isolation units, where lights are kept on 24 hours a day. Cells have a single bed and a metal toilet. There is a coat hanger on the wall, but more than a few pounds of weight on the hanger will cause it to drop like a toggle switch, so detainees cannot use it to hang themselves. A frosted window provides minimal access to natural light, but no view outside. Detainees are allowed no more than two hours of "recreation" a day. Camp 6 opened in December 2006. Detainees there are held for a minimum of 22 hours in their cells and take recreation alone in a pen surrounded by high concrete walls with a mesh covering. Detainees who try to shout to one another through the food slot in their cell door risk disciplinary action. See Amnesty International, *Cruel and Inhuman,* 5. According to Amnesty International, the isolation of prisoners in this camp is extreme: "[T]he lack of human contact in Camp 6 appears to be reinforced by other operating procedures. The cell doors are operated by remote control, and guards escorting the detainees to and from the exercise yard wear thick gloves. . . . Guards are reportedly silent during most of their contact with detainees. Detainees are also escorted in shackles whenever they leave their cells. Visits with attorneys take place in a small, windowless room, and detainees are reportedly shackled to the floor during visits." Amnesty International, *Cruel and Inhuman,* 5. The attorneys representing detainees interviewed for this study reported that their clients in Camps 5 and 6 suffered mental deterioration that makes it difficult for them to effectively participate in their legal cases. The military reportedly plans to ease some of these restrictions and allow compliant detainees to visit and exercise communally. Williams, "Guantánamo Dangles New Incentives for Detainees."

28. Williams, "Guantánamo Dangles New Incentives;" Human Rights Watch, *Locked Up Alone,* 24–40.

29. *See* Human Rights Watch, *Locked Up Alone,* 14.

30. "Guantánamo Inmates Languish," *BBC News,* Aug. 23, 2003, available at http://news.bbc.co.uk/2/hi/americas/3175501.stm (accessed August 25, 2008).

31. See "Lack of Due Process and Indeterminate Legal Status" section in Chapter IV.

32. U.S. Department of Defense, "List of Individuals Detained by the Department of Defense at Guantánamo Bay, Cuba," as updated by the Center for Constitutional Rights. Of 778 current and former detainees, the majority

have been identified as citizens of Afghanistan (221), Saudi Arabia (140), Yemen (110), Pakistan (70), Algeria (26), China (22), or Morocco (15). No other country has been represented by more than 15 detainees.

33. For example, of the 62 detainees interviewed, one-third (20) had no education while another one-third (20) finished secondary school. Five respondents had at least some post-secondary education. While all were Muslim, ten said that they only began practicing their faith recently. There was wide linguistic diversity among detainees. Over half (32) spoke Pashto (one of the languages spoken in Afghanistan); only twelve reported being fluent in Arabic and nine others reported fluency in English (an additional ten said they speak "a little bit" of English).

34. Global Security.org, "Joint Task Force GTMO," http://www.global security.org/military/agency/dod/jtf-gtmo.htm (accessed August 25, 2008).

35. Erving Goffman, *Asylums: Essays on the Social Situation of Mental Patients and Other Inmates* (New York: Anchor Books, 1961), 7; see also Stanford Prison Experiment, http://www.prisonexp.org (accessed August 25, 2008).

36. 2004 SOP §6-21(a): "Military and civilian staff members will address detainees by the detainee's cell number or ISN."

37. She also said that attitudes "softened" as the guards began to differentiate between detainees.

38. Goffman, *Asylums*, 94.

39. 2004 SOP §1-7(7).

40. Article 42 of the *Standard Minimum Rules for the Treatment of Prisoners* states that "[s]o far as practicable, every prisoner shall be allowed to satisfy the needs of his religious life by attending the services provided in the institution and having in his possession the books of religious observance and instruction of his denomination." The Minimum Standards were adopted by the First United Nations Congress on the Prevention of Crime and the Treatment of Offenders, held at Geneva in 1955, and approved by the Economic and Social Council by its resolution 663 C (XXIV) of 31 July 1957 and 2076 (LXII) of 13 May 1977. A copy of the Minimum Rules is available at http://www.unhchr.ch/html/ menu3/b/h_comp34.htm (accessed August 25, 2008).

41. Geneva Convention IV, art. 34.

42. 2004 SOP §16-14.

43. 2004 SOP §6-4 (b).

44. The database consisted of 1,215 articles about 219 released Guantánamo detainees published in seven prominent news outlets between January 1, 2002, and December 31, 2006. See Chapter 1 for details about database methods and

detainee matching. Of 219 former detainees in the media database, 14 (6%) volunteered to at least one major media source that praying was made difficult or impossible by the guards at Guantánamo.

45. U.S. Dept. of Justice, Office of the Inspector General, *A Review of the FBI's Involvement in and Observations of Detainee Interrogations in Guantánamo Bay, Afghanistan, and Iraq*, May 2008 [hereinafter OIG/DOJ Report], available at http://www.dodig.osd.mil/fo/Foia/ERR/06-INTEL-10-PublicRelease.pdf (accessed August 22, 2008), states that two FBI agents directly observed disrespectful treatment of the Quran during interrogations. Further, 31 FBI agents reported they were aware of allegations of mistreatment of the Quran outside of interrogation, for example, during cell searches. Ibid., 187–88.

46. Yee, *For God and Country*.

47. Ibid., 110–12.

48. Ibid., 115–16.

49. Xinhua News Agency, "Ex-Pakistan Guantánamo prisoner hopes to win legal battle against US," July 20, 2003.

50. "Guantánamo Bay: The Testimony," *BBC*, March 4, 2006, available at http://news.bbc.co.uk/2/hi/americas/4773396.stm (accessed August 26, 2008).

51. Christopher Cooper, "Detention Plan: In Guantánamo, Prisoners Languish in Sea of Red Tape, Inmates Waiting to Be Freed Are Caught in Uncertainty," *Wall Street Journal*, January 26, 2005.

52. Larry C. James (with Gregory A. Freeman), *Fixing Hell: An Army Psychologist Confronts Abu Ghraib* (New York: Grand Central Publishing, 2008), 57.

53. Army psychologist Larry James, in his book *Fixing Hell*, describes an interaction with an interrogator in which he encouraged him to work with guards to make a detainee more cooperative. Ibid., 60–62.

54. Headquarters, Dept. of the Army, *FM 34-52*, *Intelligence Interrogation* (Sept. 1992), Chapter 8 [hereinafter FM 34-52] (requiring compliance with the Geneva Conventions concerning the treatment and care of sources); Headquarters, Dept. of the Army, *FM 2-22.3 (FM 34-52)*, *Human Intelligence Collector Operations* (Sept. 2006) §5-75 [hereinafter FM 2-22.3] (detailing "prohibited [interrogation] actions"); FBI Report, 59, 63.

55. OIG/DOJ Report, 179–181.

56. *Memorandum for the General Counsel of the Department of Defense from Secretary Rumsfeld, Re: Detainee Interrogation*, January 15, 2003, reprinted in Karen J. Greenberg and Joshua L. Dratel, *The Torture Papers: The Road to Abu Ghraib* (Cambridge: Cambridge University Press, 2005), 238–39. The memo

allowed for the use of the now proscribed techniques with the permission of the Secretary. The military did not consider "short-shackling to be a prohibited 'stress position' until May 2004" when the commander of the base explicitly prohibited the practice. OIG/DOJ Report, 180.

57. Media interviews with detainees who were released well after 2003 confirm that they were forced to endure stress positions and short shackling at various times throughout their period of incarceration at Guantánamo.

58. OIG/DOJ Report, 170; Admiral Albert T. Church III, *Review of Department of Defense Detention Operations and Detainee Interrogation Techniques: Executive Summary*, March 11, 2005, 168 [hereinafter Church Report]; Army Regulation 15-6: *Final Report, Investigation into FBI Allegations of Detainee Abuse at Guantánamo Bay, Cuba Detention Facility*, April 1, 2005, amended June 9, 2005, 12 [hereinafter Schmidt-Furlow Report].

59. OIG/DOJ Report, 179.

60. See Schmidt-Furlow Report, 9–10 (clarifying that environmental manipulation was approved as an interrogation tactic at Guantánamo through a memorandum released by the Secretary of Defense on April 16, 2003); see also OIG/DOJ Report, 58–59 (explaining that environmental manipulation was first approved as an interrogation technique by the Secretary of Defense in a memorandum dated April 16, 2003, and that the memorandum remained in effect until September 2006, when the United States Army released a new field manual that delineated the scope of permissible interrogation techniques). See also FM 2-22.3.

61. OIG/DOJ Report, 58 (citing the DOD's "April 2003 GTMO Policy").

62. Secretary Donald Rumsfeld, "Memorandum for the Commander, U.S. Southern Command: Counter Resistance Techniques in the War on Terrorism," April 16, 2003, available at http://www.gwu.edu/~nsarchiv/NSAEBB/NSAEBB 127/03.04.16.pdf (accessed July 30, 2008).

63. OIG/DOJ Report, 63–64, 184.

64. In the media database, 19 of 219 respondents specifically mentioned to a journalist that they were subjected to extreme hot or cold temperatures while at Guantánamo.

65. Schmidt-Furlow Report, 9–10.

66. OIG/DOJ Report, 190.

67. Ibid., 190–191.

68. Schmidt-Furlow Report, 7–9.

69. Ibid., 16–17.

70. OIG/DOJ Report, 188.

71. Ibid., 189–90. Two other FBI agents said "that an FBI Intelligence Analyst told them a female military interrogator named 'Sydney' had exposed her breasts and performed sexual lap dances on detainees to make them uncomfortable and ashamed." Ibid., 190.

72. U.N. Convention Against Torture and Other Cruel, Inhuman, or Degrading Treatment or Punishment, G.A. Res. 39/46, UN GAOR, 39th Sess. Supp. No. 51, *entered into force* June 26, 1987, U.N. Doc. A/Res/39/46, available at http://www.unhchr.ch/html/menu3/b/h_cat39.htm (accessed September 12, 2008).

73. International Covenant on Civil and Political Rights, December 16, 1966, 999 U.N.T.S. 171, *entered into force* March 23, 1976.

74. European Convention for the Protection of Human Rights and Fundamental Freedoms §1, art. 3 (Nov. 4, 1950): "No one shall be subjected to torture or to inhuman or degrading treatment or punishment."

75. Article 3 in each of the conventions ("Common Article 3") prohibits "violence to life and person, in particular murder of all kinds, mutilation, cruel treatment and torture" and "outrages upon personal dignity, in particular humiliating and degrading treatment." See, for example, Geneva Convention IV, art. 3.

76. Hernán Reyes, "The Worst Scars Are In the Mind: Psychological Torture," *International Review of the Red Cross* 89, no. 867 (2007): 591–617.

77. *Prosecutor v. Krnojelac*, No. IT-97-25 (ICTY Trial Chamber), March 15, 2002, ¶ 182.

78. Reyes, "The Worst Scars Are In the Mind," 616.

79. Mayer, *The Dark Side*, 187.

80. The United States government videotaped hours of interrogations conducted by representatives of Guantánamo detainees' home countries. Permitting the questioning of detainees by foreign governments was contingent on such videotaping, which was conducted in part to help the United States gather additional intelligence. Such videotapes may ultimately confirm detainee allegations that such interrogations were often abusive, and sometimes included death threats and torture. See, for example, "Guantánamo detainees' foreign interrogations were recorded," *Los Angeles Times*, August 5, 2008, available at http://www.latimes.com/news/nationworld/nation/la-na-gitmo5-2008aug05,0, 4654363.story (accessed September 13, 2008); see also Center for Constitutional Rights, *Foreign Interrogators in Guantánamo Bay*, available at http://ccrjustice.org/ files/Foreign%20Interrogators%20in%20Guantánamo%20Bay_1.pdf (accessed September 13, 2008).

CHAPTER 4. GUANTÁNAMO: NO EXIT

1. Camp Delta Standard Operating Procedures (March 1, 2004) §9-1(4) [hereinafter 2004 SOP].

2. Solitary confinement is defined as "the physical isolation of individuals who are confined to their cells for twenty-two to twenty-four hours a day. In many jurisdictions prisoners are allowed out of their cells for one hour of solitary exercise. Meaningful contact with other people is typically reduced to a minimum. The reduction in stimuli is not only quantitative but also qualitative. The available stimuli and the occasional social contacts are seldom freely chosen, are generally monotonous, and are often not empathetic." "The Istanbul Statement on the Use and Effects of Solitary Confinement," *Torture* 18 (2008): 63–65 (adopted December 9, 2007, at the International Psychological Trauma Symposium, Istanbul) [hereinafter: "The Istanbul Statement"].

3. See Amnesty International, *United States of America: Cruel and inhuman: Conditions of isolation for detainees at Guantánamo Bay*, April 5, 2007, 19 (AI Index: AMR 51/051/2007), citing to Joint Task Force 170, Department of Defense, *Memorandum for Record: Subject: ICRC Meeting with MG Miller on 09 Oct 03, Guantánamo Bay, Cuba.* Also see William Glaberson, "Red Cross Monitors Barred from Guantánamo," *New York Times*, November 16, 2007, available at http://www.nytimes.com/2007/11/16/washington/16gitmo.html?_r=1&oref=slogin&ref=world&adxnnlx=1195330242-K/tH1ClxRqCZd%20GtREMw%20A&pagewanted=print (accessed August 1, 2008).

4. See Human Rights Watch, *Locked Up Alone: Detention Conditions and Mental Health at Guantánamo*, June 10, 2008.

5. Leila Zerrougui et al., *Situation of the Detainees at Guantánamo*, UN Doc. E/CN.4/2006/120 (2006) (report of the Chairperson-Rapporteur of the Working Group on Arbitrary Detention; the Special Rapporteur on the independence of justices and lawyers; the Special Rapporteur on torture and other cruel, inhuman or degrading treatment or punishment; the Special Rapporteur on freedom of religion or belief; and the Special Rapporteur on the right of everyone to the enjoyment of the highest attainable standard of physical and mental health).

6. See Stuart Grassian, "Psychiatric Effects of Solitary Confinement," *Washington University Journal of Law and Policy* 22 (2006): 325–83.

7. "The Istanbul Statement," 63.

8. See generally Grassian, "Psychiatric Effects." See also Peter Scharff Smith, "The Effects of Solitary Confinement on Prison Inmates: A Brief History of the Literature," *Crime and Punishment* 34 (2006): 441–528. A longitudinal study of

prisoners in Denmark found that the incidence of psychiatric disorders developed "was significantly higher in SC [solitary confinement] prisoners (28%) than in non-SC prisoners (15%)." See H.S. Anderson et al., "A Longitudinal Study of Prisoners on Remand: Psychiatric Prevalence, Incidence, and Psychopathology in Solitary v. Non-Solitary Confinement," *Acta Psychiatrica Scandinavica* 102 (2001): 19–25.

9. "The Istanbul Statement," 63.

10. Kieran McEvoy, *Paramilitary Imprisonment in Northern Ireland: Resistance, Management, and Release* (Oxford: Oxford University Press, 2001), 74.

11. Ibid., 82–83.

12. Of the remaining strikers, one had refused food "for more than eight hundred days, and another for nine hundred days." Jeffrey Toobin, "Camp Justice," *The New Yorker,* April 14, 2008.

13. Larry C. James (with Gregory A. Freeman), *Fixing Hell: An Army Psychologist Confronts Abu Ghraib* (New York: Grand Central Publishing, 2008), 66–67.

14. The remaining respondents did not explicitly discuss healthcare at Guantánamo.

15. U.S. Dept. of Justice, Office of the Inspector General, *A Review of the FBI's Involvement in and Observations of Detainee Interrogations in Guantánamo Bay, Afghanistan, and Iraq,* May 2008, 193–194 [hereinafter OIG/DOJ Report], available at http://www.dodig.osd.mil/fo/Foia/ERR/06-INTEL-10-PublicRelease.pdf (accessed August 22, 2008).

16. Our media database also contains reports regarding the deprivation of medical care at Guantánamo. The most frequently cited case was that of a detainee who alleged that he had been sent to Egyptian prisons for six months of torture prior to his arrival at Guantánamo, a practice known as "secret or extraordinary rendition." Fellow former detainees reported that he was in "catastrophic shape" when he arrived at Guantánamo. "Most of his fingernails were missing, and while sleeping he regularly bled from his nose, mouth and ears, but U.S. officials denied him treatment." Dana Priest and Dan Eggen, "Terror Suspect Alleges Torture; Detainee Says U.S. Sent Him to Egypt Before Guantánamo," *The Washington Post,* January 6, 2005, A1.

17. See James, *Fixing Hell.* Also see the leaked copy of the Department of Defense memorandum relating to an October 2003 meeting between Guantánamo authorities and members of the ICRC. Department of Justice, Joint Task Force 170, "Memorandum for Record: Subject: ICRC Meeting with MG Miller on 09 Oct 03, Guantánamo Bay, Cuba."

18. Thirteen detainees profiled in the media database reported that they forcibly had been given medication, often prior to interrogation. For example, a Pakistani detainee alleged that the Americans had given him injections and tablets prior to interrogations. "They used to tell me I was mad. I was given injections at least four or five times as well as different tablets. I don't know what they were meant for." Haroon Rashid, "Pakistani relives Guantánamo ordeal," *BBC*, May 22, 2003, available at http://news.bbc.co.uk/2/hi/south_asia/3051501.stm (accessed August 26, 2008).

19. See Mona Lynch, "The Disposal of Inmate #85271: Notes on a Routine Execution," *Studies in Law, Politics and Society* 20 (2000): 14–15.

20. NCIS Statement on Suicide Investigation, available at http://www.dod.mil/pubs/foi/detainees/NCISstatement_suicide_investigation.pdf (accessed September 13, 2008).

21. The Center for Constitutional Rights and others have raised questions about the responsibility of the U.S. government for the deaths of detainees and its handling of these incidents. On May 30, 2007, military officials at Guantánamo announced the "apparent suicide" of a detainee, Abdul Rahman Ma'ath Thafir al-Amri. He was reportedly found unresponsive in his cell. A hunger striker, he dropped over 60 pounds during his detention. The military promised to complete an autopsy before returning his body to Saudi Arabia but have yet to release the findings. William Glaberson, "Guantánamo Prisoner Cuts His Throat With Fingernail," *New York Times*, December 5, 2007; Center for Constitutional Rights, "Government Conclusions on Guantánamo Deaths Do Not Absolve Government of Responsibility," available at http://ccrjustice.org/newsroom/press-releases/government-conclusions-Guantánamo-deaths-do-not-absolve-government-responsib (accessed October 1, 2008).

22. Center for Constitutional Rights, "Government Conclusions on Guantánamo Deaths"; Mahvish Rukhasana Khan, *My Guantánamo Diary: The Detainees and the Stories They Told Me* (New York: PublicAffairs, 2008), 153–165.

23. *The Oxford Dictionary of Islam*, ed. John L. Esposito (New York: Oxford University Press, 2003), s.v. "Suicide."

24. Mark P. Denbeaux et al, *June 10th Suicides at Guantánamo: Government Words and Deeds Compared*, Seton Hall Law School, 2006, 13–14.

25. See "23 Detainees Attempted Suicide in Protest at Base, Military Says," *Associated Press*, January 25, 2005; *GlobalSecurity.org*, "Guantánamo Bay Detainees," http://www.globalsecurity.org/military/facility/Guantánamo-bay_detainees.htm (accessed August 26, 2008).

26. "Guantánamo Suicides 'Acts of War,'" *BBC News*, June 11, 2006, available at http://news.bbc.co.uk/2/hi/americas/5068606.stm (accessed August 26, 2008).

27. See Khan, *My Guantánamo Diary*, 163 (quoting forensic pathologist Dr. Patrice Mangin).

28. According to the 2004 SOPs, guards are required to secure surrounding detainees when responding to suicide attempts. 2004 SOP §32-1(e)(2). The safety and security of the guards are the top priority. 2004 SOP §32-(e)(1); §30-4(c)(10). During mass suicide attempts, especially, guards are expected to take precautions against any potential "clandestine plan[s] to overpower the guard[s] and psych staff." 2004 SOP §30-4(c)(14).

29. Jane Mayer, *The Dark Side: The Inside Story of How the War on Terror Turned into a War on American Ideals* (New York: Doubleday, 2008), 183; see also Tim Golden and Don Van Natta, "The Reach of War: U.S. Said to Overstate Value of Guantánamo Detainees," *New York Times*, June 21, 2004; Christopher Cooper, "Detention Plan: In Guantánamo, Prisoners Languish in Sea of Red Tape," *Wall Street Journal*, Jan. 26, 2005.

30. Mayer, *The Dark Side*, 183.

31. Ibid., 184.

32. Ibid., 187.

33. Mayer, *The Dark Side*, 183–212; Golden and Van Natta, "The Reach of War."

34. OIG/DOJ Report, 187.

35. The Combatant Status Review Tribunals were charged with determining whether a detainee fit the criteria of enemy combatant, defined as "an individual who was part of or supporting Taliban or Al Qaeda forces, or associated forces that are engaged in hostilities against the United States or its coalition partners. This includes any person who has committed a belligerent act or has directly supported hostilities in aid of enemy armed forces." Secretary of Defense, *Memorandum for Secretaries of the Military Departments, Chairman of the Joint Chiefs of Staff, Undersecretary of Defense for Policy, Combat Status Review Tribunal Process* (July 14, 2004).

36. Secretary of the Navy Gordon England announced the results of the review tribunals and explained the significance of the "No Longer an Enemy Combatant" (NLEC) determination: "It should be emphasized that a CSRT determination that a detainee no longer meets the criteria for classification as an enemy combatant does not necessarily mean that the prior classification as EC [Enemy Combatant] was wrong." Gordon England, *Defense Department Special Briefing on Combatant Status Review Tribunals* (March 20, 2005), available at

http://www.defenselink.mil/utility/printitem.aspx?print=http://www.defenselink .mil/transcripts/transcript.aspx?transcriptid=2504 (accessed September 13, 2008). By the end of November 2006, all 38 designated NLECs had been transferred from Guantánamo.

37. Secretary of Defense, *Memorandum for Secretaries of the Military Departments, Chairman of the Joint Chiefs of Staff, Undersecretary of Defense for Policy,* July 14, 2006, available at http://www.defenselink.mil/news/Aug2006/d20060809ARBProceduresMemo.pdf (accessed August 26, 2008).

38. *Boumediene v. Bush,* 553 U.S. __, *58 (2008).

39. Ibid., 41–42.

40. The government was only obligated to bring witnesses to testify who are "reasonably available." However, the organization that oversaw the review process, the Office for the Administrative Review of the Detention of Enemy Combatants (OARDEC), did not have a budget to bring witnesses to testify at panels, according to former Tribunal Officer Stephen Abraham. And no other government organization was obligated to pay to bring witnesses.

41. U.S. Dept. of Defense, "News Release: Detainee Transfer Announced," October 8, 2008, available at http://www.defenselink.mil/releases/release. aspx?releaseid=12275 (accessed October 8, 2008); Human Rights Watch, *Locked Up Alone,* 24–40.

CHAPTER 5. RETURN: THE LEGACY OF GUANTÁNAMO

1. U.S. Dept. of Defense, "News Release: Detainee Transfer Announced," October 8, 2008, available at http://www.defenselink.mil/releases/release. aspx?releaseid=12275 (accessed October 8, 2008).

2. Declaration of Clint Williamson, Ambassador-at-Large for War Crimes Issues, U.S. Department of State, ¶2, *Rimi v. Bush,* No. 1:05-cv-02427-RJL (D.D.C. 2008), Status Report In Response to Court's July 3, 2008 Order, filed July 14, 2008; Declaration of Sandra L. Hodgkinson, Deputy Assistant Secretary of Defense for Detainee Affairs, U.S. Department of Defense, ¶3, *Rimi v. Bush,* No. 1:05-cv-02427-RJL (D.D.C. 2008), Status Report In Response to Court's July 3, 2008 Order, filed July 14, 2008.

3. According to data collected by attorneys representing detainees, "a significant number of men have been transferred out of Guantánamo without [ever] having been officially cleared" by an annual review board. For more information on the Annual Review Boards (ARB) at which such determinations were made, see Chapter Four of this book, "Lack of Due Process and Indeterminate Legal Status."

4. Center for Constitutional Rights, *Background Information: Relevance of the Administrative Determination that a Detainee is "Cleared" for Transfer,* June 2008, 3.

5. Declaration of Sandra Hodgkinson ¶5.

6. Declaration of Clint Williamson ¶9.

7. Declaration of Sandra Hodgkinson ¶5.

8. U.S. Dept. of Defense, "News Release: Detainee Transfer Announced," October 8, 2008, available at http://www.defenselink.mil/releases/release.aspx?releaseid=12275 (accessed October 8, 2008).

9. Declaration of Sandra Hodgkinson ¶¶3–5. As of June 2005, the United States had transferred at least 65 detainees to other countries for "further detention, investigation, and prosecution, as appropriate." Declaration of Matthew C. Waxman, Deputy Assistant Secretary of Defense for Detainee Affairs, U.S. Department of Defense, ¶4, *Zalita v. Bush,* No. 1:05-cv-01220-UNA (D.D.C. 2005), Response to Petitioner's Motion for Preliminary Injunction Preventing Transfer, filed January 20, 2007. Several transferred detainees have been subsequently tried by their home countries. For example, in 2007, French courts convicted four French detainees and acquitted one on charges of "criminal association with a terrorist enterprise" in Afghanistan. Pierre-Antoine Souchard, "France convicts 5 ex-Guantánamo inmates," *USA Today,* December 19, 2007. The men had served provisional sentences upon their return to France and were released by the time the trial concluded.

10. Declaration of Clint Williamson ¶6.

11. See, for example, Human Rights Watch, *Ill-fated Homecomings: A Tunisian Case Study for Reparations,* September 2007; "Russia 'abused returned suspects,'" *BBC News,* March 29, 2007; "Former Detainees Abused Back Home: 'I'd Rather Return to Guantánamo,'" *Spiegel Online International,* September 6, 2007.

12. Seven Russian detainees were flown home in March 2004, and were immediately jailed on criminal conspiracy charges and subsequently released for lack of evidence. Human Rights Watch, *The "Stamp of Guantánamo": The Story of Seven Men Betrayed by Russia's Diplomatic Assurances to the United States,* March 2007, 20. Since then, three have fled the country or remain in hiding. Three others have been rearrested on suspected terrorism charges. A jury unanimously found two of these men, Ravil Gumarov and Timur Ishmuratov, innocent in September 2005, only to have the verdict annulled by the Supreme Court of Russia. The men were later convicted by a three-judge panel. Ibid., 38. The third, Rasul Kudaev, was detained on charges related to an attack on a government building that killed 150 people. His lawyer reported that he emerged from

the detention facility with a broken right leg, a swollen and misshapen head, and his eye full of blood. Ibid., 23. He remains in custody and no charges have been filed. The final former detainee was killed in June 2007 in a police raid. C.J. Chivers, "Russian Freed From Guantánamo Is Killed by Police Near Chechnya," *New York Times,* June 28, 2007.

13. Human Rights Watch, *Ill-fated Homecomings.*

14. Sworn Statement of Samir Ben Amor, Attorney (July 29, 2007), ¶¶18–19.

15. Ibid., 1.

16. Human Rights Watch, *Libya: Rights at Risk,* March 2008, available at http://hrw.org/english/docs/2008/01/03/libya17674_txt.htm (accessed August 28, 2008).

17. Declaration of Sandra Hodgkinson ¶5.

18. In April 2007, Australian detainee David Hicks entered into a plea agreement with U.S. military officials; Hicks pleaded guilty to one charge of material support of terrorism in exchange for a nine-month sentence, which he completed in Australia. Scott Horton, "The Plea Bargain of David Hicks," *Harper's Magazine,* April 2007, available at http://harpers.org/archive/2007/04/horton-plea-bargain-hicks (accessed August 28, 2008). Hicks was released from Australian prison on December 29, 2007. Attorney General for Australia, "Media Release: David Hicks Is Released from Yatala Labour Prison," available at http://www.attorneygeneral. gov.au/www/ministers/RobertMc.nsf/Page/RWPFC12EBADA9ACAC55 CA2573C00018B1A3 (accessed August 28, 2008). Salim Hamdan, one of Osama bin Laden's former drivers, was convicted of providing "material support for terrorism" at the conclusion of his military trial in August 2008. He was given a five-and-a-half-year sentence, five years and one month of which had already been served during his time at Guantánamo. Amnesty International, "Hamdan Convicted at Guantánamo," August 6, 2008, available at http://www.amnesty.org/en/news-and-updates/news/hamdan-convicted-Guantánamo-20080806 (accessed October 2, 2008); Associated Press, "Hamdan Gets 5 Years on Terror Charge," *MSNBC.com,* August 7, 2008, available at http://www.msnbc.msn.com/id/26055301/ (accessed October 2, 2008). Hamdan remains in Guantánamo.

19. U.S. Dept. of Defense, "List of Individuals Detained by the Department of Defense at Guantánamo Bay, Cuba," as updated by the Center for Constitutional Rights.

20. Neil Arun, "Albanian Fix for Guantánamo Dilemma," *BBC News,* January 11, 2007, available at http://news.bbc.co.uk/2/hi/europe/6189517.stm (accessed August 28, 2008).

21. In the case of Afghan detainees returned home, recent developments have increased the role that the U.S. government plays in determining their fate. Prior to April 2007, Afghan detainees were released through participation in the Peace and Reconciliation Commission. As part of a U.S.-Afghan agreement reached in 2005, the U.S. financed construction of a special security wing at a Pul-i-Charki prison outside Kabul. Finished in April 2007, it was used to house detainees transferred to Afghan custody from U.S. detention at Bagram and Guantánamo for trial under Afghan law. A U.S.-Afghan team makes joint determinations of whether a detainee should be prosecuted or released through the Peace Commission. Human Rights First, *Arbitrary Justice: Trials of Bagram and Guantánamo Detainees in Afghanistan*, April 2008, 3. Since the Pul-i-Charki prison wing opened, at least 32 detainees from Guantánamo have been transferred to the facility, in addition to hundreds from Bagram. Tim Golden, "Foiling U.S. Plan, Prison Expands in Afghanistan," *New York Times*, January 7, 2008; Human Rights First, *Arbitrary Justice*, iii. By April 2008, 160 Pul-i-Charki prisoners (of over 250 total) had been referred for prosecution; 65 defendants were convicted and 17 were acquitted. Ibid., 7. The others were not charged. Ibid., ii. Human rights groups criticized the proceedings, spotlighting detainees' lack of access to effective counsel and their inability to cross-examine witnesses. Ibid., ii–iii. None of the Afghan respondents interviewed for this study were held at the facility.

22. Western media has reported very little on the lives of detainees after their release, but four articles in the media database reported financial losses and increased debt among former detainees. In the most frequently reported case, a Pakistani detainee and father of nine children who had run a sawmill business prior to his arrest, returned home to find his mill collapsed because his sons had spent all their time looking for him. Kathy Gannon, "Pakistani prisoner freed from Guantánamo threatens to sue U.S. government for compensation," *Associated Press Worldstream*, December 28, 2002.

23. Judith Herman, *Trauma and Recovery: The Aftermath of Violence—from Domestic Abuse to Political Terror* (New York: Basic Books, 1997), 86.

24. The media database contained articles on the cases of ten former detainees that gave second-hand reports of lingering mental anguish and shock. For example, the lawyer of a former detainee from Kuwait said that he was "suffering a nervous breakdown due to his imprisonment. He has been shouting and out of control." Haitham Haddadin, "Five Kuwaitis head home from Guantánamo," *Reuters News*, November 3, 2005.

25. Post-Traumatic Stress Disorder (PTSD) is an anxiety disorder that may develop after experiencing a terrifying event. Symptoms may include reliving

the traumatic experience, emotional numbing and detachment, and hypervigilance and chronic arousal. American Psychiatric Association, *Diagnostic and Statistical Manual of Mental Disorders*, 4th ed., text rev. (Washington, D.C.: American Psychiatric Association, 2000).

26. A recent report documents the effects of torture and ill-treatment on 11 former detainees held in U.S. custody in Guantánamo and Iraq. All but one of these individuals exhibited symptoms of PTSD. Physicians for Human Rights, *Broken Laws, Broken Lives: Medical Evidence of Torture by US Personnel and Its Impact*, June 2008.

27. *The Oxford Dictionary of Islam*, ed. John L. Esposito (USA: Oxford University Press, 2003), s.v. *"Qismah;"* Reza Aslan, *No God but God: The Origins, Evolution, and Future of Islam* (Random House, 2005), 154–55.

28. Researchers have found that Islamic faith and practice give meaning to the trauma and suffering of Muslims. Marwa Shoeb, Harvey Weinstein, and Jodi Halpern, "Living in Religious Time and Space: Iraqi Refugees in Dearborn, Michigan," *Journal of Refugee Studies* (2007).

29. During a January 27, 2002, visit to Guantánamo, Secretary of Defense Donald Rumsfeld remarked that the facility houses "among the most dangerous, best-trained, vicious killers on the face of the earth." Gerry J. Gilmore, "Rumsfeld Visits, Thanks U.S. Troops at Camp X-Ray in Cuba," *American Forces Press Service*, January 27, 2002.

30. The Military Commissions Act, which Congress passed in October 2006, bars suits by "enemy combatants" against United States officials for mistreating the combatants while in detention. Military Commissions Act of 2006, Pub. L. No. 109-366, 120 Stat. 2600 §7a (2006).

31. *Rasul v. Myers*, 512 F.3d 644 (D.C. Cir. 2008), *petition for cert. filed* (U.S. Aug. 22, 2008) (No. 06-5209). The plaintiffs in *Rasul* are four British former detainees at Guantánamo who allege that they were tortured, abused, and denied their rights to practice their religion while they were incarcerated. The plaintiffs have filed a petition for certiorari seeking review by the U.S. Supreme Court.

32. Joint Intelligence Task Force—Combating Terrorism, *Defense Analysis Report—Terrorism*, December 4, 2007 (unclassified). By comparison, the recidivism rate for violent offenders in the United States is approximately 60%. U.S. Dept. of Justice Bureau of Justice Statistics, *Reentry Trends in the U.S.*, available at http://www.ojp.usdoj.gov/bjs/reentry/recidivism.htm (accessed August 29, 2008) (providing statistics from a recidivism study dated June 2002).

33. See Mark P. Denbeaux et al., *The Meaning of 'Battlefield': An Analysis of the Government's Representations of 'Battlefield Capture' and 'Recidivism' of the*

Guantánamo Detainees, Seton Hall Law School, December 10, 2007; Mark P. Denbeaux et al., *Justice Scalia, the Department of Defense, and the Perpetuation of an Urban Legend: The Truth about Recidivism of Released Guantánamo Detainees*, Seton Hall Law School, August 4, 2008.

34. Tom Lasseter, "Militants Found Recruits among Guantánamo's Wrongly Detained," *McClatchy Newspapers*, June 17, 2008.

35. Herman, *Trauma and Recovery*, 207–211.

CHAPTER 6. CONCLUSIONS AND RECOMMENDATIONS

1. These include (1) a secret directive by President Bush on September 17, 2001, granting the Central Intelligence Agency the authority to employ "an alternative set of interrogation procedures;" (2) a directive by Secretary of Defense Donald Rumsfeld on December 2, 2002, authorizing 24-hour interrogations, isolation for 30 days at a time, and the exploitation of "individual phobias (such as fear of dogs) to induce stress," which was later rescinded on January 15, 2003; and (3) a directive by the Secretary of Defense on April 16, 2003, authorizing the use of 24 interrogation methods, including environmental manipulation, sleep adjustment, and extended solitary confinement. These directives were largely based on legal memoranda prepared by staff at the Department of Justice. See *Memorandum from Deputy Assistant Attorney General John Yoo to General Counsel of Department of Defense*, January 9, 2002, reprinted in Karen J. Greenberg and Joshua L. Dratel, *The Torture Papers: The Road to Abu Ghraib* (Cambridge: Cambridge University Press, 2005), 38–79; *Memorandum from Assistant Attorney General Jay S. Bybee to White House Counsel Alberto Gonzalez*, January 22, 2002, reprinted in Greenberg and Dratel, *The Torture Papers*, 81–117; and *Memorandum from White House Counsel Alberto Gonzalez to President George W. Bush*, January 25, 2002, reprinted in Jameel Jaffer and Amrit Singh, *Administration of Torture: A Documentary Record from Washington to Abu Ghraib and Beyond* (New York: Columbia University Press, 2006), A-1–3; *Memorandum from Assistant Attorney General Jay S. Bybee to White House Counsel Alberto Gonzalez*, August 1, 2002, reprinted in Greenberg and Dratel, *The Torture Papers*, 172; *Memorandum from Deputy Assistant Attorney General John Yoo to White House Counsel Alberto Gonzalez*, August 1, 2002, reprinted in Greenberg and Dratel, *The Torture Papers*, 218.

2. Cofer Black, head of the CIA's counterterrorist center, told a September 16, 2002, Congressional hearing, "After 9/11, the gloves came off." *Joint Investigation Into September 11th: Hearing Before the Joint House-Senate Intelligence Committee*, 109th Cong. (2002) (statement of Cofer Black, Former Chief of the Counterterrorist Center, Central Intelligence Agency).

3. See the International Covenant on Civil and Political Rights, December 16, 1966, art. 7, 999 U.N.T.S. 171, *entered into force* Mar. 23, 1976, and UN Convention Against Torture and Other Cruel, Inhuman, or Degrading Treatment or Punishment, G.A. Res. 39/46, UN GAOR. 39th Sess. Supp. No. 51, *entered into force* June 26, 1987, UN Doc. A/Res/39/46, available at http://www.unhchr .ch/html/menu3/b/h_cat39.htm (accessed September 30, 2008). See also Article 3 of the Geneva Conventions of 1949 [hereinafter Common Article 3], which prohibits "violence to life and person, in particular murder of all kinds, mutilation, cruel treatment and torture" and "outrages upon personal dignity, in particular humiliating and degrading treatment." See, in particular, Geneva Convention Relative to the Treatment of Prisoners of War, incl. Annexes I–V, art. 3, August 12, 1949, 6 U.S.T. 3316, 75 U.N.T.S. 135 [hereinafter Geneva Conventions III], available at http://www.unhchr.ch/html/menu3/b/91.htm (accessed October 8, 2008).

4. On January 19, 2002, Secretary of Defense Donald Rumsfeld sent an order to the Joint Chiefs of Staff declaring that the military no longer needed to follow the Geneva Conventions in their handling of Al Qaeda and Taliban prisoners. The next day, he rescinded an earlier order by General Tommy Franks, commander of the Coalition Forces in Afghanistan, which had set up Article 5 hearings to screen captives. Now that the United States was no longer following the Geneva Conventions, there would be no need for Article 5 hearings. See Donald Rumsfeld, *Memorandum for Chairman of the Joint Chiefs of Staff*, January 19, 2002, available at http://www.defenselink.mil/news/Jun2004/d20040622doc1.pdf (accessed September 30, 2008). See Article 5 of Geneva Conventions III, available at http://www.unhchr.ch/html/menu3/b/91.htm (accessed September 30, 2008).

5. President George W. Bush, "Military Order of November 13, 2001: Detention, Treatment, and Trial of Certain Non-Citizens in the War Against Terrorism," available at http://www.law.uchicago.edu/tribunals/exec_order.html (accessed September 30, 2008).

6. Jane Mayer, *The Dark Side: The Inside Story of How the War on Terror Turned into a War on American Ideals* (New York: Doubleday, 2008), 183; see also Tim Golden and Don Van Natta, "The Reach of War: U.S. Said to Overstate Value of Guantánamo Detainees," *New York Times*, June 21, 2004; Christopher Cooper, "Detention Plan: In Guantánamo, Prisoners Languish in Sea of Red Tape," *Wall Street Journal*, Jan. 26, 2005.

7. Mayer, *The Dark Side*, 183.

8. Ibid., 184.

9. Ibid., 187.

10. On October 7, 2008, a judge ordered the government to produce a group of 17 detainees in his courtroom for their release into the United States, but no hearing to adjudicate their claims has been held as of the date of the writing of this book (October 13, 2008). Minute Entry for Proceedings Held Before Judge Ricardo M. Urbina: Motion Hearing held on 10/7/2008, *In re: Guantánamo Bay Detainee Litigation*, No. 1:05-cv-1509 (D.D.C. 2008). See also Duel Quentin Wilber, "Judge Orders Release of Chinese Muslims into U.S.," *Washington Post*, October 7, 2008. The detainees were Uighurs, an ethnic minority group in China persecuted by that government. The court ordered their release because the government no longer considered them "enemy combatants." The government immediately appealed the judge's ruling. Wilber, "Judge Orders Release."

11. U.S. Dept. of Defense, *News Release: Detainee Transfer Announced*, October 8, 2008, available at http://www.defenselink.mil/releases/release .aspx?releaseid=12275 (accessed October 8, 2008).

12. These detainees remain "stuck" either because the U.S. has been unable to negotiate release conditions with home governments or they are at risk of being tortured or persecuted if returned to their country of origin and the U.S. has not been able to reach agreement for resettlement with a third country.

13. A Department of Defense list available online includes information for a total of 759 detainees detained between January 2002 and May 12, 2006. U.S. Dept. of Defense, "List of Individuals Detained by the Department of Defense at Guantanamo Bay, Cuba, from January 2002 through May 12, 2006," available at http://www.defenselink.mil/pubs/foi/detainees (accessed October 8, 2008). However, a more recent version of the list, updated by the Center for Constitutional Rights through October 9, 2008, includes information for 778 detainees.

The U.S. government has stated that it will bring war crime charges against 60 or more of the almost 800 detainees who have been held in Guantánamo since January 2002. Associated Press, "Fast pace set for US war-crimes trials," *Military Global Allied Forces*, August 8, 2008, available at http://www.military global.com/forum/index.php/topic,5268.0.html (accessed September 13, 2008). The Department of Defense has prepared or filed charges against 23 detainees. U.S. Dept. of Defense, "Military Commission: Commission Cases," http://www.defenselink.mil/news/commissionsCo-conspirators.html (accessed October 12, 2008).

However, on October 21, 2008, the Department of Defense announced it was dropping charges against 5 detainees, but was prepared to re-file charges at a later date. Andrew O. Selsky, "US drops charges against 5 at Guantanamo after prosecutor complains about withheld evidence," Associated Press, October 21, 2008, available at http://www.newsday.com/news/nationworld/wire/sns-ap-cb-guantanamo-charges-dropped,0,191295.story (accessed October 21, 2008).

14. The *Rasul* decision prompted the U.S. government to create Combat Status Review Tribunals and Annual Review Boards as a means to determine whether a detainee should continue to be considered an "unlawful enemy combatant." Litigation challenging the status review system and its Congressionally created review procedure led to the Supreme Court 2008 decision in *Boumediene v. Bush*, 553 U.S. __ (2008).

15. In late 2003, the International Committee of the Red Cross (ICRC) informed the U.S. Administration that the totality of the conditions under which detainees were held at Guantánamo, including their indefinite confinement, had led to a worrying deterioration in the psychological health of many detainees. See Neil A. Lewis, "Red Cross Finds Detainee Abuse in Guantánamo," *New York Times*, November 30, 2004.

16. Ibid. Several studies report similar mental disturbances among prisoners placed in solitary confinement. See Stuart Grassian, "Psychiatric effects of solitary confinement," *Journal of Law and Policy* 22 (2006): 327–380. Grassian notes that mental disturbances can include "an agitated confusional state, characteristics of a florid delirium, [with] severe paranoid and hallucinatory features and also by intense agitation and random, impulsive, often self-directed violence." Also see Hernán Reyes, "The worst scars are in the mind: psychological torture," *International Review of the Red Cross* 89, no. 867 (September 2007): 606–608. Again, in 2006, the ICRC expressed its concern that "uncertainty about the prisoners' fate has added to the mental and emotional strain experienced by many detainees and their families." ICRC, *Operational Update*, December 31, 2006, quoted in Amnesty International, *United States of America, Cruel and Inhuman: Conditions of Isolation for Detainees at Guantánamo Bay*, April 5, 2007, 19 (AI Index: AMR 51/051/2007).

17. See American Medical Association Council on Ethical and Judicial Affairs, *Statement on Interrogation of Prisoners*, July 7, 2006, available at http://pn.psychiatryonline.org/cgi/content/full/41/13/4-a (accessed July 30, 2008). The AMA statement provides: "Physicians must neither conduct nor directly participate in an interrogation, because a role as physician-interrogator undermines the physician's role as healer and thereby erodes trust in both the individual physician-interrogator and in the medical profession. Physicians should not monitor interrogations with the intention of intervening in the

process, because this constitutes direct participation in interrogation. Physicians may participate in developing effective interrogation strategies that are not coercive but are humane and respect the rights of individuals." Also see American Psychiatric Association, *Psychiatric Participation in Interrogation of Detainees*, May 21, 2006, available at http://pn.psychiatryonline.org/cgi/content/full/41/12/1-b (accessed July 30, 2008). The APA resolution states: "No psychiatrist should participate directly in the interrogation of persons held in custody by military or civilian investigative or law enforcement authorities, whether in the United States or elsewhere. Direct participation includes being present in the interrogation room, asking or suggesting questions, or advising authorities on the use of specific techniques of interrogation with particular detainees. However, psychiatrists may provide training to military or civilian investigative or law enforcement personnel on recognizing and responding to persons with mental illnesses, on the possible medical and psychological effects of particular techniques and conditions of interrogation, and on other areas within their professional expertise."

18. The referendum prohibits psychologists from working in settings where "persons are held outside of, or in violation of, either International Law (e.g., UN Convention Against Torture and the Geneva Conventions) or the U.S. Constitution, where appropriate," unless they represent a detainee or an independent third party. The Association's bylaws require that it institute the policy at the next annual meeting in August 2009. See Benedict Carey, "Psychologists Vote to End Interrogation Consultations," *New York Times*, September 18, 2008.

19. Military psychologists developed interrogation techniques based on the "reverse engineering" of Survival, Evasion, Resistance, and Escape (SERE) tactics. SERE is a program developed to train U.S. military personnel to resist torture and abusive interrogation. See, for example, Physicians for Human Rights, *Break Them Down: Systematic Use of Psychological Torture by U.S. Forces*, 2005; M. Gregg Bloche and Jonathan H. Marks, "Doctors and Interrogators at Guantánamo Bay," *New England Journal of Medicine* 353 (2005): 6–8. Also see Larry C. James (with Gregory A. Freeman), *Fixing Hell: An Army Psychologist Confronts Abu Ghraib* (New York: Grand Central Publishing, 2008).

20. See Army Regulation 15-6: *Final Report, Investigation into FBI Allegations of Detainee Abuse at Guantánamo Bay, Cuba Detention Facility*, April 1, 2005, amended June 9, 2005, 9–10 [hereinafter Schmidt-Furlow Report] (clarifying that environmental manipulation was approved as an interrogation tactic at Guantánamo through a memorandum released by the Secretary of Defense on April 16, 2003); see also U.S. Dept. of Justice, Office of the Inspector General,

A Review of the FBI's Involvement in and Observations of Detainee Interrogations in Guantánamo Bay, Afghanistan, and Iraq (May 2008), 58–59 [hereinafter OIG/DOJ Report] (explaining that environmental manipulation was first approved as an interrogation technique by the Secretary of Defense in a memorandum dated April 16, 2008, and that the memorandum remained in effect until September 2006, when the United States Army released a new field manual that delineated the scope of permissible interrogation techniques). See Headquarters, Dept. of the Army, FM 2-22.3 (FM 34-52), Human Intelligence Collector Operations (September 2006) [hereinafter FM 2-22.3].

21. Geneva Conventions III, art. 3. See also *Memorandum from President George W. Bush*, February 7, 2002, reprinted in Jaffer and Singh, *Administration of Torture*, A-6, also available at http://www.pegc.us/archive/White_House/bush_memo_20020207_ed.pdf (accessed October 8, 2008) (declaring that Al Qaeda and Taliban detainees do not qualify as prisoners of war for purposes of Geneva Conventions III).

22. McClatchy Newspapers has compiled profiles of 64 former Guantánamo detainees and published several articles on the camp and former detainees based on interviews in 2007 and 2008, available at http://www.mcclatchydc.com/259/story/40334.html (accessed September 12, 2006).

23. FM 2-22.3 § 5-76.

SELECTED BIBLIOGRAPHY OF REPORTS AND MEDIA ACCOUNTS OF DETAINEE TREATMENT

GOVERNMENT REPORTS

Army Regulation 15-6: Final Report, Investigation into FBI Allegations of Detainee Abuse at Guantánamo Bay, Cuba Detention Facility, April 1, 2005, amended June 9, 2005.

Admiral Albert T. Church, III, *Review of Department of Defense Detention Operations and Detainee Interrogation Techniques: Executive Summary,* March 11, 2005.

Department of the Army, *Article 15-6 Investigation of the 800th Military Police Brigade,* May 2, 2004.

LTC Joseph Felter and Jarret Brachman, *CTC Report: An Assessment of 516 Combatant Status Review Tribunal (CSRT) Unclassified Summaries,* July 25, 2007.

Final Report of the Independent Panel to Review DoD Detention Operations, August 2004.

Joint Intelligence Task Force—Combating Terrorism, *Defense Analysis Report—Terrorism,* December 4, 2007.

Office of the Inspector General of the Department of Defense, *Review of DOD-Directed Investigations of Detainee Abuse,* August 25, 2006.

Hon. James R. Schlesinger et al., *Final Report of the Independent Panel to Review DoD Detention Operations,* submitted August 24, 2004.

U.S. Dept. of Justice, Office of the Inspector General, *A Review of the FBI's Involvement in and Observations of Detainee Interrogations in Guantánamo Bay, Afghanistan, and Iraq,* May 2008.

BOOKS AND INDEPENDENT REPORTS

Amnesty International, *United States of America: Cruel and inhuman: Conditions of isolation for detainees at Guantánamo Bay*, April 5, 2007, 19 (AI Index: AMR 51/051/2007).

Amnesty International, *Cruel, Inhuman, Degrades Us All: Stop Torture and Ill-Treatment in the "War on Terror,"* 2005.

Moazzam Begg (with Victoria Brittain), *Enemy Combatant: My Imprisonment at Guantánamo, Bagram, and Kandahar* (New York: The New Press, 2006).

Mark P. Denbeaux et al., *June 10th Suicides at Guantánamo: Government Words and Deeds Compared*, Seton Hall Law School, 2006.

Denbeaux et al., *Report on Guantánamo Detainees: A Profile of 517 Detainees Through Analysis of Department of Defense Data*, Seton Hall Law School, 2006.

Denbeaux et al., *The Meaning of 'Battlefield': An Analysis of the Government's Representations of 'Battlefield Capture' and 'Recidivism' of the Guantánamo Detainees*, Seton Hall Law School, December 10, 2007.

Denbeaux et al., *Justice Scalia, the Department of Defense, and the Perpetuation of an Urban Legend: The Truth about Recidivism of Released Guantánamo Detainees*, Seton Hall Law School, August 4, 2008.

Bill Gertz, *Breakdown: How America's Intelligence Failure Led to September 11* (Dover, United Kingdom: Regency Press, 2002).

Alex Gibney (director), *Taxi to the Dark Side* (2006), documentary film (transcript on file with the Human Rights Center, University of California, Berkeley and the International Human Rights Law Clinic at the University of California, Berkeley).

Karen J. Greenberg and Joshua L. Dratel, *The Torture Papers: The Road to Abu Ghraib* (Cambridge: Cambridge University Press, 2005).

Human Rights First, *Arbitrary Justice: Trials of Bagram and Guantánamo Detainees in Afghanistan*, April 2008.

Human Rights First, Hina Shamsi, *Command Responsibility: Detainee Deaths in U.S. Custody*, 2006.

Human Rights Watch, *U.S. Operated Secret 'Dark Prison' in Kabul*, December 19, 2005.

Human Rights Watch, *By the Numbers: Findings of the Detainee Abuse and Accountability Project*, April 2006.

Human Rights Watch, *Ghost Prisoner: Two Years in Secret CIA Detention*, February 2007.

Human Rights Watch, *The "Stamp of Guantánamo": The Story of Seven Men Betrayed by Russia's Diplomatic Assurances to the United States*, March 2007.

Human Rights Watch, *Ill-Fated Homecomings: A Tunisian Case Study of Guantánamo*, September 2007.

Human Rights Watch, *Locked Up Alone: Detention Conditions and Mental Health at Guantánamo*, June 2008.

International Committee of the Red Cross, *Visiting detainees: "The results don't happen overnight. . . ,"* August 13, 2004.

Jameel Jaffer and Amrit Singh, *Administration of Torture: A Documentary Record from Washington to Abu Ghraib and Beyond* (New York: Columbia University Press, 2007).

Larry C. James (with Gregory A. Freeman), *Fixing Hell: An Army Psychologist Confronts Abu Ghraib* (New York: Grand Central Publishing, 2008).

Mahvish Rukhsana Khan, *My Guantánamo Diary* (New York: PublicAffairs, 2008).

Murat Kurnaz, *Five Years of My Life, An Innocent Man in Guantánamo* (New York: Palgrave Macmillan, 2008).

Chris Mackey and Greg Miller, *The Interrogators: Task Force 500 and America's Secret War Against Al Qaeda* (New York: Back Bay Books, 2005).

Jane Mayer, *The Dark Side: The Inside Story of How the War on Terror Turned into a War on American Ideals* (New York: Doubleday, 2008).

Steven H. Miles, "Medical Investigations of Homicides of Prisoners of War in Iraq and Afghanistan," *Medscape General Medicine*, http://www.pubmedcentral .nih.gov/articlerender.fcgi?artid=1681676.

Pervez Musharraf, *In the Line of Fire: A Memoir* (New York: Free Press, 2006).

Physicians for Human Rights, *Break Them Down: Systematic Use of Psychological Torture by U.S. Forces*, 2005.

Physicians for Human Rights, *Broken Laws, Broken Lives*, June 2008.

Philippe Sands, *Torture Team: Rumsfeld's Memo and the Betrayal of American Values* (New York: Palgrave Macmillan, 2008).

Andy Worthington, *The Guantánamo Files: The Stories of the 774 Detainees in America's Illegal Prison* (London: Pluto Press, 2007).

James Yee, *For God and Country: Faith and Patriotism Under Fire* (New York: PublicAffairs, 2005).

John Yoo, *War By Other Means: An Insider's Account of the War on Terror* (New York: Atlantic Monthly Press, 2006).

Leila Zerrougui et al., *Situation of the Detainees at Guantánamo*, UN Doc. E/CN.4/2006/120, 2006.

Philip Zimbardo, *The Lucifer Effect: Understanding How Good People Turn Evil* (New York: Random House, 2007).

ARTICLES

H.S. Anderson et al., "A Longitudinal Study of Prisoners on Remand: Psychiatric Prevalence, Incidence, and Psychopathology in Solitary v. Non-Solitary Confinement," *Acta Psychiatrica Scandinavica* 102 (2001).

Associated Press, "Fast pace set for US war-crimes trials," *Military Global Allied Forces*, August 8, 2008.

M. Gregg Bloche and Jonathan H. Marks, "Doctors and Interrogators at Guantánamo Bay," *New England Journal of Medicine* 353 (2005).

Benedict Carey, "Psychologists Vote to End Interrogation Consultations," *New York Times*, September 18, 2008.

CBS, "The Court-Martial of Willie Brand," *60 Minutes*, March 5, 2006.

Christopher Cooper, "Detention Plan: In Guantánamo, Prisoners Languish in Sea of Red Tape," *Wall Street Journal*, Jan. 26, 2005.

Paisley Dodds, "Lawyers Seek Damages for Guantánamo Detainees Who Were Allegedly Abused," *Associated Press Worldstream*, October 27, 2004.

Omar El Akkad, "We Don't Have Prisoners Here," *Globe and Mail*, April 19, 2008.

Mohamed Fadhel, "Guantánamo ex-prisoners claim abuse, Koran desecration," *Agence France Presse*, November 17, 2005.

"Former Detainees Abused Back Home: 'I'd Rather Return to Guantánamo,'" *Spiegel Online International*, September 6, 2007.

Kathy Gannon, "Pakistani prisoner freed from Guantánamo threatens to sue U.S. government for compensation," *Associated Press Worldstream*, December 28, 2002.

James F. Gebhardt, "The Road to Abu Ghraib: U.S. Army Detainee Doctrine and Experience," *Military Review* (January–February 2005).

Gerry J. Gilmore, "Rumsfeld Visits, Thanks U.S. Troops at Camp X-Ray in Cuba," *American Forces Press Service*, January 27, 2002.

William Glaberson, "Red Cross Monitors Barred from Guantánamo," *New York Times*, November 16, 2007.

Tim Golden, "U.S. Report, Brutal Details of 2 Afghan Inmates' Deaths," *New York Times*, May 20, 2005.

Tim Golden and Don Van Natta, "The Reach of War: U.S. Said to Overstate Value of Guantánamo Detainees," *New York Times*, June 21, 2004.

Stuart Grassian, "Psychiatric Effects of Solitary Confinement," *Washington University Journal of Law and Policy* 22 (2006).

"Guantánamo Bay: The Testimony," *BBC News*, March 4, 2006.

"Guantánamo Inmates Languish," *BBC News*, August 23, 2003.

"Guantánamo Suicides 'Acts of War,'" *BBC News*, June 11, 2006.

"Guantánamo's New Jail," *BBC News*, April 30, 2002.

Haitham Haddadin, "Five Kuwaitis head home from Guantánamo," *Reuters News*, November 3, 2005.

Peter Jan Honigsberg, "Chasing Enemy Combatants and Circumventing International Law: A License for Sanctioned Abuse," *UCLA J. Int'l L. & Foreign Aff.* 12 (2007).

"The Istanbul Statement on the Use and Effects of Solitary Confinement," *Torture* 18 (2008).

Tom Lasseter, "Militants Found Recruits Among Guantánamo's Wrongly Detained," *McClatchy Newspapers*, June 17, 2008.

Lasseter, "U.S. Abuse of Detainees was Routine in Afghanistan Bases," *McClatchy Newspapers*, June 17, 2008.

Neil A. Lewis, "Red Cross Finds Detainee Abuse in Guantánamo," *New York Times*, November 30, 2004.

Eric Lichtblau and Scott Shane, "Report Details Dissent on Guantánamo Tactics," *New York Times*, May 21, 2008.

Mona Lynch, "The Disposal of Inmate #85271: Notes on a Routine Execution," *Studies in Law, Politics and Society* 20 (2000).

Jane Mayer, "The Memo," *The New Yorker*, February 27, 2006.

Richard J. McNally, *Remembering Trauma* (Cambridge, MA: Harvard University Press, 2003).

PBS, "A Question of Torture," *Frontline*, October 18, 2005.

Dana Priest and Dan Eggen, "Terror Suspect Alleges Torture; Detainee Says U.S. Sent Him to Egypt Before Guantánamo," *The Washington Post*, January 6, 2005.

Priest and Scott Higham, "At Guantánamo, a Prison within a Prison: CIA Has Run a Secret Facility for Some Al Qaeda Detainees, Officials Say," *Washington Post*, December 17, 2004.

Haroon Rashid, "Pakistani relives Guantánamo ordeal," *BBC News*, May 22, 2003.

Hernán Reyes, "The Worst Scars Are in the Mind: Psychological Torture," *International Review of the Red Cross* 89, no. 867 (September 2007).

Kathleen T. Rhem, "Detainees Living in Varied Conditions at Guantánamo," *American Forces Press Service*, February 16, 2005.

David Rose, "They Tied Me Up Like a Beast and Began Kicking Me," *The Observer*, May 17, 2004.

Peter Scharff Smith, "The Effects of Solitary Confinement on Prison Inmates: A Brief History of the Literature," *Crime and Punishment* 34 (2006).

Eric Schmitt and Tim Golden, "U.S. Planning Big New Prison in Afghanistan," *New York Times*, May 17, 2008.

Scott Shane, "China Inspired Interrogations at Guantánamo," *The New York Times*, July 2, 2008.

Katherine Shrader, "U.S. Has Detained 83,000 in War on Terror," *Associated Press*, November 16, 2005.

Craig Smith and Souad Mekhennet, "Algerian Tells of Dark Term in U.S. Hands," *New York Times*, July 2, 2006.

Jeffrey Toobin, "Camp Justice," *The New Yorker*, April 14, 2008.

Del Quentin Wilber, "Judge Orders Release of Chinese Muslims into U.S.," *Washington Post*, October 7, 2008.

Carol J. Williams, "Guantánamo Dangles New Incentives for Detainees," *Los Angeles Times*, August 3, 2008.

Bob Woodward, "CIA Told to Do 'Whatever Necessary' to Kill Bin Laden," *Washington Post*, October 21, 2001.

Xinhua News Agency, "Ex-Pakistan Guantánamo Prisoner Hopes to Win Legal Battle Against US," July 20, 2003.

AUTHORS AND ACKNOWLEDGMENTS

Laurel Fletcher and Eric Stover were the lead authors of the book and principal investigators of the study. Laurel Fletcher; Eric Stover, Stephen Paul Smith, Alexa Koenig, Zulaikha Aziz, Alexis Kelly, Sarah Staveteig, and Nobuko Mizoguchi authored the book. Andrew Moss, Rachel Shigekane, Jamie O'Connell, Neelam Ihsanullah, Emil Ray, and Reem Salahi contributed to the research for the book. Jonathan Cobb edited the book. Camille Crittenden provided further editorial assistance. Barbara Grob provided technical and editorial support during the research phase of the project. Samuel Miller, Shayana Kadidal, Emi MacLean, and Deborah Popowski of the Center for Constitutional Rights provided invaluable comments. Carolyn Patty Blum, Emeritus Clinical Professor of Law, University of California, Berkeley, deserves special thanks for her commentary on multiple drafts of the book and collaboration on and support of the project. Dean Christopher Edley, Jr. provided generous support to this project. The research librarians at Berkeley Law School offered invaluable assistance throughout the project. The authors thank Reed Malcolm and Marilyn Schwartz at University of California Press for guiding the manuscript through the final phases of production and publication.

LAUREL E. FLETCHER is Director of the International Human Rights Law Clinic and Clinical Professor of Law at the University of California, Berkeley, School of Law.

ERIC STOVER is Faculty Director of the Human Rights Center and Adjunct Professor of Law and Public Health at the University of California, Berkeley.

STEPHEN SMITH is a Ph.D. Candidate in Sociology and J.D. Candidate in Law, University of California, Berkeley.

ALEXA KOENIG is an attorney and Ph.D. student in Jurisprudence and Social Policy, University of California, Berkeley.

ZULAIKHA AZIZ is a 2008 graduate of University of California, Berkeley, School of Law.

ALEXIS KELLY is a 2008 graduate of University of California, Berkeley, School of Law.

SARAH STAVETEIG is a Ph.D. Candidate in Sociology & Demography, University of California, Berkeley.

NOBUKO MIZOGUCHI is a Ph.D. Candidate in Demography, University of California, Berkeley.

The following team of UC Berkeley students entered the data into the media database: Amir Abadi, Stephanie Ahn, Lei Deng, Sangita Devaskar, Sam Heft-Neal, Rosha Jones, Hiraa Khan, Christine Russell, Daniel Saver, Charles Taylor, Albert Wang, and Jing Wang.

Several organizations and individuals provided invaluable assistance to researchers in the field, including Claire Tixeire and Isabelle Brachet of International Federation for Human Rights (FIDH); Marie-Agnès Combesque at the Ligue Française des Droits de l'Homme et du Citoyen (LDH); staff at the Afghanistan Human Rights Organization (AHRO), including Lal Gul "Lal," AHRO Chairman, Ghulam Farooq "Safi," AHRO Consultant, Dr. Ibne Amin "Khalid," AHRO Advisor, AHRO Investigators Dost Mohammad and Mohammad Jamil, and AHRO volunteers Dr. Nangiali "Ibrahimi" and Noorrahman Rahmani Totakhil; Maryam Hassan, Moazzam Begg, and Asim Qureshi at Cageprisoners; staff at Reprieve; staff at the National Organization for Defending Rights and Freedoms (HOOD); and Nabeel Rajab, President of the Bahrain Center for Human Rights.

Research for this book was supported, in part, by grants from the Nathan Cummings Foundation, and generous contributions from Greg and Liz Lutz, and Werner and Mimi Wolfen. The National Security and Human Rights Campaign of the Open Society Institute provided additional support to the project.

ABOUT THE ORGANIZATIONS

HUMAN RIGHTS CENTER, UNIVERSITY OF CALIFORNIA, BERKELEY

THE HUMAN RIGHTS CENTER promotes human rights and international justice worldwide and trains the next generation of human rights researchers and advocates. We believe that sustainable peace and development can be achieved only through efforts to prevent human rights abuses and hold those responsible for such crimes accountable. We use empirical research methods to investigate and expose serious violations of human rights and international humanitarian law. In our studies and reports, we recommend specific policy measures that should be taken by governments and international organizations to protect vulnerable populations in times of war and political and social upheaval. For more information, please visit hrc.berkeley.edu.

INTERNATIONAL HUMAN RIGHTS LAW CLINIC, UNIVERSITY OF CALIFORNIA, BERKELEY, SCHOOL OF LAW

THE INTERNATIONAL HUMAN RIGHTS LAW CLINIC (IHRLC) designs and implements innovative human rights projects to advance the struggle for justice on behalf of individuals and marginalized communities through advocacy, research, and policy development. The IHRLC employs an interdisciplinary model that leverages the intellectual capital of the university to provide innovative solutions to emerging human rights issues. The IHRLC develops collaborative partnerships with researchers, scholars, and human rights activities worldwide. Students are integral to all phases of the IHRLC's work and acquire unparalleled experience generating knowledge and employing strategies to address the most urgent human rights issues of our day. For more information, please visit www.humanrightsclinic.org.

CENTER FOR CONSTITUTIONAL RIGHTS

THE CENTER FOR CONSTITUTIONAL RIGHTS is dedicated to advancing and protecting the rights guaranteed by the United States Constitution and the Universal Declaration of Human Rights. Founded in 1966 by attorneys who represented civil rights movements in the South, CCR is a non-profit legal and educational organization that has led the legal battle over Guantánamo for more than six years. For more information, please visit www.ccrjustic.org.

INDEX

Page numbers in italics denote illustrations.

Text: 10/15 Janson
Display: Akzidenz Grotesk, Gotham
Compositor: International Typesetting and Composition
Indexer: Ruth Elwell
Printer and binder: Sheridan Books, Inc.